D0213944

THE BIG LIES OF SCHOOL REFORM

The Big Lies of School Reform provides a critical interruption to the ongoing policy conversations taking place around public education in the United States today. By analyzing the discourse employed by politicians, lobbyists, think tanks, and special interest groups, the authors uncover the hidden assumptions that often underlie popular statements about school reform, and demonstrate how misinformation or half-truths have been used to reshape public education in ways that serve the interests of private enterprise.

Through a thoughtful series of essays that each identify one "lie" about popular school reform initiatives, the authors of this collection reveal the concrete impacts of these falsehoods—from directing funding to shaping curricula to defining student achievement. Luminary contributors including Deborah Meier, Jeannie Oakes, Gloria Ladson-Billings, and Jim Cummins explain how reform movements affect teachers and administrators, and how widely-accepted mistruths can hinder genuine efforts to keep public education equitable, effective, and above all, truly public. Topics covered include common core standards, tracking, alternative paths to licensure, and the disempowerment of teachers' unions. Beyond critically examining the popular rhetoric, the contributors offer visions for improving educational access, opportunity, and outcomes for all students and educators, and for protecting public education as a common good.

Paul C. Gorski is an Associate Professor of Integrative Studies, teaching in the Social Justice and Education concentrations, at George Mason University and the founder of EdChange.

Kristien Zenkov is an Associate Professor at George Mason University, where he teaches courses in secondary and literacy education and serves as co-director of the "Through Students' Eyes" project.

THE BIG LIES OF SCHOOL REFORM

Finding Better Solutions for the Future of Public Education

Edited by Paul C. Gorski and Kristien Zenkov

Routledge
Taylor & Francis Group

NEW YORK AND LONDON

First published 2014
by Routledge
711 Third Avenue, New York, NY 10017

and by Routledge
2 Park Square, Milton Park, Abingdon, Oxon, OX14 4RN

Routledge is an imprint of the Taylor & Francis Group, an informa business

© 2014 Taylor & Francis

The right of the editor to be identified as the author of the editorial
material, and of the authors for their individual chapters, has been asserted
in accordance with sections 77 and 78 of the Copyright, Designs and
Patents Act 1988.

All rights reserved. No part of this book may be reprinted or reproduced
or utilized in any form or by any electronic, mechanical, or other means,
now known or hereafter invented, including photocopying and recording,
or in any information storage or retrieval system, without permission in
writing from the publishers.

Trademark Notice: Product or corporate names may be trademarks or
registered trademarks, and are used only for identification and explanation
without intent to infringe.

Library of Congress Cataloging-in-Publication Data

The big lies of school reform : finding better solutions for the future of
  public education / edited by Paul C. Gorski and Kristien Zenkov.
    pages cm
  Includes bibliographical references and index.
  1. School improvement programs—United States.   2. Public schools—
United States.   3. Education—Aims and objectives—United States.
4. Education—Standards—United States.   5. Educational accountability—
United States.   6. Educational change—Government policy—United
States.   I. Gorski, Paul C., author, editor of compilation.   II. Zenkov,
Kristien, author, editor of compilation.
  LB2822.82.B595 2014
  371.2'07—dc23
  2013042694

ISBN: 978-0-415-70793-0 (hbk)
ISBN: 978-0-415-70794-7 (pbk)
ISBN: 978-1-315-88636-7 (ebk)

Typeset in Bembo
by Apex CoVantage, LLC

Paul: In memory of Wendy Amosa and Dan Balón, good friends and great educators who fought the good fight and left us far too early.

Kristien: To the youth who tell the truth—about their lives, their school experiences, and how we might best serve them as teachers—here's hope that this book might enable others to see through even one of these lies.

CONTENTS

FOREWORD

A few years ago, the pace at which states debated and implemented legislation that would evaluate teachers in part on the basis of whether the average scores of their students on standardized tests went up over time began to quicken. The rationale was quite seductive: if scores went up, didn't that mean that the students were learning and that the teachers of those students were effectively teaching them (alternatively, if the scores did not go up, didn't that mean that the students were not learning and that their teachers were failing to teach?)? Never mind that testing experts were arguing that standardized tests were never designed to measure teacher effectiveness and were already proving to be invalid and unreliable for such use. Debates among policymakers and in the media swirled around whether, for example, student test scores should count for 25 percent of teacher performance evaluations or 40 percent. What we were not debating was whether student test scores should count at all.

I remember wondering with my follow education researchers and advocates about how to intervene in this debate, given what seemed to be two sizable problems with how this debate was framed. First, we were concerned about what the debate masked. The question of whether test scores should be 25 percent or 40 percent already limited our intervention to a debate over percentage. Anyone entering the debate had to first agree with the more foundational assumption that test scores indeed tell us what we want to know about student learning and teacher effectiveness. The framing of this debate, in other words, masked the deeper question about what such tests can and do actually tell us—which is the more important question that we should have been debating.

Second and perhaps more insidious was what the debate asserted. The rhetoric around school reform did not address broader systemic problems such as inequitable funding, historic segregation, narrowed curriculum, and the increasing frequency of implementing "reforms" that lack sound research bases. No, the rhetoric continued to focus on the individual teacher—the good ones who lift up their students against all odds or the bad ones whose laziness and incompetence cause the failure of entire populations of children. This individualization of the "problem" of education fuels the desire to see the teacher or school leader or parent or even student held accountable. Hence the need for testing, the need to link test scores with teacher performance, and in the end, the commonsensical idea that if you care about children, you will support high-stakes testing.

So, in this debate on teacher evaluation, the "lie" was not merely that the tests tell us what we want to know; more significant, the "lie" was that the people who care about underserved children are the ones pushing for high stakes. This was the genius behind the framing of this debate—either you buy into the first lie or you get dismissed by the second, but, either way, the very terms of the debate silence a real debate on the real issues.

So-called reforms in education today are plagued by these types of strategic lies that mask the real problems, silence alternative perspectives, and hinder progress toward more equity and justice in our nation's schools. Many of us feel, at a gut level, that these "reforms" are problematic, but I know that I often find myself wishing that I had more historical and policy context, more data and analysis to help me see the picture differently and to enter the conversation differently and to challenge what has become the commonsense of schooling today. And for these reasons, this smart, accessible, well-researched, usable book by Gorski, Zenkov, and colleagues could not come at a better time. Tackling the most significant of problems and lies, this book helps us to see behind the masks, revealing the power of rhetorical strategies and confronting us with the realities that lie beneath. This book provides essential resources to reframe the debate and reclaim public education. Read this, share this, and join the movement.

Kevin Kumashiro
Dean of the University of San Francisco School of
Education, and author of *Bad Teacher!: How Blaming
Teachers Distorts the Bigger Picture*

INTRODUCTION

Paul C. Gorski and Kristien Zenkov

In their book, *Merchants of Doubt,* Naomi Oreskes and Erik M. Conway describe how a relatively small group of privately funded, pro-industry scientists, lobbyists, and think tanks have managed to stunt public discourses and, as a result, affect public policy, through information campaigns meant to misinform the public about a wide range of social concerns, from the health effects of smoking to the realities of climate change. Among their chief strategies is to propagate lies ("the earth is in a *cooling* phase") or half-truths ("the earth is warming, but it's just part of a natural cycle") in order to gain popular support for public policy initiatives that reflect industry economic interests—by, for instance, redirecting resources from public schools to private enterprise—rather than the common good.

We believe that a similar phenomenon is under way and making increasingly dangerous strides in the sphere of public education in the United States. We are sold school reforms supposedly meant to strengthen public education for *all students* with language that suggests a commitment to equity or democracy (e.g., *merit* pay, school *choice*); we are told these reforms will ensure that we leave no child behind, that they'll bolster all students' access to "the top" of, well, *something*. The propaganda appears to be convincing to a great number of people, including some advocates for educational equity, who continue to buy into all manner of illogical school reform initiatives.

A few years ago, for example, during a keynote address at a national conference on educational equity, the director of President Barack Obama's initiative on "Hispanic education" implored the audience to do all we could do to support Latino students, particularly recent immigrants, to achieve in school. Strangely, at least to us, his discussion of "achievement" revolved entirely around raising standardized test scores. He never mentioned actual learning or what it meant to create an equitable learning environment. He didn't urge us to rethink the elimination of bilingual education programs or the growing prevalence of repressive, irrational English-only policies, even in the face of national studies demonstrating the harm these policies do to students who are learning English. He never mentioned the legacy of racism Latina/o families have experienced—continue to experience—in U.S. schools. His remarks essentially appeared to draw on a series of bad assumptions about effective and equitable schooling—bad and very, very *popular* assumptions. He received a standing ovation from an audience of hundreds of people who had gathered to talk about creating and sustaining equitable and just schools.

At the root of his assumptions, as well as the suppositions driving a good portion of contemporary conversations on school reform, we believe, is a series of lies or mistruths that are meant to misdirect genuine efforts to protect and strengthen a version of public education that is truly public and to reshape public education in ways that serve the interests of private enterprise. Public conversations about achievement, accountability, teachers' qualifications, teacher preparation, and other aspects of schooling often appear to be mired in the resulting misinformation, as the authors in this volume discuss in great detail.

It is in this climate, in response to these troubling conditions, that we decided to assemble this edited volume, *The Big Lies of School Reform*. One purpose of the book is to uncover the lies that misdirect conversations about school improvement and educational equity, to describe what is motivating those lies (and to whose benefit), to reveal how these deceptions appeal, often illogically, to rhetoric that appears to support our grandest goals for students, teachers, and society, and to describe how popular reform movements *actually* affect a broad range of educational stakeholders. We were very intentional about selecting the term "lie" to frame the policies and practices the authors in this volume detail; these are conscious, intentional, popular deceptions that are being foisted upon the U.S. public and, more important, that uniformly harm our schools, students, and citizens. These are not matters of opinion or issues for debate: they are bold, dishonest attempts at shifting the very assumptions upon which our nation's notions of "public" and "public education" are founded.

Another purpose of this book is to imagine other possibilities for striving toward equitable schools. We were determined not to allow this project to become yet another volume of dark critical analysis lacking a direction forward, absent hope. The chapter authors were asked to provide both an analysis and a direction forward, a vision. They responded, as you will see, with a powerful combination of the two, using a mixture of anecdote, examinations of research, and detailed policy breakdowns. The result is what we consider to be an accessible collection of poignant and pointed analysis grounded in everyday practicalities of schools and clearing a path toward a more equitable vision for the present and future of public education.

Speaking of the authors, when we started this project, we sought out the voices of a wide range of people who have been involved in education in a variety of ways. They are activists, scholars, educators, combinations of these, all with long histories of work in and with schools. Some, like Gloria Ladson-Billings, Deborah

Meier, and Jeannie Oakes, are well-established voices in support of equitable public schools. Others, like Wayne Au and Katy Swalwell, are among the most thoughtful, deeply informed emerging voices. At the earliest stages of conceiving this book, we started with a list of lies and a "best-case-scenario" list of authors, each of whom we mentally preassigned to one of those lies. To our most pleasant surprise, virtually everybody to whom we reached out as potential contributors— Gloria, Deborah, Jeannie, Wayne, Katy, and the rest—found the project compelling and important enough to lend it their perspectives.

A final note about the lies discussed in *The Big Lies of School Reform:* by no means do we consider this book a complete analysis of every lie bouncing around in school reform conversations and debates. We realize that some important and compelling lies about merit pay, vouchers, charter schools, and a whole host of other contemporary initiatives warrant the kind of attention authors in this volume give to the issues they address. We understand that this is, in essence, a sort of sampler of lies rather than the whole kit and caboodle. In the end, though, we felt it was more important that we ensure that the book illustrates different ways of raising questions and rethinking the school reform discourse than to make sure we cover every possible deception.

Preview of the Rest of the Book

Many editors either begin or end a book project with an eye to the organization of the chapters. Somewhat strangely, perhaps, we approached this task of considering how to order this volume's chapters only long after we had received most drafts and worked with authors to make revisions and finalize their contributions. It was only when we at last stepped back from the full collection of these chapters that we appreciated what now impresses us as a quite nifty logic. The chapters in this text fit quite nicely into four sections that move us from lies related to the bigger picture of the contexts of today's schools, to deceptions about our schools' curriculum and their assessment practices, to duplicitous ideas about teachers, and, finally, to lies about schools and policy reforms.

The Big Lies of School Reform includes a foreword by Kevin Kumashiro, a distinguished colleague and critical voice who introduces us to the rhetorical ploys that have twisted our notions of "public" and "public education." Following this introduction, the first section, "The Big Picture," opens with a chapter by Gloria Ladson-Billings, who explores some of the recent and recently historical deceptive characterizations of poor children and policies and practices that neoliberal reformers suggest will best serve them in our schools. Rochelle Gutiérrez examines two of biggest lies upon which our nation's diminishing vision of "public" education is currently founded: the absolute necessity of high-stakes testing and the troubling notion of the "achievement gap."

Of course, these deceptive big-picture reforms and practices must take shape in the everyday content of our schools' lessons and evaluations. Chapters in the second section of this volume, "Curriculum and Assessment," detail the lies behind four of these elements. Anthony Cody opens this section with an exploration of the grand lie of the Common Core: the curricular standards that threaten, yet again, to alter and delimit the very content of what students learn. Curt Dudley-Marling intelligently examines the seemingly age-old notion of "direct instruction," detailing how these narrow, reductive notions of pedagogy are damaging for teachers and students. Jim Cummins follows with a consideration of how the fastest-growing—and potentially most vulnerable—demographic in our schools, immigrant and English-language-learning youth, are least well served by neoliberal deceptions. And Deborah Meier closes this section with a discussion of the unavoidable risks behind the lies of our nation's current assessment addiction.

In "Teachers and Teaching," the third section of our book, we offer two chapters that put faces to the important and shifting sets of individuals who engage with our students, enact these curricula, implement these assessments, and are frequently the subjects of some of the greatest abuses of these lies. Kristien Zenkov explores the deceptions behind the now almost universally accepted notions that anyone can teach and that teacher education is no longer necessary. Then Katy Swalwell cogently details the troubling and flawed idea that teachers' unions are inherently damaging for our students and schools.

In the closing section of this volume, "Schools and Policy," we include four chapters that take two steps back from the classroom-level implications of these lies, first examining school-level impacts and then considering federal- and policy-level effects. Lauren Anderson and Jeannie Oakes provide an incisive exploration of one of the most deeply rooted deceptions in our schools: the idea that tracking students is educationally effective and has a place in a democracy's school system. Paul C. Gorski provides a detailed exploration of some of the ways that misguided assumptions about individuals and communities living in poverty detrimentally impact their school and life prospects. Wayne Au reveals how our increasingly competition-oriented, capitalism-driven approach to schooling is too easily—and erroneously—conflated with effective school reforms. And the chapter by Michelle Renée and Tina Trujillo closes our volume with a keen exploration of how current federal-level education policies not only are rooted in reform effort lies but also result in long-term damage to our students, schools, and communities.

PART I
The Big Picture

1

THE PEDAGOGY OF POVERTY

The Big Lies about Poor Children

Gloria Ladson-Billings

The year 1983 marked a kind of education reform renaissance in the United States with the publication of the now-famous report "A Nation at Risk," prepared by then-President Ronald Reagan's National Commission on Excellence in Education. This document essentially implicated our entire public education system, warning of the dangerous road we were traveling and the seemingly fatal education and economic ends we would meet. It wagged its finger at many aspects of schooling in the United States: the curriculum, schools' organizational structures, and teachers, to name just a few. However, as the resulting so-called reform movement picked up steam, we quickly seemed to shift away from discussing our joint destinies and shared responsibilities to identifying individual culprits. We went from a *nation* at risk to a place where only *certain children* were "at risk." This notion became so pervasive that "at risk" rapidly evolved into a code phrase for poor students, immigrants, and students of color. Indeed, we began talking about poverty as a "culture" rather than a socioeconomic state of being or injustice (Gorski, 2008).

The big lie that emerged from these events was that poor children were a different breed of human being who could not benefit from expansive curricula and innovative pedagogical strategies. Instead, we were told that "at-risk" children needed "basic skills" and classroom instruction that helped bring "order" to their lives. As a consequence, we began to see education "reforms" that tightly regulated the schooling experiences of poor children, particularly in urban schools. In this chapter, I will provide several examples of the kinds of specific restructuring measures that emerged in urban and other schools serving working-class, poor, and increasingly diverse children that reinforced the notion that they needed regimentation to succeed in school.

At Least They Can Look the Part

One of the early "reforms" that took place in urban schools was the introduction of "school uniforms." On the surface, a practical and policy shift focused on students' garb may seem benign. After all, in schools throughout the world—including in the United Kingdom, Japan, Kenya, and Australia—children wear uniforms. Often undocumented is the fact that in what policymakers and now the general public identify as "developing" countries the inability to purchase a uniform often *keeps* students from attending school. The United States has always prided itself on the notion of freedom of individual expression and appreciated that wearing whatever we want is an expression of that freedom. It is true that private schools and church-sponsored schools in the United States have long required their students to wear uniforms. But public schools have almost always operated with a "common school" orientation, where parents and families maintained control over personal decisions—such as whether or not to participate in a school lunch program, whether to grant permission for a student to attend a field trip, or how to dress their individual child (within the boundaries of the school dress code).

The movement to require public school children to wear uniforms seemed to have reasonable justifications. Advocates claimed that wearing uniforms would help minimize the competitiveness to wear certain styles and brands that made poor students feel less worthy (Gursky, 1996). Wearing a school uniform was supposed to help students focus on their studies instead of becoming preoccupied with superficial concerns like clothing (Brunsma & Rockquemore, 2003). Other claims suggested that wearing uniforms would minimize unruly behavior because all children would just "look like students." Unfortunately, none of these claims was supported by research (Brunsma & Rockquemore, 1998). They just sounded like good ideas.

What too few people have considered is the way in which corporate interests benefited from the move to have millions of students in public schools wear mandatory school uniforms. Companies like Sears, J.C. Penney's, and Kohl's turned the push for school uniforms into a very profitable enterprise ("School Uniforms Make the Grade," 1997). In cities like Philadelphia, each school was able to choose its own uniforms. Of course, because Philadelphia serves a large number of working-class and poor students, many families are transient—often moving several times in the course of a year. Each move might mean a shift to a new school, and each new school would likely require the purchase of another school uniform. Yes, corporate interests loved the decision to require school uniforms.

In many of these schools, policing uniform compliance became an administrative preoccupation. In one school in Mobile, Alabama, the teachers complained that much of their time was consumed with determining whether students were wearing their uniforms appropriately. Were the skirts long enough, were the boys wearing belts, and were the uniforms complete (e.g., with the shirt and bottom)? No schools that previously had discipline problems reported marked improvements in student behavior because of these new uniform requirements. But, of course, the prevailing belief was that poor children needed the regimentation of the school uniform to regulate their behavior and, the argument went, allow them to focus more on their academic tasks (Brunsma & Rockquemore, 1998).

What's the Next Line?

As this and other crisis-minded state and national reform efforts took hold, one of the major and most troubling curriculum "innovations" in high-poverty urban schools was the scripted curriculum. Here teachers were given a "script" of every-thing they were to say during a reading lesson (Ede, 2006). No innovation or cre-ativity on the part of the teacher was needed or desired. Instead of being thinking, ethical intellectuals, teachers were reduced to state functionaries who did whatever the teacher's guide prescribed. This form of "teaching" was similar to monitoring a standardized test wherein teachers read verbatim a text that is similar to the fol-lowing: "You will have 20 minutes to complete this section. Please stop at the end of the section. Fill in the bubbles completely. Erase all stray marks on the page."

Hearing teachers speaking in that automaton-like manner once a year is some-thing with which most students have become familiar and to which they are even inured. However, the expectation that teachers teach this way every day further reduced them to low-skilled technicians and downgraded low-income students to apparently empty receptacles that did not need to be engaged like their wealthier peers. This kind of "teaching" could not accommodate students' questions or even the most reasonable and relevant tangents. The learning for poor children in many contexts became prepackaged, predetermined, and rote.

The reduction to scripted curricula was emblematic of the general contraction of the curriculum poor children were to receive. And the imposition of mandated standardized testing for grades 3 through 8 meant that poor children generally had access to a barebones curriculum that focused on reading, writing, and mathemat-ics (Jones et al., 1999). That which was tested was taught. Gone from the typical curriculum taught at schools serving poor children were social studies, science, art, music, physical education, and any form of enrichment (Ede, 2006). The new "script" was determined by the test.

This restriction of the curriculum was a direct response to the call in "A Nation at Risk" for what was euphemistically described as curriculum "coher-ence." According to the report, the curriculum had become unwieldy and out of control, resulting in a buffet of offerings with no central core or commonalities. For poor children it was especially important to teach "the basics" or "fundamen-tals" through stripped-down curricula that were controlled largely by textbook companies and curriculum committees. Individual teachers could no longer be trusted to make curriculum decisions; poor children were entitled to nothing more than rudimentary concepts and pedagogies. This shift was extraordinary in its austerity. Such approaches flew in the face of even compensatory programs such as Head Start or *Sesame Street,* which provided poor children with context and cultural experiences linked to basic skills such as reading and mathematics (Austin, 1977; Minton, 1975).

Now poor children were confined to a steady stream of "drill and kill" routines in their classrooms. Their entire curriculum and schooling experience were tied to preparing for "the test." Their schools, their teachers, and their intellectual identities became synonymous with their performances on standardized tests. Schools, which should provide opportunities for *widening* the world for poor children, were becoming places where their worlds became increasingly *constrained* and *narrow.*

Attention!

Largely but not exclusively the result of the school uniform requirements and the narrowing of the curriculum, schools serving students in poverty became places of strict regimentation. Additionally, students in many of the neoliberal-inspired charter school programs were required to walk down the hallways in absolute silence on black lines painted on the floors (Livingston, 2013). In some schools, children and youth were supposed to hold their hands together behind their backs as they moved about the building or waited to travel from classroom to classroom. In the classroom they were regularly called upon to "track" the teacher—a method of always keeping one's eyes on the teacher (Lemov, 2010). This "methodology" seems almost Skinnerian as teachers hold their hands in the air and ask students to "track."

The sad thing about this kind of regimentation is that it is reminiscent of only one other type of institution: prison. Neoliberal notions of educating the poor rely heavily on keeping them managed and under control. There is no belief in the intellect or imagination of economically impoverished children as the keys to their educational futures. And we could certainly *never* consider their cultures as resources for promoting academic achievement. They are being prepared for a life of compliance while their upper- and upper-middle-class peers engage in higher-level thinking and innovation. Upper-middle-class children are groomed to be entrepreneurs and innovators (or at least technically sophisticated enough to hold good-paying jobs), while poor children are coached and drilled to continue occupying low-skilled, poor-paying, service-sector jobs (Wilson, 1987).

The insistence on strict regimentation and order reinforces the notion that poor children are living chaotic and unruly lives and that schools are their last hope for redemption—the one place that could bring order to their lives. The contrasts between U.S. society's acceptance of these lies and other industrialized nations' embrace of vastly different assumptions and practices are stark. In a recent visit to Sweden I went to a school for "newcomers" (the term for recent immigrants). I was struck by the freedom with which students moved through the corridors. No one asked if they had hall passes. In the cafeteria, small children were allowed to serve themselves from the steam tables. Despite the students' poor performance on the state tests—owing primarily to their lack of fluency in the Swedish language—the teachers offered a full curriculum that included science, social studies, the arts, physical education, sewing, and shop classes. The humanity of the children remained intact despite the trauma of fleeing from war-torn (e.g., Afghanistan, Syria, Somalia) or economically weak (e.g., Greece) nations. These students were seen not as prisoners in their new country but rather as children with the same developmental needs as their wealthier peers.

Does Your Mother Love You?

Another feature of schooling for poor children relates to the ways that their parents and families are regarded. Many of the schooling opportunities available to urban students treat poor parents as if they do not love or know how to care for their own children. Evidence of this perspective is seen in the requirement for parents to sign "contracts" regarding the monitoring and supervision of their children's schoolwork (Coeyman, 1999). It is hard to imagine asking middle-class White parents to sign a document attesting to their willingness to manage and oversee their children's school-related activities. Neoliberal schooling strategies presume that poor parents and families need lessons about how to be responsible, caring adults rather than tutorials about how to deal with hostile and inflexible bureaucracies.

Sadly, the not-so-subtle ways that schools discriminate against the poor is not lost on the children themselves. A few years ago I was in a school composed of poor, working-class, and middle-class students and witnessed a little Black boy crying in the corner of the cafeteria. When I asked him what the problem was, he sobbed, "I don't want to be in that line." His reference was to the fact that children receiving free lunch were required to get in one line, while those who brought a lunch from home were to get in a different line. Bringing a lunch from home symbolized the fact that you had someone at home who cared enough to pack you a meal. A lunch from home made you special.

In another instance, a local newspaper ran a story about an upper-middle-class woman who fixed a hot lunch for her teenaged children and 10 or 12 of their friends every day because the school cafeteria was "too chaotic." Not surprisingly, her children's friends were all also White and middle class. The "chaos" emanated from the Black, brown, and Southeast Asian immigrant students who were making up an increasing proportion of the school's population. The newspaper article was lauding this mother for being a "good" parent.

The idea that poor parents or poor children's extended family members do not know how to parent has a long tradition in education research. Early childhood research suggested that poor mothers did not know how to talk to their children. Comparisons of how many words poor parents utter and the number spoken by middle-class parents to their children have long been conflated with evaluations of "good" parenting. "Good" parents negotiate with their children and offer them choices, and "bad" parents are seen as too directive and authoritarian. "Good" parents ask if children would like to take a seat. "Bad" parents tell children to sit down!

These Children Can't

Lies about poor children are framed by assumptions about their intellectual lives: poor children are defined by what schools believe they *cannot* do rather than by their *potential*. Both anecdotal and research reports are filled with descriptions of thoughtful teachers attempting to do innovative and creative curriculum projects with poor children (Boykin & Noguerra, 2011), only to be thwarted by others who insist that "These children can't do that!" These unchecked assumptions of student incompetence echo throughout urban school systems and those serving poor and increasingly diverse children and turn classrooms into no more than high-cost babysitting services. The presumption that children *can* learn has to be the premise on which we base our practice. When we do not hold that foundational belief in common, we are not working from a shared purpose and we fracture the social contract between citizens and their schools.

It is not enough to espouse platitudes about our confidence that all students can learn. It is important for teachers to recognize the evidence behind such declarations. Those who are familiar with child development know that African American children sit up, crawl, stand, and walk before most other children (Cook & Cook, 2007). But that "advance" does not continue as they move into schools. The early standing, crawling, and walking babies fall quickly behind in the average classroom. What has happened? Now, it is true that not all African American children are poor, but clearly a larger proportion of Black children are poor than of their White counterparts. In social science language, race and poverty "co-vary." But, if African American children, on average, are "ahead" of their White peers in their physical development, what happens to them as they enter school? How do they slip behind their White peers after starting out ahead?

The close connection between race and poverty often leads people to think of them as absolutely synonymous. Thus, even African American children who are from middle-class families are painted with the same brush as their poorer brethren. There is an inherent belief that they cannot perform because they are all thought to be "poor"—economically, intellectually, and culturally.

One of the premises of school desegregation is that it is important to break up concentrations of poverty, not because poor children are incapable of learning but because in an environment of extreme poverty, too many education professionals may presume that the students *cannot* learn (Chavous, 2012). At least in environments in which teachers push students to their maximum potential (as is often the case in middle-class communities), poorer children who are included may have an opportunity to advance along with their middle-class peers.

They Just Don't Want to Work

The belief that the children are *incapable* of learning is too often accompanied by a competing, if similarly unarticulated, conviction that they do not want to work (Ferguson, 2007). This presumption of "laziness" and "slovenliness" extends beyond school-aged children to societal conceptions of poor adults (Quane & Rankin, 1998). However, most of the labor-intensive, backbreaking work done in a society is performed by people in poverty. Many do menial jobs—sometimes two or three at a time. They work long hours, often for minimum wage, yet we claim that they are lethargic or even slothful. This analysis is reminiscent of a time in U.S. history when African slaves worked from sunup to sundown and yet were described as "lazy."

These stereotypes promote a notion that poor children are not succeeding in school because they lack the requisite "work ethic." This is an utterly paradoxical notion precisely because most poor children have seen nothing but work from the time they could understand what it means to live in a family. In poor families it is not unusual for very young children to have work responsibilities such as caring for babies, doing the laundry, or washing the dishes. Whereas middle-class children have the luxury of clubs, teams, and special lessons, most poor children are required to contribute to their families' well-being and survival.

They Don't Value Education

A frequently heard—and often explicit—neoliberal stance intimates that poor children (and their families) do not value education. This is perhaps one of the more egregious lies about poor people. Nothing could be further from the truth. Poor people have a deep devotion to education as the vehicle for advancement—economic, social, and cultural. Rather, poor children (and their families) do not value the "schooling" they are receiving because they are smart enough to realize its inferiority to the education offered to their wealthier peers. The kind of schooling most poor children receive will not open any doors to social and economic advancement. Many of their schools do not prepare them for postsecondary educational opportunities or provide workplace readiness. It is this experience they do not value.

The understanding that children were receiving a substandard education is part of what engendered the modern civil rights movement. People marched, lost jobs, and were beaten, jailed, and killed in order to receive an education. The idea that poor people do not value education is contradicted by almost everything in their history. Unlike their wealthy counterparts, poor people actually believe that education might *improve* their circumstances. Wealthier people tend to understand education or, more specifically, *schooling* as a credentialing mechanism. They realize it is important for their children to get into the "right" schools with the "right" teachers so that they can be admitted into the "right" colleges and universities and ultimately take their "rightful" place in society. This is always a place that advantages them and maintains the status quo.

It's Their Own Fault

Perhaps the biggest and most pernicious lie about poor people is that their poverty is their own faults. As a nation, the United States is not empathic toward the poor. We can sometimes seem sympathetic toward them when we provide a modicum of charity, but, in truth, such charity primarily makes the *donor* feel good. Middle- and upper-income citizens often are happy to write a check or even champion a charitable cause that purports to help the poor. However, few are willing to support major social policy and structural changes that would actually *benefit* the poor.

One of the major examples of our less-than-empathic view of the poor is the major shift in welfare policies that occurred in the early 1990s (Sawhill, 1995). During this time, both individual states and the federal government (at the initiation of the Clinton administration) decided we needed to move poor families (mostly households headed by single mothers) from "welfare to work." Such a slogan sounds good—as if we are making it possible for people to obtain or regain the dignity of being contributing members of society. What such a policy masks is the fact that most welfare recipients lack the marketable skills to move into anything more than minimum-wage jobs and the reality that childcare costs generally eat up a large share of low-wage workers' earnings.

Taking people off welfare makes politicians look good. There is little discussion of the actual impact of attempting to add thousands of low-skilled people to the labor market. Instead, the public discourse typically highlights one egregious case of welfare fraud to bolster the notion that most welfare recipients are undeserving and that their poverty is their own fault. But declaring that poor people are poor solely because of their own bad decisions and unwillingness to work ignores the reality that income disparity has grown more in the past 30 years than at any other time in our nation's history (Waldron & Peck, 2012). Our tax policies are skewed toward the wealthy, and our school financing and segregated communities ensure that poor children will never have access to quality schools. Even the so-called neoliberal education reforms are designed to *remove* quality education from poor communities and to turn the one thing that the poor depend on into a for-profit enterprise.

Logically, poor education for poor people produces poor outcomes. If poor children persist in school, they are less likely to have a quality postsecondary outcome (Webley, 2013). Few have had the opportunity to earn the kind of academic record that makes a four-year college a real option. Some will go on to two-year community or technical colleges, where they are more likely to choose a terminal degree program such as "Certified Nurse Assistant" or "Administrative Assistants" than a liberal arts transfer option that would allow them to move into a four-year institution and enjoy the improved academic and employment prospects that would offer.

And they are the lucky ones. Most will not continue on to postsecondary schooling but instead will end up in a series of low-skilled jobs, mostly in the service sector. These jobs will pay the minimum wage, and even when these young adults attempt to follow society's life patterns that dictate marriage and children, they will not make enough to lift the next generation out of poverty. So, once again, they will produce children who follow the blueprint set for them by the structural inequality that is a part of our society.

Of course, a few poor children will break free of this cycle. These few are held up as evidence that our current system, with its increasing reliance on neoliberal distortions, works. Unfortunately, those exceptions only serve as further grounds for condemning the many who are unable to break free of the grip of structural poverty and social inequity (Fisher, 2012) They allow us to look at those who continue to struggle and surmise that, once again, their poverty is their own fault.

Coda

Throughout this chapter I have attempted to point to some of the persistent myths about education and poor children. I have briefly explored the notions that superficial changes like school uniforms, scripted curricula, prison-like regimentation, and intervention in parenting choices are what A. Wade Boykin calls "transactional" change as opposed to "transformational" change (Boykin, 2009). These modifications and adjustments give the appearance that schools are doing something—but this "something" rarely results in real change for students and their families.

I focused next on the discursive practices that encapsulate our sense of poor children and their families. Some observers argue that poor children are incapable of mastering school tasks, that they do not value education, and that their poverty is their own fault. Neither the remedies mentioned nor these discursive explanations are helpful in moving forth an agenda for truly improving the education of poor children. If we are to take serious our commitment to educate all children, we must recognize the lies, deceptions, and distortions that limit our willingness to create educational experiences that serve all children well.

References

Austin, G., et al. (1977). Some perspectives on compensatory education and inequality. *Contemporary educational psychology, 2,* 311–320.

Boykin, A. W. (2009). What it really takes to improve student outcomes. Retrieved from www.doe.virginia.gov/special_ed/tech_asst_prof_dev/self_assessment/disproportionality/boykin_presentation_9_30_09.ppt

Boykin, A. W., & Noguera, P. (2011). Creating the opportunity to learn: Moving from research to practice to close the achievement gap. Alexandria, VA: ASCD.

Brunsma, D. L., & Rockquemore, K. A. (1998). Effects of student uniforms on attendance, behavior problems, substance use, and academic achievement. *Journal of Educational Research, 92*(1), 53–62.

Brunsma, D. L., & Rockquemore, K. A. (2003). Statistics, sound bites, and school uniforms: A reply to Bodine. *Journal of Educational Research, 97*(2), 72–77.

Chavous, K. P. (2012, October 23). Kids in poverty can still learn. [Web log post]. Retrieved from www.huffingtonpost.com/kevin-p-chavous/poverty-education-children-_b_2003928.html

Coeyman, M. (1999, November 2). Schools make a contract—with parents. *Christian Science Monitor.* Retrieved from www.csmonitor.com/1999/1102/p13s1.html

Cook, J. L., & Cook, G. *The world of children.* (2007). Upper Saddle River, NJ: Pearson.

Gursky, D. (1996). "Uniform" improvement? *The Education Digest, 61*(7), 46–48.

Ede, A. (2006). Scripted curriculum: Is it a prescription for success? *Childhood Education, 83*(1), 29–32. doi:10.1080/00094056.2006.10522871

Ferguson, R. F. (2007). *Toward excellence with equity.* Cambridge, MA: Harvard Education Press.

Fisher, D. (2012, May 5). Poor students are the real victims of college discrimination. [Web log post]. Retrieved from www.forbes.com/sites/danielfisher/2012/05/02/poor-students-are-the-real-victims-of-college-discrimination/

Gorski, P. (2008). The myth of the "culture of poverty." *Educational Leadership, 65*(7), 32–36.

Jones, M. G., Jones, B. D., Hardin, B., Chapman, L., Yarbrough, T., & Davis, M. (1999). The impact of high-stakes testing on teachers and students in North Carolina. *Personality and Individual Differences, 81*(3), 199–203.

Lemov, D. (2010) *Teach like a champion.* San Francisco: Jossey-Bass.

Livingston, D. (2013, September 3). I CAN charter schools directors work to show their model can turn out college-ready kids. *Akron Beacon Journal Online.* Retrieved from www.ohio.com/news/local/i-can-charter-schools-directors-work-to-show-their-model-can-turn-out-college-ready-kids-1.425646

Minton, J. H. (1975). The impact of *Sesame Street* on readiness. *Sociology of Education, 48*(2), 141–151. doi:10.2307/2112472

Quane, J. M., & Rankin, B. H. (1998). Neighborhood poverty, family characteristics, and commitment to mainstream goals: The case of African American adolescents in the inner city. *Journal of Family Issues, 19*(6), 769–794. doi:10.1177/019251398019006006

Sawhill, I. V. (1995). Welfare reform: An analysis of the issues. [Research report]. Retrieved from Urban Institute, www.urban.org/publications/306620.html

"School uniforms make the grade" (1997). *Discount Store News, 36*(16), A36–A38.

Waldron, T., & Peck, A. (2012, November 16). Why income inequality has skyrocketed in the last 30 years. [Web log post]. Retrieved from http://thinkprogress.org/economy/2012/11/16/1204871/why-income-inequality-has-skyrocketed-in-the-last-30-years/

Webley, K. (2013, May 9). We're doing a lousy job of getting poor kids to college. Retrieved from http://nation.time.com/2013/05/09/were-doing-a-lousy-job-of-getting-poor-kids-to-college/

Wilson, W. J. (1987). The obligation to work and the availability of jobs: A dialogue between Lawrence M. Mead and William Julius Wilson. *Focus, 10*(2), 11–19.

2

IMPROVING EDUCATION AND THE MISTAKEN FOCUS ON "RAISING TEST SCORES" AND "CLOSING THE ACHIEVEMENT GAP"

Rochelle Gutiérrez

The United States is one of the most developed countries in the world, yet our students consistently perform poorly or in a mediocre fashion on international comparisons of achievement (AIR, 2005). The results are particularly bleak for Latin@s,[1] Black Americans,[2] English-language learners, American Indians, and students living in poverty, for whom the schooling system has failed. Even when students across the nation make overall gains, as they did in 2011, significant gaps between racial groups remain (Aud et al., 2012). Many Americans are wondering: *How will we improve the state of public education?*

As you read this, millions of students across the nation are being prepared to perform better on standardized tests. They sit and listen while teachers describe how best to prepare for a test: sleep well, eat a good breakfast, work slowly, read test questions several times, and check your answers. Testing consultants regularly visit to offer strategies for raising scores. These consultants remind teachers to focus on "bubble kids," those who are on the brink of passing, in order to help bolster schools' chances for meeting Adequate Yearly Progress requirements. Students take practice tests so that they can identify the kinds of knowledge they possess and the kinds of knowledge they still need to develop in order to pass the tests; they make posters of important information that are then displayed on classroom walls, where they can refer to them while they take the tests. This process seeks to ensure that *all* students are supported fully in order to score as high as possible. In turn, schools, districts, and states use test scores to highlight "student achievement" on publicly available school report cards so that parents can make decisions about which schools are the most rigorous or have the greatest impact on students. Schools that show lower student achievement return to the drawing board and focus again on preparing their students for the next round of tests.

This is good news, right? Student achievement is one of the primary goals of schooling. And teachers, who are juggling many goals, need guidance on how best to use their time. Schools *should* boast about their students' achievement when they get good results, right? Also, as community members, we want to know which schools do not perform well so that we can avoid sending our children to them or figure out a way to make them better. It is encoded in our morals: we need to raise the floor for students who are not faring well in school.

This approach to reforming education might appear to be on target until we come to recognize that doing well on a test does not necessarily mean a student has learned. In fact, we are preoccupied with test scores—in particular the gap between White and Black students—and stuck in the unbridled belief that these scores measure academic success (Gutiérrez, 2008). Liberals and conservatives alike strongly support the goal of closing the test-score gap between low-income youth (often conflated with students of color) and their wealthy (Whiter) peers. However, when we explore further, we see that the "achievement gap" is an attractive distracter, keeping us from addressing gaps in actual *learning*.

In considering this argument, I turn to mathematics, a subject that receives the bulk of testing and that is often the focus of school reform. Understanding the impact of testing on mathematics learning is important because mathematics is the basis of our highly technological society. Mathematics operates as a gatekeeper for other subjects (e.g., the sciences) and for high-earning careers and also serves as a proxy for intelligence in society. So, even people who do not intend to pursue mathematics-related careers find that the consequences of not doing well in mathematics last long into the adult years (Martin, 2006). Let us explore how a focus on test scores and the achievement gap may be the wrong direction for our society.

What's Wrong with Focusing on the Achievement Gap?

First, let us consider what we understand about learning by approaching it from an achievement-gap perspective. Most achievement-gap studies offer little more than a static picture of inequities between broadly defined groups. These studies rely primarily on one-time responses from students and teachers; they do not capture the history or the contexts that created these inequities. Even when researchers identify the factors most associated with the achievement gap (e.g., income, family background), these factors often are outside the spheres of influence of teachers, administrators, and policymakers. That is, teachers cannot change the backgrounds of students they teach. Moreover, because the data are collected during target years (e.g., fourth grade, eighth grade), we never learn how any individual student does over a given period of time—the growth she or he makes after having spent a year in one or more classrooms. Instead, we learn how this year's eighth graders compare to last year's eighth graders, despite the fact that they are not the same students and might not be taking the same test. So, making such comparisons and claiming that schools have "increased" the percentage of students scoring at a particular level may not be accurate; it certainly isn't very precise. Before entering school, the second batch of eighth graders might have already known more mathematics than the previous group of eighth graders. Even longitudinal data tend to be based upon correlations and inferences; researchers never really can pinpoint what *causes* "achievement gaps."

Although researchers have studied the gap extensively, the resulting understandings have not translated into significant progress for students of color and students living in poverty (Lee, 2002; Porter, 2005). In fact, researchers erroneously assume that the factors that cause differences *between* groups can help us improve the situation for a *specific* group. That may not be the case (Lubke, Dolan, Kelderman, & Mellenbergh, 2003). For instance, understanding the factors that cause the economic achievement gap will not necessarily bolster the educational outcomes of low-income students. So any policies we create that are based on those false assumptions (e.g., based on large-scale data sets like the National Assessment of Educational Progress) are wrongheaded.

The main problem with an achievement-gap perspective is not just that it tends to rely on quantitative studies, as there are ways of using quantitative data to inform strategies for bolstering learning, as in longitudinal studies of successful Latin@ students or examinations of their achievement across different contexts. The problem with an achievement-gap perspective is that it relies in many ways on a theoretical lens that supports deficit thinking and negative stereotypes about Latin@s, Black Americans, English-language learners, American Indians, and students living in poverty, among other groups of students. First, an achievement-gap perspective perpetuates the myth that there is more variation in the scores between groups, say between Black and White students, than there is within groups. This myth depicts the achievement gap as the normal state of things, a kind of truth about different racial, language, or economic groups (Herrnstein & Murray, 1994). Yet, research on the malleability of intelligence (Aronson, Lustina, Good, & Keough, 1999) and problems with testing (Gierl, Bisanz, Bisanz, Boughton, & Khaliq, 2001; Wiliam, Bartholomew, & Reay, 2004) suggest that this hierarchy is socially constructed, more an indication of bias than reality. Moreover, most people are unaware that while mean values for these groups may differ, a significant percentage of individual performances overlap. That is, many Latin@s, Black, and White students perform at the same level.

A variety of other equity concerns surround the achievement-gap paradigm:

- The paradigm draws on a static notion of student identity as quantifiable in terms of race, class, gender, language, and other identities. It ignores students' multiple identities and the extra work that marginalized students must do to manage the negative stereotypes about mathematics ability that circulate about their groups (McGee & Martin, 2011; Stinson, 2013).

- The achievement-gap discourse sends an unintended message that marginalized students are not worth studying in their own right—a comparison group is necessary, and it always seems to be the most privileged group. Such a framing further engrains whiteness and middle- to upper-income identities as norms, positioning other groups as "the other."
- The paradigm places groups in opposition to each other. One's gain is the other's loss, potentially fueling insecurities among White and middle- or upper-income families when the gap narrows.
- Concepts like "the gap" (like the term "urban education") serve as safe proxies for discussions about particular groups of students without naming them. It is not the gap but rather specific populations with which we should be concerned. There are many gaps we could choose to focus on that we do not. For example, when White students are compared with Asian and Asian American students, they "underperform," yet the media do not report on White students as deficient or talk about how to get them to be more like Asians.

Hilliard (2003) argues that we should pay more attention to the gap between Black Americans and excellence (as defined within the group) than between Black and White students. Rarely do we acknowledge that even our highest-performing students may not model the excellence we want (Boaler, 1997). That is, some communities may value a tight connection between doing mathematics and the values and practices in their culture as opposed to mere achievement that is measured in school (Meaney, Trinick, & Fairhall, 2013). In fact, a drive for excellence, not parity with Whites, is at the heart of most programs that have produced substantial gains in racially marginalized students' learning (Triesman, 1992). Current gap studies in mathematics education allow researchers to talk about and unconsciously normalize the "low achievement" of Black, Latin@, American Indian, English-language learners, and working-class students without acknowledging racism in society, school-level resources and tracking policies, the low numbers of teachers of color, the fact that the least-qualified teachers are teaching racially and economically marginalized students, or the ways students are reduced to a particular race in schools through disciplinary policies and surveillance. Some researchers have referred to the accumulation of these negative historical, economic, and sociopolitical effects on Black and Latin@ students as the "opportunity gap" (Flores, 2007) or the "education debt" (Ladson-Billings, 2006) to show that the problem lies within our system as opposed to individuals or cultural groups. In the end, although some measures of student progress are sensible, it is irresponsible to continue to frame achievement primarily from a gap perspective.

Adding to this list of concerns is the problem that an achievement-gap perspective on learning has perpetuated the misunderstanding that the problem underlying the gaps (and therefore the solution) is "technical." Most studies attempting to identify factors associated with the achievement gap and therefore potential levers for school improvement are overly focused on tangible character- istics or behaviors: teacher knowledge, use of technology, and pedagogical strate- gies. Because of this narrow focus, these studies suggest that all that is needed to improve learning for *all* students is a better list of good teaching practices (Bartolomé, 2003). These findings tend to ignore big, important systemic factors that underlie educational outcome inequalities, such as the nation's unwillingness to invest sufficient resources in public education, increasingly underappreciated and overworked teachers, the pressures of high-stakes accountability, growing poverty as well as deepening wealth and income gaps, and larger social condi- tions (Ladson-Billings, 2006; Lipman, 2003). In many ways, discrepancies in stan- dardized achievement test scores mirror discrepancies in opportunities and life chances that students from different backgrounds experience in their everyday lives. But how often do we talk about those discrepancies in experiences when trying to understand the achievement gap? How often do we talk about them when we start discussing solutions?

In the end, achievement-gap studies tie us to narrow definitions of learning and equity that ignore these contextual factors. Most professionals, including teachers, would agree that mathematical proficiency constitutes much more than can be measured on standardized tests (National Research Council, 2001), but gap studies tend to be based on measures of basic skills mastery.

Why are we so preoccupied with the achievement gap? Some researchers have suggested we should pay more attention to the kinds of skills that are important in life, such as perseverance, curiosity, conscientiousness, optimism, and self-control (Tough, 2012). They remind us that kids who have not faced real challenges will not be prepared to navigate obstacles later in life. Yet, we continue to turn to rais- ing test scores as our approach to improving schools because the data are readily available and because testing companies and college boards have a vested interest in keeping the status quo.

Wealthy students often attend private or independent schools that do not nec- essarily focus on testing. However, such students still tend to score well on stan- dardized tests and therefore reap the benefits of a system that values those scores. However, even parents of high-performing test takers should be wary. Standardized tests are a limited measure of what students actually know. My experience with many selective and magnet schools in the Midwest suggests that their mathemat- ics curriculum is still quite traditional, preparing students primarily for Advanced Placement tests, rather than fostering creative thinking in mathematical problems, an understanding of the connections between mathematics and other disciplines, a knowledge of how mathematics has been practiced throughout history or in different parts of the world today, or awareness of new (more humanistic) ways to use mathematics in society. In essence, a focus on the achievement gap dis- tracts us from larger goals we should want for our students, including expanding themselves intellectually, having meaningful interactions with peers, understand- ing content in a broader context of history or society, and being able to apply ideas learned in school to out-of-school contexts in order to solve problems in life. In this sense, the gap-gazing fetish affects the learning opportunities of *all* students, not just students of color or students living in poverty.

Students are not the only losers in an education system that focuses obsessively on raising test scores and closing the achievement gap. Teachers also are casualties. The media, through focused news stories and movies like *Waiting for Superman,* have started depicting teachers as the problem underlying the achievement gap. Perhaps as a result, standardized test scores have begun making their way into teacher evaluations. For example, one Washington-based advocacy organization, Data Quality Campaign, is suggesting that we assign teachers, like students, a unique code that ties them to their "training" and then track how well their students perform on standardized tests (Iorio & Adler, 2013). This form of reducing teachers to numbers is similar to reducing students to test scores.

Unfortunately, tying teachers' evaluations and salaries to students' test scores has proved ineffective in impacting real learning. Across the United States, teachers and administrators have felt pressured to help their students cheat on standardized tests or alter their answers after tests have been turned in. Thirty-eight states and the District of Columbia have had confirmed cheating incidents (Schaeffer, 2013). Some researchers have suggested that teachers are beginning to leave the profession as a result of the testing craze (Bagnall, 2013). Certainly, it is affecting teacher and student morale. And, schools of education have seen the number of applicants for teaching credentials decline over the past few years. Moreover, because most schools test almost exclusively in the areas of mathematics and English/reading, some teachers are being evaluated on students whom they have not even taught (Sawchuck, 2013). Rather than rethinking the emphasis on testing, policymakers have suggested we need to create tests in more subjects to cover all of those that teachers teach. The pressure for mathematics and English teachers to pull up their schools' average scores is likely to keep instruction in these subjects from ever moving beyond preparing students for the tests.

A Different Possible Future

If scores on standardized achievement tests capture only a fraction of the issues we think are important to learning, where else should we turn our attention? Elsewhere, I have proposed a framework for thinking about learning and equity (figure 2.1).[3] It contains four dimensions: access, achievement, identity, and power. Achievement is still part of the overall picture. However, standardized test scores contribute less than one-fourth of the components of learning for which we strive.

Access refers mainly to students' opportunities to learn (Nasir & Cobb, 2007). It includes the kinds of material and resources that are available to students, such as teachers being available before, during, and after school; updated and rigorous textbooks and learning materials; advanced technology as a tool for learning;

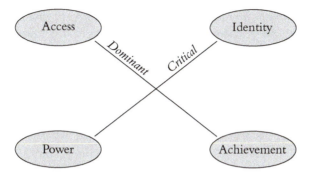

FIGURE 2.1 Dimensions of Equity

teachers who are credentialed in their subjects and engaged in ongoing professional development; classroom environments that invite deep learning; reasonable class sizes; and supports for learning outside class hours. Access is a necessary but insufficient condition for learning, partly because people tend to strive for equal (the same for everybody) access rather than equitable (fair) access. That is, if some students are not performing well in a classroom, they may need greater or different kinds of attention than students who are performing well.

More than just opportunities to learn, we also should concern ourselves with tangible student outcomes, or what I refer to as *achievement*. Although measures of achievement may include standardized test scores, they also should consist of broader student outcomes such as the level of participation in a given class, what types of mathematics courses a student takes and the content covered in those courses, and whether a student continues to participate in a mathematics-based field or career after finishing schooling. Some have referred to this participation as the Science-Technology-Engineering-Mathematics (STEM) pipeline. Course-taking patterns are especially important to consider for older students because those who continue to take mathematics courses after they have fulfilled their requirements for graduation may be experiencing a connection to mathematics or may value the kinds of patterns that mathematics allows us to see in the world around us. Moreover, the type of content covered in courses is also an important measure because many schools have altered their curriculum to include algebra courses that last two years instead of one, giving us a false sense of accomplishment when we see students have passed two math courses.

Access and achievement are the dimensions of learning most touted by policymakers, the media, and mainstream society. Certainly, these dimensions are important, as there are economic and social consequences for not having enough math credits to graduate from high school, not scoring high enough on a standardized test to gain entrance into a college, or not doing well enough in math courses to consider a math-based career that can confer a high salary and prestige.

However, if students are required to park their identities at the classroom door in order to achieve in mathematics, they are not necessarily growing. Students should be able to become better people in their own eyes, not just in the eyes of others (Gutiérrez, 2007).

This is why another important dimension of learning is *identity*, the image students have of themselves while doing mathematics. Identity relates to the fact that mathematics is a cultural practice, that people have been developing mathematics throughout time for centuries. In fact, educational researchers (D'Ambrosio, 2006) and the national professional society for mathematics education (NCTM, 2008) argue in their equity position statement that teachers need to "empower all students to build a relationship with mathematics that is positive and grounded in their cultural roots and history." Measures of success here do not consist merely of recognizing that one's ancestors have contributed to mathematics. They include the extent to which students think they are doers of mathematics, are able to do mathematics in their dominant language, use algorithms from their home countries or cultures, and/or do mathematics problems that build on the expertise they have in their own communities. Identity does not mean that students are treated in essentialistic ways, presuming, for example, that all Latin@s will be motivated to know that Mayans invented the concept of zero. In the end, identity should measure how well a student feels "whole" while doing mathematics.

However, even if students have access to quality mathematics, achieve a high standard of academic outcomes as defined by the status quo, and have opportunities to "be themselves and better themselves" while doing mathematics, there remains more to consider from the point of view of students themselves. This is why a final piece of the equity puzzle involves *power*. This dimension is concerned with voice in the classroom (who gets to talk, who decides the curriculum, and so on), opportunities for students to use mathematics as an analytical tool to critique the world around them. Using an approach referred to as "social justice mathematics," some teachers have had their students survey their communities' experiences with the police to calculate the likelihood that Blacks, Latin@s, and Whites will be pulled over while driving a car (Gutstein, 2006). The students are then able to use mathematics to represent these data and to offer suggestions for change to the local police department. In this way, students are becoming literate citizens and may be more likely to conceptualize the field of mathematics as a humanistic practice that can address real problems.

Access and achievement combined are referred to as the *dominant axis* because they measure how well students "play the game" of mathematics as it currently stands. Identity and power are referred to as the *critical axis* because they challenge the static formalism embedded in traditions of the West; acknowledge that mathematics is not a politically neutral enterprise (see mathematics as a human practice that reflects the agendas, priorities, and framings that people bring to it); and seek to help build critical citizens. This axis relates to students' ability to "change the game." If we care about larger goals than test taking, it is not enough for students to play the game as it currently exists; they must also be able to change it. However, in order to make changes, they must be able to play it well enough (i.e., do mathematics that is recognized by mathematicians). As such, there is a tension inherent in addressing all of these goals—both playing and changing the game.

Addressing all four dimensions simultaneously may not be possible. At times, teachers may need to address goals that help students play the game and at other times goals they may need to help students change the game. For instance, in studying the likelihood of being pulled over by the police, the form of mathematics may involve simple ratios or fractions and can be seen as less rigorous than developing a geometric proof or finding the equation of a line. However, what is required of students in this kind of problem solving involves reasoning and making meaning of the data, connecting the data to one's previous experiences and beliefs about what is fair. If we want our students to be engaged in meaningful and powerful learning, they need to have all four of the dimensions addressed over time.

If we gave as much attention to the dimensions of identity and power as we currently do to achievement, we would see calls for very different instruction. As it stands, an emphasis on increasing test scores and closing the achievement gap leads to more of the same: students sitting at desks as opposed to working in groups or out in the community, teachers lecturing as opposed to kids exploring with one another, a continued focus on getting the right answer as opposed to understanding why something works, getting Black and Latin@ students as well as students living in poverty to measure up to the levels of their White and wealthier peers as opposed to achieving a level of excellence by their own standards. If, on the other hand, we refuse to be distracted by achievement-gap headlines and calls for new reforms that promise to raise test scores, we can redefine student success in ways that are worth striving for all of our students.

Notes

1. I use the @ sign to indicate both an "a" and an "o" ending (Latina and Latino). The presence of both endings decenters the patriarchal nature of the Spanish language, where it is customary for groups of males (Latinos) and females (Latinas) to be written in the form that denotes only males (Latinos). I write the term Latin@ with the "a" and "o" intertwined (as opposed to the more commonly used Latina/o), as a sign of solidarity with individuals who identify as lesbian, gay, bisexual, transgender, questioning, and queer (LGBTQ).

2. I prefer the term Black American, as opposed to African American, to highlight the fact that many Black students living in the United States have ancestry in the Caribbean, South America, and Asia, among other places. Nonetheless, Black students who attend schools and live in the United States are racialized in similar ways, regardless of country of origin.

3. For other goals of mathematics learning, see Martin's (2006) description of *literacy for freedom*, Gutstein's (2006) distinction between *functional literacy* and *critical literacy*, Boaler's

(2006) notion of *relational equity*, the National Council on Education in the Discipline's (2001) focus on *quantitative literacy*, and Keitel and Kilpatrick's (2005) push for *common sense* in mathematics education.

References

American Institutes for Research (AIR). (2005). *Reassessing US international mathematics performance: New findings from the 2003 TIMSS and PISA.* Washington, DC: American Institutes for Research.

Aronson, J., Lustina, M. J., Good, C., & Keough, K. (1999). When white men can't do math: Necessary and sufficient factors in stereotype threat. *Journal of Experimental Social Psychology, 35,* 29–46.

Aud, S., Hussar, W., Johnson, F., Kena, G., Roth, E., Manning, E., Wang, X., and Zhang, J. (2012). *The condition of education 2012 (NCES 2012–045).* U.S. Department of Education, National Center for Education Statistics. Washington, DC. Retrieved March 20, 2013, from http://nces.ed.gov/pubsearch

Bagnall, J. (2013). Too many teachers are quitting, experts warn. *The Montreal Gazette,* February 1, 2013. Retrieved March 10, 2013, from www.canada.com/mobile/iphone/story.html?id=7907873

Bartolomé, L. (2003). Beyond the methods fetish: Toward a humanizing pedagogy. In A. Darder, M. Baltodano, & R. D. Torres (Eds.), *The critical pedagogy reader* (pp. 408–429). New York: RoutledgeFalmer.

Boaler, J. (1997). Setting, social class and survival of the quickest. *British Educational Research Journal, 23*(5), 575–595.

Boaler, J. (2006). Promoting respectful learning. *Educational Leadership, 63*(5), 74–78.

D'Ambrosio, U. (2006). *Ethnomathematics: Link between traditions and modernity.* London: Sense Publishers.

Flores, A. (2007). Examining disparities in mathematics education: Achievement gap or opportunity gap? *The High School Journal, 91*(1), 29–42.

Gierl, M. J., Bisanz, J., Bisanz, G. L., Boughton, K. A., & Khaliq, S. N. (2001). *Illustrating the utility of differential bundle functioning analyses to identify and interpret group differences on achievement tests.* Paper presented at the meeting of the American Educational Research Journal, Seattle. Retrieved October 1, 2007, from www.education.ualberta.ca/educ/psych/crame/

Gutiérrez, R. (2007). Context matters: Equity, success, and the future of mathematics education. In T. Lamberg & L. R. Wiest (Eds.), *Proceedings of the 29th annual meeting of the North American Chapter of the International Group for the Psychology of Mathematics Education* (pp. 1–18). Stateline (Lake Tahoe), Nevada. University of Nevada, Reno.

Gutiérrez, R. (2008). A "gap gazing" fetish in mathematics education? Problematizing research on the achievement gap. *Journal for Research in Mathematics Education, 39*(4), 357–364.

Gutstein, E. (2006). Driving while Black or Brown: The mathematics of racial profiling. In J. Masingila (Ed.), Teachers engaged in research: Inquiry into mathematics practice in grades 6–8 (pp. 99–118). Reston, VA: National Council of Teachers of Mathematics.

Herrnstein, R. J., & Murray, C. (1994). *The bell curve: Intelligence and class structure in American life.* New York: Free Press.

Hilliard, A. G., III (2003). No mystery: Closing the achievement gap between Africans and excellence. In T. Perry, C. Steele, & A. G. Hilliard (Eds.), *Young, gifted, and black: Promoting high achievement among African American students* (pp. 131–165). Boston: Beacon Press.

Iorio, J. M., & Adler, S. M. (2013). Take a number, stand inline, better yet, be a number, get tracked: The assault of longitudinal data systems on teaching and learning. *Teachers College Record.* Published online at www.tcrecord.org/Content.asp?ContentID=17051. Downloaded on March 10, 2013.

Keitel, C., & Kilpatrick, J. (2005). Mathematics education and common sense. In J. Kilpatrick, C. Hoyles, & O. Skovsmose (Eds.), *Meaning in mathematics education* (pp. 105–128). New York: Springer.

Ladson-Billings, G. (2006). From the achievement gap to the education debt: Understanding achievement in U.S. schools. *Educational Researcher, 35*(7), 3–12.

Lee, J. (2002). Racial and ethnic achievement gap trends: Reversing the progress towards equity? *Educational Researcher, 31*(1), 3–12.

Lipman, P. (2003). *High stakes education: Inequality, globalization, and urban school reform.* New York: Routledge.

Lubke, G., Dolan, C. V., Kelderman, H., & Mellenbergh, G. J. (2003). On the relationship between sources of within- and between-group differences and measurement invariance in the common factor model. *Intelligence, 31,* 543–566.

Martin, D. (2006). Mathematics learning and participation as racialized forms of experience: African American parents speak on the struggle for mathematics literacy. *Mathematical Thinking and Learning, 8*(3), 197–229.

McGee, E. O., & Martin, D. (2011). You would not believe what I have to go through to prove my intellectual value!: Stereotype management among successful black mathematics and engineering students. *American Educational Research Journal, 48*(6), 1347–1389.

Meaney, T., Trinick, T., & Fairhall, U. (2013). One size does not fit all: Achieving equity in Maori mathematics classrooms. *Journal for Research in Mathematics Education, 44*(1), 235–263.

Nasir, N. S., & Cobb, P. (Eds.). (2007). Improving access to mathematics: Equity and diversity in the classroom. New York: Teachers College Press.

National Council of Teachers of Mathematics (NCTM). (2008). Equity in mathematics education. Retrieved March 20, 2008, from www.nctm.org/about/content.aspx?id=13490

National Council on Education in the Disciplines. (2001). *Mathematics and democracy: The case for quantitative literacy.* Washington, DC: Author.

National Research Council. (2001). *Adding it up: Helping children learn mathematics.* Washington, DC: National Academy Press.

Porter, A. (2005). Prospects for school reform and closing the achievement gap. In C. A. Dwyer (Ed.), *Measurement and research in the accountability era* (pp. 59–98). Mahwah, NJ: Lawrence Erlbaum.

Sawchuck, S. (2013). Florida unions sue over test-score-based evaluations. *Education Week.* Retrieved April 16, 2013, from www.edweek.org/ew/articles/2013/04/16/29lawsuit.h32.html

Schaeffer, B. (2013). *Standardized exam cheating confirmed in 37 states and DC: New report shows widespread test score corruption.* National Center for Fair and Open Testing. Retrieved March 27, 2013, from www.fairtest.org/2013-Cheating-Report-PressRelease

Stinson, D. (2013). Negotiating the "white male math myth": African American male students and success in school mathematics. *Journal for Research in Mathematics Education, 44*(1), 69–99.

Tough, P. (2012). *How children succeed: Grit, curiosity, and the hidden power of character.* New York: Houghton Mifflin.

Treisman, U. (1992). Studying students studying calculus: A look at the lives of minority mathematics students in college. *College Mathematics Journal, 23,* 362–372.

Wiliam, D., Bartholomew, H., & Reay, D. (2004). Assessment, learning, and identity. In P. Valero & R. Zevenbergen (Eds.), *Researching the socio-political dimensions of mathematics education: Issues of power in theory and methodology* (pp. 43–61). Norwell, MA: Kluwer.

PART II

Curriculum and Assessment

3

THE COMMON CORE

Engine of Inequity

Anthony Cody

The people and organization advancing the Common Core suggest that a common set of standards, with assessments to match, will deliver equitable outcomes from our schools. This is the same siren call that was sung more than a decade ago for No Child Left Behind.

As No Child Left Behind was becoming one of the most unpopular laws in the nation, around 2006 or 2007, political leaders sought ways to rescue standards and tests from their ignominy. NCLB had been faulted for several things. First, because it allowed each state to select its own set of tests and set its own proficiency levels, more than 80 percent of the students in Kentucky were rated as "proficient" while fewer than half the students in Massachusetts achieved this mark. Arne Duncan, Secretary of Education under President Barack Obama, has made it clear that his goal is not to remove pressure to perform well on tests but to make them more efficient, rational, and pervasive.

Another irrational aspect of NCLB has been its focus on math and reading as the chief basis for school accountability. This has led many low-income schools to focus almost exclusively on these two subjects at the expense of physical education, art, history, and even science. The Department of Education's solution for this is to greatly expand the subjects that will be tested. As of 2013, new tests covering almost every subject at almost every grade level were being scheduled to be rolled out over the next few years. As Duncan promised in 2010, schools will get new tests that will be "smarter" than those dumb old bubble tests. In his speech "Beyond the Bubble Tests," he explained:

> For the first time, teachers will consistently have timely, high-quality formative assessments that are instructionally useful and document student

growth—rather than just relying on after-the-fact, year-end tests used for accountability purposes.

For the first time, state assessments will make widespread use of smart technology. They will provide students with realistic, complex performance tasks, immediate feedback, computer adaptive testing, and incorporate accommodations for a range of students.

(Duncan, 2010)

The new tests will be so "smart" that students will have to take them on computers. And the computers are even smarter and can grade them for us! So teachers can give the tests more often, and that will allow us to track student progress more accurately than ever. And we can pay teachers more for better results, which will reward the good teachers and weed out the bad ones. And everyone, from California to New York to Mississippi, will be subject to the same standards, assessments, and curriculum, so all students will have the same opportunity to show how smart they are, and we will at last reach that promised land of equity for all.

Each fall, the introduction of a battery of tests to allow for the measurement of "growth" at the level of the individual teacher will effectively double the amount of testing. In addition, "formative" tests are in the works, designed to be given at regular intervals through the year. Teachers in Seattle have experienced this innovation firsthand in the form of the Measures of Academic Progress (MAP) assessments. These are among the "Next Generation" tests touted by Duncan several years ago. They are "computer-adapted tests," meaning that as students begin answering questions, the test gauges their ability and gives them easier or harder questions going forward. While ideally this allows for a more accurate test, in practice many students discover that if they intentionally do poorly on the first batch of questions, the rest of the test is a breeze.

The fundamental premise driving all of this is that students in poverty suffer because of the low standards that have been set for them. They suffer because the "bar" has been set too low, and if we can just manage to set one bar across the land and all get on the same page, we will pull everyone up to the same level. There is also an implied promise that technological innovations, usually computer based, will allow for great leaps forward, once a national market has been created.

We've Got Problems

The root source of this idea is businesspeople like Bill Gates, who made it clear in his 2013 annual letter that, for him, the most valuable thing schools can do to improve is to measure and set goals for improvement (Gates, 2013). This is hardly a new idea. It has its roots in the work of Frederick Taylor, who brought us a whole new realm of endeavor in the 1920s: the measurement of efficiency in production. Charlie Chaplin's 1936 movie *Modern Times* provided a satirical treatment of this endeavor, depicting a factory worker whose every movement has been studied and predetermined for maximum efficiency. Our current generation of Gatesian technocrats has added a patina of innovation to this concept through the magic of "data." Instead of time-motion studies, we have ever-finer-grained analysis of student performance and ever tighter links to teacher behaviors to help us to all to improve.

It is clear why business leaders are attracted to this sort of thinking. In business, the relentless search for internal efficiency in production and management is key to beating one's competitors. But what is good for assembly lines and sales associates is not necessarily good for growing children.

There is not much evidence that the Common Core will achieve what proponents claim. To start, this is hardly the first time we have tried to lift all students through common academic standards. Many U.S. states are as large as or large than, many nations. Each state has a set of standards that all students are expected to meet and that shape assessments and curriculum. If a common high bar will deliver equitable outcomes nationwide, why have we not seen equitable outcomes within states with standardized systems?

When Duncan suggests that the formative tests he advocates are an innovation, he demonstrates his ignorance of the true nature of formative assessment. Experienced teachers do *not* lack the means to carry out formative assessments of their students, which are best done in the context of classroom instruction. But the plan is to externalize *all* assessment, to make the teacher a technician who passively delivers the "expertly designed" curriculum and assessments.

We are moving toward an educational process that is mediated every step of the way by assessments and benchmarks, so that all students are led through a carefully prescribed sequence of lessons, with benchmarked expectations frequently measured and reported on and teacher pay meted out like so many food pellets to a trained pigeon.

The Promise of a National Market

One promise that Common Core proponents appear to be delivering on is the creation of a national market for tests and curricula. In 2011, Arne Duncan's chief of staff, Joanne Weiss, wrote this:

> The development of common standards and shared assessments radically alters the market for innovation in curriculum development, professional development, and formative assessments. Previously, these markets operated on a state-by-state basis, and often on a district-by-district basis. But the adoption of common standards and shared assessments means that education entrepreneurs will enjoy national markets where the best products can be taken to scale.
>
> (Weiss, 2011)

In 2009, Bill Gates said,

> In terms of standards, the state-led Common Core State Standards initiative is developing clear, rigorous standards that will match the best in the world. Last month, 46 governors and chief state school officers made a public commitment to embrace those standards. This is encouraging; but identifying common standards is just the starting point. We'll only know if this effort has succeeded when the curriculum and tests are aligned to these standards. . . . For the first time there'll be a large uniform base of customers looking at using products that can help every kid learn and every teacher get better.
>
> (Gates, 2009)

Any perusal of education-industry trade journals reveals this market in full effect, with professional organizations such as the ASCD (formerly the Association for Supervision and Curriculum Development) enthusiastically on board as expert implementers. The designers of this system have intentionally created a positive feedback loop. Opportunities are created for companies to make money from curriculum, tests, and professional development, and then this money is used to promote more of the same, with the illusion that real learning is being served. They are creating something akin to the military-industrial complex President Eisenhower warned us of fifty years ago—a test-driven machine fueled by profits.

Hopes Raised, Then Dashed

Many teachers are excited by the prospect of new standards and assessments. We are weary of the bubble tests aligned with state standards. The new standards talk of critical thinking, and the new tests, we are told, will be so much better. In many places teachers are being invited to participate in the creation of new curricula aligned with the standards. Adam Heenan, a teacher in Chicago, reported to me that over the summer of 2012, teachers were asked to develop performance assessments aligned with the Common Core standards. However, when the teachers returned to work in August, they were given boxes of canned Common Core curricula and assessments that had been purchased from Pearson. The work they had done, just like that, was undone (Heenan, 2012).

The promoters of the Common Core assert that the standards offer only a framework and that teachers are still responsible for designing lessons and delivering instruction. But as our colleagues in Chicago discovered, in the top-down world driven by high-stakes assessments, standards become mandates, and these mandates are best served by packaged curricula. Teacher autonomy becomes a quaint relic. That is the experience of many teachers, particularly in high-poverty districts and schools.

Preparing for College in Kindergarten

The Common Core also brings a greater emphasis on "college readiness." This drive is already being used to justify tests for students beginning as early as kindergarten, because schools must meet annual benchmarks. In order to meet all the benchmarks, the Common Core pushes skills and concepts into lower grade levels than ever before, a process that is termed "rigor." Unfortunately, this results in a curriculum that is beyond what is appropriate for young children. The Common Core in effect "backwards maps" skills and content on the assumption that we intend to prepare everyone for college. This winds up pushing some very high benchmarks down into kindergarten. As Carol Burris, a New York principal, noted,

> The Common Core Standards expect that four- and five-year-olds will count to 100 by ones and tens and will write the numbers from 0 to 20. However, childhood learning experts not only stress that each child will develop differently, they set counting skills for five year olds not from 1 to 100, but to 20 at age 5 and to 30 between the ages of 5 and 6.
>
> (Burris, 2013)

Kris Nielsen, a teacher, last year quit his job over concern about the ways tests have become central to our schools. In his book, *Children of the Core,* he shares this passage from a *third-grade* reading assignment aligned to the Common Core:

> Mount Everest is considered the highest mountain—above sea level—in the world, but it's not really the tallest. Measured from its base on the floor of the ocean, Mauna Kea, in Hawaii, is 33,476 feet tall. Only the top 13,796 feet of Mauna Kea are above sea level.

The reading alone is more than challenging for most third graders, but look at the question prompt that came with it (Neilsen, 2013):

1. Mount Everest is the highest mountain, but Mauna Kea is the tallest mountain. Write the reason that the tallest and the highest mountain are not the same. Provide evidence to support your answer. (p. 57) (Neilsen, 2013)

Those administering the test seem to be cognizant of the stress it is likely to cause. Administrators in New York distributed guidelines for parents of elementary-school students taking the tests described, telling them:

> Let your child know that these tests are meant to be really hard. That's because they are designed to measure whether students are on track for college and a good job when they finish high school.
>
> (New York City Department of Education, 2013)

The state administrators want parents to understand—if the test is "really hard," it is necessary, because this will whip the students into shape for the job market of 2025.

Doubling the Number of College Graduates

The Common Core has been sold as part of a grand plan to increase the number of students "college and career ready." Bill Gates has a goal of doubling the number of students who graduate from college, and the rhetoric of education reform suggests this will somehow translate into economic prowess for our country (Kamanetz, 2013). However, there does not appear to be a strong economic basis for this push. The story goes that the reason for rising unemployment is that the people graduating from our schools are not prepared for college and careers. But when we look at the best projections available for where jobs will be in the coming decade, we find a different story.

Recent Bureau of Labor Statistics projections of job openings going forward to 2018 suggest that 23 percent of jobs will require a bachelor's degree or a more advanced degree. Approximately 67 percent of job openings will require a high school diploma or less (Lacey & Wright, 2009). The Chicago branch of the Federal Reserve studied the demand for workers at various skill levels and in a 2012 report found no particular demand for skilled workers (Faberman & Mazumder, 2012). Research by Marc Levine at the University of Wisconsin confirms this. Levine states:

> The consensus among top economists is that the skills gap is a myth. High unemployment is mainly the result of a deficiency in aggregate demand and slow economic growth, not because workers lack the right education or skills. The skills of the labor force did not suddenly erode between 2007 and 2009, when the unemployment rate more than doubled, so it makes no sense to claim that high unemployment in 2009 and through today has been caused by a soaring number of "unqualified" workers.
>
> (Levine, 2013)

So the urgency with which the Common Core has been promoted is largely false. Our economy is not lagging because of a lack of college graduates, and, in fact, it will have great difficulty absorbing a significant increase in college graduates looking for jobs that reflect their educational attainment. If laws of supply and demand remain in effect, an increase in the number of people with college degrees may actually reduce their level of pay and job security, because there will be such a surplus of applicants. But that is not a prospect likely to disturb the corporate sponsors of the project. There are reasons beyond employment for students to attend college, of course—but the economic rationale driving the Common Core is weak indeed.

Raising the Bar and Lowering the Boom on Students

How is this rising pressure to perform on tests affecting our students? According to a report from the Alliance for Childhood (2011) for which more than 4,000 U.S. teachers were surveyed, three- and four-year-old children are being expelled at three times the national rates for K–12 students, and 4.5 times more boys than girls were being expelled. Amazingly, the rate of expulsion at these schools was related to the amount of play encouraged at the schools: more play equaled fewer expulsions. This same report reveals how, in Germany, when researchers compared students in kindergartens focused on cognitive achievement and those from play-based schools, they found that children who had played at school were much better off—more advanced in reading and math and better adjusted socially and emotionally. They were more creative and expressive, as well. As a result of this study, German kindergartens brought play back to its preschools (Almon & Miller, 2011).

When Kyung Hee Kim studied creativity among children, she found a disturbing trend downward (Bronson & Merryman, 2010). This decline in creativity corresponds with warnings from Yong Zhao, who has pointed out that the United States is in danger of killing the creative goose that laid our golden egg. As we are embracing testable standards as the route to success, educators in China are doing their best to escape the trap of high-stakes tests. And, as Yong Zhao also points out, high scores on the international PISA test have not yielded economic growth but actually correlate with diminished innovation and entrepreneurship (Zhao, 2012). Insofar as the Common Core represents an extension and enhancement of our emphasis on improvement via standards and associated tests, it is likely to extend this decline in creativity.

The Promise of Failure

The early returns are already in from Common Core tests in Kentucky, where proficiency levels dropped by 30 percent in the first couple years of testing (Morella, 2012). In New York, there are similar projections of a rising level of failure from the new Common Core–aligned tests being taken in 2013.

Given the fact that this entire project has been carefully engineered by advocates of free-market reform whose aim is to "disrupt" the public school monopoly, it is not a stretch to suggest that failure is actually their desired outcome for our students and schools. A recent report on National Public Radio lent credence to this theory. After having Gates Foundation–funded experts inform listeners about how states had become adept at lowering proficiency standards to avoid negative consequences under NCLB, reporter Cory Turner suggested:

> Now, under the more rigorous Common Core standards, it will be harder for states to hide their failing schools. But what has Common Core watchers

nervous is not that states will cheat but that the first round of student scores in 2015 will be honest, and bad—so bad they shock parents and strike fear into politicians.

(Turner, 2013)

After all, the dismal indictment from No Child Left Behind has worn a bit thin. People have decided the multiple-choice tests were flawed and have begun to question the wisdom of closing schools on the basis of their performance on the NCLB tests. What better way to convince the public that the public schools are to blame for our problems than to introduce a whole new set of standards and tests to nail down the verdict?

The False Promise of Technocracy

New technology is unlikely to solve the problems the previous generation of testing technology created. Promoters of the Common Core have suggested that the new tests will take us "beyond the bubble tests," but the problem is not within the bubbles or the Scantron forms. The problem is that we are trying to improve teaching in the backwards way that an overly simplistic, data-driven system requires. Instead of challenging teachers to find the best ways to engage their students, we are giving them lists of standards and scripted curricula to use to meet them. We replace the expectation that teachers will excite and inspire their students to take on new challenges with the expectation that they will deliver a predetermined lesson in which even student responses are anticipated.

Technology arriving with the "Next Generation" of assessments allows student essays to be almost instantly scored by a computer, using an algorithm that looks at the vocabulary and sentence structure and even provides students with detailed and specific feedback about these things. But the computer cannot actually understand the real meaning of what the students have written. It is not a genuine audience with the ability to form a meaningful relationship with students. In this paradigm, writing has become a technical exercise to be perfected, not a means of communicating ideas or thoughts.

An Alternative Vision: Accountability Based in Our Communities

Doug Christensen was the Commissioner of Education in Nebraska, which resisted the grips of NCLB longer than any other. It did this through a system of assessments that were developed at district and regional levels. In Dr. Christensen's view,

Assessment and accountability must have their locus of action and policy at the local level and in the hands of educators and local policy leaders. Name a profession that is not in charge of their [sic] own metrics of success and the metrics of what is good practice? Lawyers are in charge of theirs. Medical doctors are in charge of theirs. So are accountants, nurses, bankers, and even morticians. Why aren't educators? Why aren't the local folks in charge and accountable?

(Cody, 2010)

Julian Vasquez Heilig has applied a similar framework in developing what he terms "Community Based Accountability" (CBA). According to the Executive Summary of the CBA framework, "CBA involves a process where superintendents, school boards, school staff, parents, students and community stakeholders create a plan based on set short-term and long-term goals based on their local priorities" (Cody, 2013). This locally designed plan would take the place of the current intrusive federal supervision.

This approach is also embedded in recent steps taken by California governor Jerry Brown to return more autonomy to local school districts, using a framework he terms "subsidiarity," which is "the idea that a central authority should only perform those tasks which cannot be performed at a more immediate or local level." Higher levels of government should be there to assist and support, but they should respect the jurisdiction of local school districts and the autonomy of teachers and students. In other words, higher or more remote levels of government, such as the state, should render assistance to local school districts but always respect their primary jurisdiction and the dignity and freedom of teachers and students (Brown, 2013).

Conclusion

In the end, the Common Core offers a series of educational promises that are false, balanced by marketing promises that are rapidly coming true. Our schools do not suffer from any lack of rigor, and pushing skills downward toward kindergarten will not yield better outcomes. Instead, we will produce students and schools once again labeled failures for no sound reason. We have the stick for students and schools and plenty of carrots for vendors of curricula, tests, data systems, and training services aligned with the standards.

We need to reexamine our goals and realize that students ought not to be driven by the demand to perform on tests. Teachers should not be driven to prepare everyone for the future our technocrats have preordained. Some curricular guidelines might be appropriate, but these should be defined as close to our communities as possible. Our communities should play a strong role in supporting schools and making sure that the curriculum is preparing students well for life beyond school. Schools should be accountable to parents, students, and their communities, not to a national testing system, no matter how technologically advanced.

Five years from now, we will look back on the Common Core much as we now look back on No Child Left Behind, as yet another exercise in social engineering gone awry. Just like NCLB, the Common Core is an engine of inequity. The technocrats rarely see the flaws in their plans, so it will be up to teachers, students, and parents to turn the page and begin creating a new chapter in our schools, driven not by standardized test scores but by human imagination and creativity. That is a book waiting to be written.

References

Alliance for Childhood. (2011). *The crisis in early education.* New York, NY: Author.

Almon, J., & Miller, E. (2011). The Crisis in Early Education; A Research-based Case for More Play and Less Pressure. Alliance for Childhood. Retrieved from www.allianceforchildhood.org/sites/allianceforchildhood.org/files/file/crisis_in_early_ed.pdf

Bronson, P., & Merryman, A. (2010). The Creativity Crisis. *Newsweek.* Retrieved from www.thedailybeast.com/newsweek/2010/07/10/the-creativity-crisis.html

Brown, J. (2013). State of the State Address. Retrieved from http://gov.ca.gov/news.php?id=17906

Burris, C. (2013, March 11). 'Storm of Reform'—Principal Details Damage Done. Retrieved from www.washingtonpost.com/blogs/answer-sheet/wp/2013/03/11/storm-of-reform-principal-details-damage-done/

Cody, A. (2010, November 15). Doug Christensen: Local Initiative, Self-determination and Leadership Are the ONLY Thing. Retrieved from http://blogs.edweek.org/teachers/living-in-dialogue/2010/11/doug_christensen_local_initiat.html

Cody, A. (2013, February 12). Could Community-Based Accountability Get the Federal Government Out of Our Schools? Retrieved from http://blogs.edweek.org/teachers/living-in-dialogue/2013/02/could_community_based_accounta.html

Duncan, A. (September 2, 2010). Beyond the Bubble Tests: The Next Generation of Assessments. Speech to state leaders at Achieve's American Diploma Project Leadership Team Meeting.

Faberman, R. J., & Mazumder, B. (2012). Is There a Skills Mismatch in the Labor Market? Letter from the Chicago Federal Reserve. Retrieved from www.chicagofed.org/digital_assets/publications/chicago_fed_letter/2012/cfljuly2012_300.pdf

Gates, B. (2013). Bill Gates 2013 Annual Letter. Retrieved from http://annualletter.gatesfoundation.org/#

Gates, Bill (2009, July 28). Bill Gates at the National Conference of State Legislatures (clip 5). [YouTube]. Gates Foundation. Retrieved from www.youtube.com/watch?v=xtTK_6VKpf4??

Heenan, A. (2012, August 24). Personal communication.

Kamanetz, A. (2013, April 15). Bill Gates on Education: 'We Can Make Massive Strides.' Retrieved from www.fastcompany.com/3007841/tech-forecast/bill-gates-education-we-can-make-massive-strides

Lacey, A., & Wright, B. (2009). Occupational Employment Projections to 2018. *Monthly Labor Review.* Retrieved from www.bls.gov/opub/mlr/2009/11/art5full.pdf

Levine, M. (2013). The Skills Gap and Unemployment in Wisconsin; Separating Fact from Fiction. University of Wisconsin–Milwaukee Center for Economic Development. Retrieved from www4.uwm.edu/ced/publications/skillsgap_2013–2.pdf

Morella, M. (2012). Common Core Standards: Early Results from Kentucky Are In. *US News and World Report.* Retrieved from www.usnews.com/opinion/articles/2012/12/04/common-core-standards-early-results-from-kentucky-are-in

Neilsen, K. (2013). *Children of the Core.* Scotts Valley, CA: CreateSpace.

New York City Department of Education (2013). *Tips for talking with your child about the Common Core Standards and changing state tests.* New York, NY: Author.

Turner, C. (July 5, 2013). Education Reform Movement Learns Lesson from Old Standards. *Morning Edition.* National Public Radio.

Weiss, J. (2011, March 31). The Innovation Mismatch: 'Smart Capital' and Education Innovation. Retrieved from http://blogs.hbr.org/innovations-in-education/2011/03/the-innovation-mismatch-smart.html

Zhao, Yong, (2012, July 17). Doublethink: The Creativity-Testing Conflict. *Education Week.* Retrieved from www.edweek.org/ew/articles/2012/07/18/36zhao_ep.h31.html

4

DIRECT INSTRUCTION

Effectively Teaching Low-Level Skills

Curt Dudley-Marling

A veteran Michigan teacher I know attended a mandatory workshop recently to learn about *Reading Mastery,* a *Direct-Instruction*-based approach to reading instruction that her district was adopting. Several days of training to implement scripted reading lessons focused on low-level skills, and the use of finger snaps to mark the call-and-response rhythm of the lessons persuaded her that the time had come for her to retire. She had no taste for the prescriptive, mind-numbing lessons that failed to treat her as a knowledgeable professional with nearly 40 years of teaching experience and did not respect her students as the thoughtful, intelligent people that they were.

There has been a proliferation of scripted, basic-skills programs in U.S. schools, particularly in reading and math, since the implementation of the No Child Left Behind Act of 2001. The attraction of such programs is that they are, presumably, efficient and effective; specifically, these programs can be implemented without expensive teacher training, and they are presumed to be "research based." In other words, school officials who adopt these programs believe that they work by achieving desirable results at relatively low costs.

In this chapter I challenge the claim that *Direct Instruction (DI)* and other scripted programs achieve better outcomes at lower costs. I conclude that prescriptive, basic-skills programs like *Direct Instruction* are neither efficient nor effective and, therefore, are not in the interests of students, teachers, or parents. These sorts of reforms do fit well within a particular policy context, however. Prescriptive curricula have especially high value in the context of market-based school restructuring that currently dominates education reform in the United States (and other English-speaking countries). Therefore, I begin with a brief discussion of the ideology of free-market schooling.

A Market-Based Approach to Schooling

Public policy in the United States and in other Western countries is increasingly being driven by free-market ideologies that are based on the belief that competition necessarily leads to the efficient and effective delivery of various goods and services. From this perspective, the ideal role of government is limited to keeping people safe from criminal behavior and foreign threats and preserving the rules of the free market. Further, governments are expected to leave to the markets services, including utilities, transportation, and education, that could be more efficiently—and profitably—delivered by the private sector (Harvey, 2005). In his seminal article on the role of government in education, the economist Milton Friedman (1955) argued for a competitive schooling system based on vouchers that parents would be free to use at any school of their choosing. In Friedman's formulation of public schooling, the role of government would be limited to ensuring that schools meet certain minimum standards.

Over the years, Milton Friedman's goal of a competitive schooling system based on vouchers has garnered the enthusiastic support of conservative politicians and many people in the business community. However, political resistance and various legal challenges[1] to vouchers have forced free-market advocates to seek alternative ways to discipline American schools in the ways of the market. No Child Left Behind (NCLB), for example, imposes a range of market-inspired reforms on American schools, including "accountability, high-stakes testing, data-driven decision making, choice, charter schools, privatization, deregulation, merit pay, and competition among schools" (Ravitch, 2010, p. 21).

The rapid expansion of charter schools represents the most significant achievement of people eager to expose public schools to the competitive forces of the free market.[2] Charters function as quasi-market schools (Whitty, Power, & Halpin, 1998) that are subject to many but not all of the regulations that govern traditional public schools, although specific regulations vary by state. Charters are presumed to offer parents (read: consumers) choice, thereby forcing traditional public schools to compete for students to survive. For-profit charters, as is apparent by the name, are also expected to make a profit. To make this system of choice work, parents require information regarding the relative effectiveness of the schools among which they are choosing. Writing in the *Washington Post,* the conservative commentator Michael Gerson (2013) observed:

> The main problem of American primary and secondary education is . . . [that] it is a market with insufficient information and choices, resulting in poor quality. We don't have standards and measurements that allow us to adequately compare the outcomes between students, between schools and between states.

The use of research-based practices offers an indirect measure of a school's potential effectiveness, but, in the context of market-based schooling, parents also require data on how effectively teachers utilize these practices. The high-stakes, standardized testing regimes that have been implemented across the United States are intended to provide both the marketing data parents require to make informed choices and the motivation teachers need to excel, since schools that cannot compete will fail to attract enough students to survive. This is the logic of the market.

The logic of the market also requires the instruction to be efficient, respecting what is claimed to be increasingly scarce taxpayer dollars. Charters, models for free-market schooling, achieve lower instructional costs by hiring less experienced teachers (Miron & Urschel, 2010; Center for Public Education, 2012) and by utilizing standardized, highly scripted programs, especially in reading, that require less experienced teachers with lower levels of training (Arsen & Ni, 2012; Garcia, Barber, & Molnar, 2009). Additionally, standardized curricula, which align expected knowledge across schools by focusing on discrete, easy-to-measure skills, are particularly useful for providing the comparative data needed to foster school choice. This is the logic of market-based schooling that extends beyond charters to traditional public schools eager to apply the principles of the free market to the education of all students.

There is little doubt that scripted instructional practices are efficient—that is, cost effective—but are they effective for teaching students? In the rest of this chapter I consider the efficacy of highly structured reading programs widely used in schools. I focus specifically on *Direct Instruction (DI)*, marketed by McGraw-Hill SRA as "Reading Mastery" (Engelmann & Carnine, 1982), because it is used in many market-based charters as well as traditional public schools serving predominantly low-income students. *Direct Instruction* also follows the behaviorist logic of other highly structured reading programs like Success-for-All (see Slavin et al., 1996) that are often found in similar contexts (e.g., Garcia, Barber, & Molnar, 2009). *Direct Instruction* (capital D, capital I) is distinguishable from direct instruction (small d, small i), which refers to the occasionally explicit instruction that all children require (throughout this chapter *Direct Instruction* or *DI* in italics refers to the instructional program). *DI* is presented as an instructional technology that can be applied to all areas of the curriculum. I chose to focus on *DI* and reading because literacy is the primary focus of my teaching and scholarship. I am confident, however, that my critique of *DI* and reading applies to prescriptive instructional programs more generally.

Is *Direct Instruction (DI)* Effective?

DI is a highly scripted reading program that focuses on isolated reading skills (e.g., sounds and letters) presumed to be prerequisites for independent reading. The National Institute for Direct Instruction (2012) describes *DI* as a "model for teaching that emphasizes well-developed and carefully planned lessons designed around small learning increments and clearly defined and prescribed teaching tasks." Advocates of *DI* point to 40 years of research that they claim demonstrate the effectiveness of the *Direct Instruction* model of reading instruction (National Institute for Direct Instruction, 2012). *DI* researcher Jean Stockard (2011), for example, cites several meta-analyses that, she concludes, indicate that "students who receive reading instruction in this approach have higher levels of reading achievement and stronger growth in reading skills over time than students in other curricula" (p. 3). A reporter for ABC's news program *20/20* was sufficiently impressed by *DI* to declare that it was a "method of teaching children how to read that [is] simple and work[s] every time" (Stossel, 1995).

Not all reading researchers have been persuaded that *DI* "works" even most of the time, much less "all the time." For example, the *What Works Clearinghouse,* created by the U.S. Department of Education to determine the effectiveness of various instructional programs, concluded that the published research showing the efficacy of *DI* was "insufficiently rigorous" to determine whether *DI* actually *works* (Education Consumer's Foundation, 2011, p. 3). My own review of the research on *DI* (see Dudley-Marling & Paugh, 2005) cites numerous studies challenging the efficacy of this approach to teaching reading. Many of these studies indicate that *DI* is most effective for teaching low-level skills but much less effective for teaching higher-level comprehension strategies.

Advocates of *DI* are unbowed by negative evidence regarding its efficacy, tending to blame poor results on a lack of teacher fidelity to program scripts or other external factors (Adams & Engelmann, 1996). When a Wisconsin study did not support the superiority of *Direct Instruction* (Ryder, Sekulski, & Silberg, 2003), for example, Siegfried Engelmann, the primary author of *DI,* blamed teachers who failed to follow the program's procedures (Manzo, 2004).[3] But claims and counter claims about whether *DI* works obscure the fundamental question: works *at what?* A hammer, for example, works, but it works to accomplish some tasks better than others; that is, a hammer is very good at pounding nails into wooden surfaces but not so useful when one is tightening or loosening screws. Even if you accept the claim that *DI* is "effective," the fundamental question remains: At what is *DI* effective?

Direct Instruction: Effective at What?

A recent study by Stockard (2011) provides a useful illustration of the effectiveness of *DI* in teaching certain reading skills and not others (see Eppley, 2011, for a thoughtful critique of the Stockard study). Stockard compared a group of students who had been taught reading using the *Reading Mastery* program (a commercial version of *DI*) (Engelmann et al., 2002) since the beginning of kindergarten with students who began the program later in their school careers. The comparisons were based on two subtests from the *Dynamic Indicators of Basic Early Literacy Skills* (*DIBELS*): Nonsense Word Fluency (NWF), which measures students' ability to read phonetic nonsense words, and Oral Reading Fluency (ORF), which measures students' speed and accuracy reading connected text. The two groups of students were also compared to the national norming sample for DIBELS. Stockard reported that the students who had received *DI* since kindergarten outperformed students who had received less *DI* and the DIBELS norming sample.

The Stockard study is typical of a body of research indicating that *DI* is an efficient and effective means of teaching the discrete skills *DI* advocates claim are basic to success in reading. Underpinning this conclusion is a developmental/behavioral model of reading that holds that learning to read is, fundamentally, about decoding words quickly and accurately. The presumption is that learning to read is a function of mastering a finite scope and sequence of discrete skills that lead directly to fluent reading and text comprehension. From this perspective, it makes perfect sense to use sounding out "nonsense words" or reading words quickly and accurately as measures of students' developing reading ability.

However, current theory in sociolinguistics, literary studies, and cultural psychology indicate that the behavioral theory of reading that informs *Direct Instruction* grossly misrepresents the reading process. Decades of research indicate that while readers utilize sound–symbol relationships in the process of reading, they use this knowledge in combination with other cues, including background knowledge and knowledge about the regularities of language (Weaver, 2002). Sounding out nonsense words is a skill, but it is a skill distinctly different from what readers actually do in the process of reading connected text, when they simultaneously use their knowledge of phonetics, their knowledge of the world, and their knowledge about the regularities of the English language to construct meaning (see Rhodes & Dudley-Marling, 1996, for a detailed discussion of a sociocultural model of reading). Moreover, people do not learn to read "once and for all" but, rather, learn to read particular texts, for particular purposes, in particular social and cultural contexts (Gee, 2011). In other words, reading is always situated in cultural contexts involving specific values, beliefs, goals, props, ways of interacting, and so on. Sounding out nonsense words *is* a reading practice, but it is a practice unique to particular school settings (such as the ones using *DI*); however, it bears only a superficial resemblance to reading practices students encounter outside school.

Back to the question: At what is *DI* effective? *DI* is effective at teaching low-level reading skills that, for most literacy educators, are insufficient for learning to read. *DI* advocates have accused their critics of willfully ignoring the data in support of DI (Carnine, 1999). Like other literacy educators, I do not ignore the research base for *DI*. Instead, I reject *DI* and the research supporting *DI*—and similar scripted reading programs—because they are based on a thoroughly discredited behavioral model of human learning (see Chomsky, 1959, for a thorough dismantling of B. F. Skinner's behavioral theory of language and behaviorism more generally). But, as Eppley and Corbett (2012) observe, "The reading wars will never . . . be over because the real war is not really a war at all, it is a disagreement about what counts as reading" (p. 1).

This is not, however, a mere disagreement over theories of reading. I believe that *DI* and other behaviorally oriented reading programs that focus early reading instruction on low-level reading skills through scripted instruction do real harm to teachers and students, especially students in high-poverty schools, who are most likely to be victimized by these approaches.

An Impoverished Practice

The evidence indicates that children in high-poverty schools tend to fall further behind as they pass through the grades "regardless . . . of their initial skill level" (Snow, Burns, and Griffin, 1998, p. 98). This finding led James Gee (2004) to question, "What is it about school that manages to transform children who are good at learning . . . regardless of their economic and cultural differences, into children who are not good at learning, if they are poor or members of certain minority groups?" (p. 10). The answer may lie in the inferior curricula provided to students attending high-poverty schools, a circumscribed "pedagogy of poverty" (Haberman, 1991) focused on low-level skill instruction that limits students' educational and vocational possibilities.

Rigid, skills-obsessed programs like *DI* harm students in at least two ways: by what they do and what they fail to do. First, *DI*'s hyper-focus on discrete, word-level skills misrepresents the reading process and denies students access to the wide range of sense-making strategies students in more affluent schools learn. The effect is that, while students in *DI* classrooms learn reading "skills," students in many other classrooms are learning what it means to make sense of challenging and interesting texts. A study by Garcia, Barber, and Molnar (2009) is illustrative. They examined Stanford Achievement Test reading scores for for-profit and nonprofit charter schools as well as for traditional public schools in Arizona. They discovered that students in the for-profit charters, which relied heavily on standardized, highly structured reading programs, including *DI* and *Success-for-All,* outperformed students in other schools on low-level "basic skills" but significantly underperformed in the complex-thinking-skills area of reading comprehension. This finding is consistent with an abundance of reading research indicating the limiting effects of reading instruction overly focused on word-level skills (see Allington, 2009).

Second, scripted reading programs like *DI* harm students by transforming teachers into mindless technicians who are expected to follow the script despite strong evidence that teachers of reading are most effective when they are both knowledgeable about reading and able to exercise a measure of professional discretion in the use of reading methods (e.g., Allington & Johnston, 2001; Pressley et al., 2001). Dick Allington (2002), an eminent reading researcher, concluded that

> Expert teachers produce readers regardless of the reading series they are mandated to use. . . . Expert teachers alter and modify reading programs to better meet the needs of their students. Expert teachers simply ignore mandates and go about teaching all their students to read.
>
> (p. 17)

Of course, teachers using *DI* are expected to faithfully execute the teaching script, denying students the benefit of their knowledge and experience. Indeed, in the context of scripted reading instruction, there is no need for teachers who are knowledgeable or experienced. The same argument can be made for scripted programs in math or other subject areas.

Ultimately, teaching is an infinitely complex activity. Reducing teaching to a scripted, technical activity devoid of artistry—in which teachers are merely conduits for distant program developers—deprives students of the high-quality teaching support they need to realize their potential as readers, writers, mathematical problem solvers, and so on.

The Antidote to *Direct Instruction:* High-Expectations Curricula

Markets will always move in the direction of forms of standardization that reduce costs. In the case of market-based schools, the use of one-size-fits-all, scripted reading programs limits the need for expensive professional development and experienced teachers. Reading programs like *DI* that focus on discrete skills are a way of achieving the efficiencies associated with standardization. But standardized learning programs ignore a fundamental reality: learners are not standardized. There is enormous variability among students in any classroom, and effective teaching requires knowledgeable teachers who are able to adapt what they do on the basis of their ongoing assessment of individual learners.

Moreover, the goal of efficient teaching and learning is illusory. *Efficient* learning is an oxymoron or, at a minimum, a notion that applies only to the lowest-level skills. Higher levels of human learning—such as learning to talk, to solve mathematical problems, or to read—are transformative and infinitely complex. Teachers can, for example, create affordances for thoughtful engagement with challenging texts. For instance, for the past two years I've worked with teachers in a high-poverty, low-achieving Boston school to help teachers learn to lead engaging, evidence-based discussions of challenging texts. In these "interpretive discussions" (Haroutunian-Gordon, 2009), students in grades 1–5 learned to respond to open-ended questions by making claims, citing textual evidence, and making explicit the link between their claims and the evidence. In very real ways, these discussions look like the kind of discussions I aim for in my graduate classes at Boston College. Similar evidence-based discussions in math (Chapin & O'Connor, 2012) and science (Sohmer, 2012) have achieved powerful results in other urban schools.

In contrast to the one-size-fits-all form of scripted lessons that characterize programs like *DI,* teachers can also offer students individualized, strategic scaffolding to help them learn how readers go about making sense of various texts. Such instruction is often explicit but, far from being scripted, emerges from teachers' pedagogical knowledge and their knowledge of individual learners, developed through careful, ongoing assessment. For example, effective teachers of readings sometimes model for their students the processes (e.g., re-reading, actively thinking about what they're reading) employed by mature readers as they make sense of texts. They might even do a quick mini-lesson for individual or small groups of students on the regularities of English orthography (e.g., d-ate, r-ate) *if* they find that students lack sufficient knowledge of sound-symbol relationships to read effectively. So-called basic skills are not ignored but taught within the context of reading authentic, engaging texts. In general, the antidote to programs like *DI* that exacerbate inequalities in schooling and the society more generally is to provide all students with the sort of rich, engaging, high-expectation curriculum commonly found in high-achieving schools and classrooms.

In the end, the conceit that reading processes can be broken down into a finite scope and sequence of discrete skills grossly misrepresents the reading process and human learning more generally. Behavioral approaches like *DI* do real harm by severely limiting students' affordances for learning. And, given the reality that *DI* and other scripted reading programs are most often found in schools serving poor children of color, these programs work to maintain inequities that mock the American dream. Through *Direct Instruction* the poor learn their place in the marketplace as obedient and *efficient* workers. As Pat Paugh and I once observed, "The rich get richer; the poor get Direct Instruction" (Dudley-Marling & Paugh, 2005, p. 156).

Notes

1. As I was writing this chapter, the Supreme Court of Louisiana ruled 6–1 against the state's proposed voucher system. A few weeks earlier, the Indiana Supreme Court upheld that state's voucher system (Strauss, 2013).
2. Market-based schooling practices such as charter schools, accountability, merit pay, and high-stakes testing have achieved support across the political spectrum, including within the Obama administration (Ravitch, 2010).
3. Englemann expressed his low regard for teachers in the following statement, published in *The New Yorker:* "We don't give a damn what the teacher thinks, what the teacher feels . . ." Engelmann said. "On the teachers' own time they can hate [*Direct Instruction*]. We don't care as long as they do it" (Radosh, 2004).

References

Adams, G. L., & Engelmann, S. (1996). *Research on Direct Instruction: 25 years beyond DISTAR.* Seattle: Educational Achievement Systems.

Allington, R. L. (2009). *What really matters for struggling readers: Designing research-based programs.* Third ed. Boston: Allyn & Bacon.

Allington, R. L. (2002). *Big Brother and the national reading curriculum: How ideology trumped evidence.* Portsmouth, NH: Heinemann.

Allington, R. L., & Johnston, P. (2001). What do we know about effective fourth-grade teachers and their classrooms? In C. Roller (Ed.), *Learning to teach reading: Setting the research agenda* (pp. 150–165). Newark, DE: International Reading Association.

Arsen, D., & Ni, Y. (2012). *Is administration leaner in charter schools? Resource allocation in charter and traditional public schools.* East Lansing, MI: Education Policy Center at Michigan State University, Working Paper #24.

Carnine, D. (1999). *Why education experts resist effective practices.* Washington, DC: Thomas B. Fordham Foundation.

Center for Public Education (2012). *Charter schools: Finding out the facts: At a glance.* Alexandria, VA: National School Boards Association. Retrieved May 13, 2013, from www.centerforpubliceducation.org/charterschools

Chapin, S. H., & O'Connor, C. (2012). Project challenge: Using challenging curriculum and mathematical discourse to help all students learn. In C. Dudley-Marling & S. Michaels (Eds.), *High-expectation curricula: Helping all students succeed with powerful learning* (pp. 113–127). New York: Teachers College Press.

Chomsky, N. (1959). Review of Skinner's *Verbal Behavior. Language, 35,* 26–58.

Dudley-Marling, C., & Paugh, P. (2005). The rich get richer; The poor get Direct Instruction. In B. Altwerger (Ed.), *Reading for profit: How the bottom line leaves kids behind* (pp. 156–171). Portsmouth, NH: Heinemann.

Education Consumers Foundation. (2011). *Direct instruction: What the research really says.* Arlington, VA: Author.

Engelmann, S., Arbogast, A., Bruner, E., Lou Davis, K., Engelmann, O., Hanner, S., et al. (2002). *SRA Reading Mastery Plus.* DeSoto, TX: SRA/McGraw-Hill.

Engelmann, S. E., & Carnine, D. (1982). *Theory of instruction: Principles and applications.* New York: Irvington Publishers.

Eppley, K. (2011). Reading mastery as pedagogy of erasure. *Journal of Research in Rural Education, 26*(13), 1–5.

Eppley, K., & Corbett, M. (2012). I'll see it when I believe it: A dialogue on epistemological difference and rural literacies. *Journal of Research in Rural Education, 27*(1), 1–9.

Friedman, M. (1955). The role of government in education. In R. A. Solo (Ed.), *Economics and the Public Interest.* New Brunswick, NJ: Rutgers University Press.

Garcia, D. R., Barber, R., & Molnar, A. (2009). Profiting from public education: Education management organizations and student achievement. *Teachers College Record, 111*(5), 1352–1379.

Gee, J. P. (2004). *Situated language and learning: A critique of traditional schooling.* New York: Routledge.

Gee, J. P. (2011). *Social linguistics and literacies: Ideology in discourses.* Fourth ed. New York: Routledge.

Gerson, M. (2013, May 21). GOP fear of Common Core education standards unfounded. *Washington Post.* Retrieved June 1, 2013, from www.washingtonpost.com/opinions/michael-gerson-gop-fear-of-common-core-education-standards-unfounded/2013/05/20/9db19a94-c177–11e2–8bd8–2788030e6b44_story.html?hpid=z2

Haberman, M. (1991). The pedagogy of poverty versus good teaching. *Phi Delta Kappan, 73,* 290–294.

Haroutunian-Gordon, S. (2009). *Learning to teach through discussion: The art of turning the soul.* New Haven, CT: Yale University Press.

Harvey, D. (2005). *A brief history of neoliberalism.* New York: Oxford University Press.

Manzo, K. K. (2004). Study challenges direct reading method. *Education Week, 23,* 3.

Miron, G., & Urschel, J. L. (2010). *Equal or fair? A study of revenues and expenditure in American charter schools.* Boulder, CO, and Tempe, AZ: Education and the Public Interest Center & Education Policy Research Unit. Retrieved May 3, 2013, from http://epicpolicy.org/publication/charter-school-finance

National Institute for Direct Instruction (2012). *Basic philosophy of direct instruction.* Retrieved July 1, 2013, from www.nifdi.org/aboutdi

Pressley, M., Allington, R. L., Wharton-McDonald, R., Collins-Block, C., & Morrow, L. (2001). *Learning to read: Lessons from exemplary first-grade classrooms.* New York: Guilford.

Radosh, D. (2004, July 26). The Pet Goat Approach. *The New Yorker,* p. 28.

Ravitch, D. (2010). *The death and the life of the great American school system: How testing and choice are undermining education.* New York: Basic Books.

Rhodes, L. K., & Dudley-Marling, C. (1996). *Readers and writers with a difference: A holistic approach to teaching struggling readers and writers.* Portsmouth, NH: Heinemann.

Ryder, R. J., Sekulski, J. L., & Silberg, A. (2003). *Results of Direct Instruction reading program evaluation longitudinal results: First through third grade 2000–2003.* Milwaukee: University of Wisconsin–Milwaukee.

Slavin, R. E., Madden, N. A., Dolan, L. J., Wasik, B. A., Ross, S., Smith, L., & Dianda, M. (1996). Success for All: A summary of research. *Journal of Education for Students Placed at Risk, 1*(1), 41–76. doi:10.1207/s15327671espr0101_6

Snow, C. E., Burns, M. S., & Griffin, P. (1998). *Preventing reading difficulties in young children.* Washington, DC: National Research Council.

Sohmer, R. (2012). The investigators club: A high-expectation alternative to textbook science. In C. Dudley-Marling & S. Michaels (Eds.), *High-expectation curricula: Helping all students succeed with powerful learning* (pp. 128–142). New York: Teachers College Press.

Stockard, J. (2011). Increasing reading skills in rural areas: An analysis of three school districts. *Journal of Research in Rural Education, 26*(8), 1–19.

Stossel, J. (1995, October 13). *20/20.* [Broadcast]. ABC Network.

Strauss, V. (2013). Louisiana Supreme Court rules school voucher funding unconstitutional. *Washington Post.* Retrieved May 7, 2013, from www.washingtonpost.com/blogs/answer-sheet/wp/2013/05/07/louisiana-supreme-court-rules-school-voucher-funding-unconstitutional/

Weaver, C. (2002). *Reading process and practice.* Third ed. Portsmouth, NH: Heinemann.

Whitty, G., Power, S., & Halpin, D. (1998). *Devolution and choice in education: The school, the state and the market.* Melbourne: Australian Council for Educational Research.

5

DETANGLING THE LIES ABOUT ENGLISH-ONLY AND BILINGUAL EDUCATION

Jim Cummins

Few educational issues in the United States in recent years have been as volatile or as ideologically loaded as bilingual education. Bilingual education has evoked passionate responses from all sectors of society, pitting those who have characterized it as a "death wish" (Bethell, 1979) on the part of federal and state governments against those who see it as fundamental to the pursuit of equality of educational opportunity for students who speak home languages other than English. In much of this debate, confusion has reigned about what exactly constitutes a bilingual program. For example, it has been argued (e.g., Porter, 1990; Rossell & Baker, 1996) that monolingual English-only programs for linguistic-minority students in the United States are supported by the success of French "immersion" programs for English-background students in Canada despite the fact that these "immersion" programs involve two languages of instruction (English and French), are taught by bilingual teachers, and aim to promote bilingualism and biliteracy. Thus, it is appropriate to clarify initially what we are talking about when we discuss bilingual education.

What Is Bilingual Education?

The term "bilingual education" refers to an organized and planned program that uses two (or more) languages of instruction. The central defining feature of bilingual programs is that the languages are used to teach subject-matter content rather than just the languages themselves. Bilingual instruction can be implemented at any grade or age level, ranging from preschool through university or college. In countries around the world, bilingual programs have been implemented both for students who come from linguistic-minority groups and for students from the majority or dominant linguistic group. Programs intended for dominant group students provide bilingual instruction in order to enable students to learn subject-matter content taught in a second language (L2) as a means of acquiring proficiency in that language while continuing to develop their home languages and literacy skills. More intensive forms of these programs are often termed "immersion programs," in which, in some grade levels, instruction is conducted for most of the day in the second language. In some cases, both majority- and minority-group students are in the same programs, with the goal of developing bilingualism and biliteracy for both groups (e.g., some "dual-language" programs in the United States).

Opposition to bilingual education is highly selective. It focuses only on the provision of home-language (L1) instruction for students from linguistic-minority backgrounds. There is virtually no controversy about the provision of bilingual programs or second-language immersion programs to children of the dominant group(s) in society. For example, French immersion programs for English-speaking students in Canada have been minimally controversial during the past 50 years because they are voluntary and serve the interests of the dominant group.

The tune changes dramatically, however, when bilingual programs are implemented for students from linguistic-minority groups, particularly groups that have been excluded from social opportunities over many generations (such as Latino/Latina communities in the United States) or who have immigrated relatively recently from other countries. In these contexts, bilingual education has become entangled in xenophobic discourses aimed at protecting imagined national identities against infiltration by alien values, languages, cultures, and religions. This vehement opposition is rooted in the accurate perception that bilingual education potentially *does* threaten established power structures. Use of a language as a medium of instruction confers recognition, status, and often economic benefits (e.g., teaching positions) on speakers of that language. Consequently, bilingual education is not simply a politically neutral instructional innovation. It is also a sociopolitical phenomenon that is implicated in the ongoing competition between social groups for material and symbolic resources.

The U.S. Bilingual-Education Debate

The U.S. Supreme Court mandated in the 1974 *Lau v. Nichols* decision that school districts were required to take active steps to ensure that instruction was meaningful to students who came to school with limited knowledge of English. The court did not mandate bilingual education or any other specific program. However, the U.S. Department of Health, Education, and Welfare subsequently issued the so-called Lau Remedies, a set of pedagogical guidelines designed to implement the Supreme Court's legal directives. The Lau Remedies mandated the use of transitional bilingual education in elementary schools where there were sufficient numbers of "limited English proficient" students from the same language background to make it feasible. Transitional bilingual education entailed using students' L1 as a temporary instructional bridge (together with English instruction) until they had acquired sufficient English proficiency to participate successfully in the mainstream English-medium classroom. Faced with oversight from the Office of Civil Rights, school districts suddenly found themselves required to make radical changes to their organizational and hiring structures in order to implement an instructional program that appeared radical and, in some ways, counterintuitive: How did it make any sense to try to develop English skills by teaching in Spanish or other minority languages? How could reduced exposure to English result in higher English achievement?

Almost 25 years of pushback from school districts and intense public and academic debate culminated in June 1998 with the passage of Proposition 227 in California by a margin of 61 to 39 percent. Proposition 227 severely curtailed the availability of bilingual instruction for linguistic-minority students. Two years later, in November 2000, Arizona voters endorsed Proposition 203, which was even more restrictive in relation to bilingual education. Massachusetts followed shortly thereafter, illustrating the fact that opposition to bilingual education cut across liberal and conservative political lines. All of these propositions were intended to eliminate the use of bilingual children's L1 for instructional purposes except in exceptional circumstances. However, they left open the option that bilingual programs could be implemented for fluent English speakers as a way of developing proficiency in an additional language.

The skepticism of politicians, media pundits, many educators, and some academics in relation to bilingual education centered around two major concerns. The first of these was sociopolitical or ideological in nature, focusing on the claim that bilingual education fosters social divisiveness and undermines social cohesion by creating permanent ethnic enclaves. This ideological concern has typically been backed up by the psychoeducational claim that bilingual education denies students access to the language they need for academic success by reducing their instructional exposure to English. As documented in the following sections, neither claim stands up to empirical scrutiny.

Opposition to Bilingual Education: A Sampling of Perspectives

Claim 6a. Bilingual education will foster social conflict because it runs counter to the American "melting pot" tradition whereby previous generations of immigrants were assimilated. As noted earlier, many commentators have objected strenuously to the implementation of bilingual-education programs on the grounds that they run counter to the American tradition of assimilating immigrant groups into the mainstream society. To these commentators, the increased status that accrues to a language such as Spanish as a result of being recognized for instructional purposes in schools appears likely to undermine the efficient operation of the melting pot. Not only will individuals who speak that language be rewarded with jobs and other incentives, but children will also be encouraged to retain their languages and take pride in their cultures. Opponents of bilingual education view the encouragement of ethnic distinctiveness with some dismay, seeing it as an invitation to the rapidly increasing Spanish-speaking population to consider Quebec-style separatism from the United States. A favorite theme of many commentators is that the melting pot worked well for previous generations of immigrants who "made it" without crutches and that Spanish-speaking students could also make it if they tried or if their parents cared about their education.

This perspective is articulated clearly in the following quotations. An early warning about political divisiveness was expressed in a *New York Times* editorial entitled "Bilingual Danger" on November 22, 1976, reprinted in 1977 by *TESOL Quarterly*:

> The disconcerting strength gathered by separatism in Canada contains a relevant lesson for the United States and its approach to bilingual education . . . it is no exaggeration to warn that the present encouragement given to making [Spanish-speaking] enclaves permanent, in the mistaken view that they are an expression of positive pluralism, points the road to cultural, economic and political divisiveness. . . . Without exaggerating the threat to America's nationhood now that English has prevailed, it nevertheless remains pertinent to warn against a misguided linguistic separatism that, while it may seem to promise its advocates limited political and ideological power, can only have the effect of condemning to permanent economic and social disadvantage those who cut themselves off from the majority culture.
>
> (pp. 109–110)

President Ronald Reagan echoed these concerns in a speech on March 2, 1981:

> But it is absolutely wrong and against American concept[s] to have a bilingual education program that is now openly, admittedly dedicated to preserving their native language and never getting them adequate in English so they can go out into the job market.
>
> (quoted in Clines, 1981)

A more paranoid warning was expressed in the fall of 1988 in a memorandum from John Tanton, chairman of *U.S. English,* an advocacy group dedicated to making English the official language of the United States:

> *Gobernar es popular* translates "to govern is to populate." In this society, where the majority rules, does this hold? Will the present majority peacefully hand over its political power to a group that is simply more fertile? . . . Can *homo contraceptivus* compete with *homo progenitiva* if borders

aren't controlled? . . . Perhaps this is the first instance in which those with their pants up are going to get caught by those with their pants down.

(quoted in Crawford, 1995, p. 68)

Even commentators widely viewed as "liberal" shared in the concern that bilingual education would fragment the United States. For example, the historian Arthur Schlesinger Jr., in his 1991 book *The Disuniting of America,* declared:

> Bilingualism shuts doors. It nourishes self-ghettoization, and ghettoization nourishes racial antagonism. . . . Using some language other than English dooms people to second-class citizenship in American society. . . . Monolingual education opens doors to the larger world . . . institutionalized bilingualism remains another source of the fragmentation of America, another threat to the dream of "one people."
>
> (1991, pp. 108–109)

Although the issue has been less volatile in recent years, partly because of the consensus among researchers discussed later, dramatic warnings still hit the headlines on a regular basis. For example, in early 2007, Newt Gingrich, former Speaker of the House of Representatives, characterized bilingual education as "stunningly destructive" and argued that American civilization will "decay" unless the government declares English the nation's official language.

Response. These claims that bilingual education will promote segregation rather than integration reveal a profound ignorance of American educational and social history. The groups that have tended to experience persistent educational difficulty (African American, Latino/Latina, Native American, and Native Hawaiian students) were never given the opportunity to "melt" into the American mainstream. Their status has been that of internal colonies insofar as they have been subordinated and regarded as inherently inferior for generations by the Euro-American dominant group. The history of social and educational exclusion experienced by Spanish speakers in the United States was clearly expressed in 1981 in the case of *United States vs. State of Texas.* The judge noted the "pervasive, intentional discrimination throughout most of this century" against Mexican American students (a charge that was not contested by the State of Texas in the trial) and noted:

> the long history of prejudice and deprivation remains a significant obstacle to equal educational opportunity for these children. The deep sense of inferiority, cultural isolation, and acceptance of failure, instilled in a people by generations of subjugation, cannot be eradicated merely by integrating the schools and repealing the "no Spanish" statutes.
>
> (1981, p. 14)

The eminent sociologist Joshua Fishman (1977) responded specifically to the claim in the *New York Times* editorial quoted earlier that bilingual education will foster Quebec-style separatism:

> The *New York Times* seems to fear that something divisive . . . might grow out of bilingual education in the USA . . . If Hispanic . . . "divisiveness" increases in the USA, it will be because of the long tradition of English-dominated inequality, such as that long practiced in Quebec, rather than because of bilingual education which functions to link together populations that might otherwise be totally estranged.
>
> (pp. 110–111)

In short, underachievement among certain social groups is a direct consequence of their exclusion from social and educational opportunity. Societal power relations operated to ensure that groups considered inferior were kept far away from the melting pot. The educational system reinforced the operation of societal power relations by punishing students for speaking their home languages, segregating students according to race, and providing educational opportunities for students from low-income racialized minorities that were vastly inferior to those provided for Euro-American students (see, for example, Kozol, 2005). Given the sociopolitical roots of the achievement gap between dominant and marginalized group students, it is logical to argue that bilingual education or any other intervention program is likely to be successful in reducing the achievement gap only to the extent that it challenges coercive relations of power. This *can* happen when bilingual instruction is embedded in culturally relevant instruction that explicitly aims to affirm student identities and challenge racist structures and interactions (Cummins, 2001; Ladson-Billings, 1995). However, the simple provision of some L1 instruction, by itself, is unlikely to reverse the legacy of educational discrimination.

Claim 6b. Bilingual education implies an unconvincing "less equals more" logic whereby less English instruction is assumed to lead to more English achievement. Rather than basing public policy on this faulty premise, it makes more sense to immerse linguistic-minority students at an early age in an English-only instructional environment in which they will have maximum opportunity to learn the language and succeed academically. Furthermore, rigorous analyses of the research data on bilingual education show that it is inferior to "structured English immersion" in developing English literacy skills.

This overall argument consists of four subparts: (a) the claim that "time on task" (or "maximum exposure") is the major variable underlying language learning and hence that immersion in English is the most effective means to ensure the learning of English; (b) the claim that under these conditions of immersion, language-minority students will quickly pick up sufficient English (within one or two years) to survive academically without further special support; (c) the claim that English immersion should begin as early as possible in students' school careers since younger children are better language learners than older children; and (d) as would be expected from the preceding claims, the claim that the research evidence shows that English-only instruction works better than bilingual education in promoting academic achievement.

Rosalie Pedalino Porter (1990) clearly articulates the "time-on-task" and "earlier-is-better: principles in stating:

> My personal experience and professional investigations together impel me to conclude that the two overriding conditions that promote the best learning of a second language are (1) starting at an early age, say at five, and (2) having as much exposure and carefully planned instruction in the language as possible. Effective time on task—the amount of time spent learning—is, as educators know, the single greatest predictor of educational achievement; this is at least as true, if not more so, for low-socioeconomic-level, limited-English students. Children learn what they are taught, and if they are taught mainly in Spanish for several years, their Spanish-language skills will be far better than their English-language ones.
>
> (pp. 63–64)

Nathan Glazer, in responding to questions posed by the editors of the journal *Equity and Choice,* also endorsed the "time-on-task" principle together with his conviction that students would be able to transition to mainstream classes after one year of intensive English-as-a-second-language support:

> all our experience shows that the most extended and steady exposure to the spoken language is the best way of learning any language. . . . How long? It depends. But one year of intensive immersion seems to be enough to permit most children to transfer to English-language classes.
>
> (Glazer & Cummins, 1985, p. 48)

Proposition 227 in California was also explicitly premised on the claim that one year of intensive English instruction would be sufficient to enable English learners to integrate into mainstream classrooms with minimal additional support. On the CNN program *TalkBack Live* (October 11, 2000), Ron Unz, who initiated Proposition 227, claimed that English learners learned English in "well under one year" when they were immersed in English-only programs. He further claimed that "all of the bilingual researchers . . . claim that it takes five to seven years for a child to learn English" and "everybody knows that's nonsense" (*TalkBack Live,* 2000).

These "commonsense" claims from commentators who clearly examined the research evidence only superficially, if at all, relied on the conclusions of two writers whose detailed analysis of the research appeared to show that bilingual education "didn't work." Since the early 1980s, Keith Baker and Christine Rossell have published several independent analyses of the bilingual-education literature aimed at demonstrating that bilingual education produced inferior outcomes to what they term "structured immersion" (e.g., Baker & de Kanter, 1981; Rossell & Baker, 1996). Structured immersion programs are essentially English-only programs that build support for second-language learning into the delivery of curriculum. A small window is opened for very limited use of students' L1, but the goal of structured immersion is to immerse students in English as a means of maximizing their opportunities to learn the language.

In the one article that they co-published, Rossell and Baker (1996) articulated the following apparently impressive advantages of structured immersion over bilingual education:

> The research evidence indicates that, on standardized achievement tests, transitional bilingual education (TBE) is *better* than regular classroom instruction in only 22% of the methodologically acceptable studies when the outcome is reading, 7% of the studies when the outcome is language, and 9% of the studies when the outcome is math. TBE is never better than structured immersion, a special program for limited English proficient children where the children are in a self-contained classroom composed solely of English learners, but the instruction is in English at a pace they can understand.
>
> (p. 1)

Furthermore, they reported that the comparisons of reading scores between TBE and structured immersion showed that structured immersion was superior in 83 percent of cases and that no differences were observed in 17 percent.

Response. The "time-on-task" argument is immediately refuted by the outcomes of virtually every bilingual program for either minority or majority students that has ever been evaluated. It has been repeatedly documented in programs from around the world that students—both minority and majority—educated for part of the day in a minority language do not suffer adverse consequences in the development of academic skills in the majority language (see August & Shanahan, 2006; Cummins, 2001; Cummins & Hornberger, 2008; Genesee, Lindholm-Leary, Saunders, & Christian, 2006). The major reason that less instruction in English results does not have adverse effects on students' English proficiency is that transfer of concepts, learning strategies, and features of languages occurs across languages. This "interdependence" hypothesis has been supported by a vast amount of research evidence (see Dressler & Kamil, 2006, for a review).

If the time-on-task hypothesis were valid, then students in *all* bilingual programs would suffer adverse consequences with respect to their proficiency in the majority language when considerably less instructional time is spent in that language. The most comprehensive review of the relevant data to date was conducted by the National Literacy Panel on Language-Minority Children and Youth (August & Shanahan, 2006), a panel of highly credible researchers appointed by the Bush administration to evaluate the scientific evidence on this issue. The panel concluded that bilingual instruction exerts a moderately positive but significant effect on minority-group students' academic achievement in the dominant school language:

> In summary, there is no indication that bilingual instruction impedes academic achievement in either the native language or English, whether for language-minority students, students receiving heritage language instruction, or those enrolled in French immersion programs. Where differences were observed, on average they favored the students in a bilingual program. The meta-analytic results clearly suggest a positive effect for bilingual instruction that is moderate in size. This conclusion held up across the entire collection of studies and within the subset of studies that used random assignment of students to conditions.
>
> (Francis, Lesaux, & August, 2006, p. 397)

This finding concurs with the results of other recent comprehensive reviews (e.g., Genesee et al., 2006; Rolstad, Mahoney, & Glass, 2005).

The argument that under conditions of English-only instruction, linguistic-minority students will, within one or two years, acquire sufficient English academic skills to thrive in the mainstream classroom is also refuted by the research evidence (e.g., Cummins, 1981; Hakuta, Butler, & Witt, 2000). Particularly relevant in light of Ron Unz's claims in the context of California's Proposition 227 is the finding that after three years of English-only instruction, a mere 12 percent of English-language learners in California had acquired sufficient academic English to be redesignated as English-proficient (Parrish, Merickel, Perez, Linquanti, et al., 2006).

How do we reconcile the contradictory interpretations of the bilingual education research advanced by Rossell and Baker as measured against the work of virtually all other researchers both internationally and within the United States? Major problems are immediately evident in Rossell and Baker's interpretation of the research. For example, when we look more closely at the research studies that supposedly demonstrate the superiority of "structured immersion" over "transitional bilingual education" it turns out that *90 percent of these studies are interpreted by their authors as supporting the effectiveness of bilingual and even trilingual education.* Seven of the 10 studies that Rossell and Baker claim support structured immersion over TBE were studies of French immersion programs in Canada (two of these involved trilingual instruction!). Typically, in these programs English-speaking students are "immersed" in French in kindergarten and grade 1, after which the program rapidly becomes 50 percent English (L1) and 50 percent French (L2). In other words, Canadian French immersion programs are bilingual programs, taught by bilingual teachers, and their goal is the development of bilingualism and biliteracy. It is, at the very least, incongruous to argue for monolingual English programs on the basis of the success of bilingual programs.

Two of the other "structured immersion" programs are actually bilingual programs involving dual-language instruction (one a large-scale study of Afrikaans-English bilingual education in South Africa and the other a kindergarten program in Texas that involved one hour of Spanish-medium instruction per day). Thus, only one of the programs that Rossell and Baker cited as evidence for monolingual education is actually a monolingual program.

Even if Rossell and Baker's (1996) claims were not ludicrously incoherent and self-contradictory, they are directly refuted by the conclusions of all other reviews of the literature. For example, Lindholm-Leary and Borsato (2006) conclude that

> [T]here is strong convergent evidence that the educational success of ELLs [English language learners] is positively related to sustained instruction through the student's first language . . . most long-term studies report that the longer the students stayed in the program, the more positive were the outcomes.
>
> (p. 201)

Deconstructing Big Lies Regarding Bilingual Education

Three types of "Big Lies" can be identified in the 40-year-old debate in the United States on bilingual education: (a) intentional dishonesty, (b) willful blindness, and (c) doublethink. Intentional dishonesty involves consciously distorting the research and attempting to persuade others (e.g., policymakers, the general public) that the claimed advantages of bilingual education are unsupported by research findings. Those who perpetuate this form of "Big Lie" adopt the stance of courtroom lawyers who advocate for their clients regardless of their guilt or innocence. Some of the opponents of bilingual education who have been cited in this chapter very likely have consciously disseminated interpretations of the research that they know are inaccurate with the goal of demonstrating that the "experts" disagree and that therefore common sense should take precedence in policy-decisions.

Willful blindness has been documented in many social spheres (e.g., Heffernan, 2011) and refers to the phenomenon whereby individuals choose to remain ignorant of information that might challenge or contradict their beliefs or convictions. Thus, many opponents of bilingual education have genuinely believed that the bulk of the research demonstrates that English-only programs yield results superior to those obtained by bilingual programs. However, they are able to sustain this belief only by choosing not to examine the research in any serious way or by choosing to believe someone else's claim that the research is, in fact, aligned with their ideological convictions. Thus, when Arthur Schlesinger Jr. (1991) suggests that "bilingualism shuts doors," one has to wonder how any intelligent human being could make such an absurd statement. Clearly, he is identifying "bilingualism" with "lack of English proficiency" and in the process demonstrating willful blindness to the fact that there is a vast amount of research showing that bilingualism enhances aspects of cognitive functions and opens doors to a far greater variety of experiences than are available to monolinguals.

Finally, "doublethink" is alive and well in the debate on bilingual education. The term was coined by George Orwell in his futuristic novel *Nineteen Eighty-Four*

(1949/1983) to refer to the simultaneous belief in two contradictory ideas. Orwell describes the process of doublethink as follows:

> *Doublethink* means the power of holding two contradictory beliefs in one's mind simultaneously, and accepting both of them. The Party intellectual knows in which direction his memories must be altered; he therefore knows that he is playing tricks with reality; but by the exercise of *doublethink* he also satisfies himself that reality is not violated. The process has to be conscious, or it would not be carried out with sufficient precision, but it also has to be unconscious, or it would bring with it a feeling of falsity and hence of guilt.
>
> (1949/1983, p. 865)

I have documented numerous instances of doublethink in the bilingual education debate (Cummins, 1999). As just one example, Porter (1990) argues strongly against transitional bilingual education on the grounds that it fails to teach children English effectively and violates the "time-on-task" principle that posits a direct relationship between time spent in the medium of English and English achievement. However, she goes on to strongly endorse two-way bilingual programs for both linguistic-majority and -minority students, asserting that they "are also considered to be the best possible vehicles for integration of language minority students, since these students are grouped with English-speakers for natural and equal exchange of skills" (p. 154). She seems oblivious to the fact that typical two-way or dual-language programs involve considerably more instruction in the minority language than is the case with short-term transitional bilingual programs and that thus linguistic-minority students will spend even *less* time "on-task" in two-way than in transitional bilingual programs.

Conclusion

All three variations of "Big Lies" involve an ethical failure on the part of those who perpetuate them. This is even more the case subsequent to the conclusions of the National Literacy Panel on Language-Minority Children and Youth (August & Shanahan, 2006). While some aspects of this report have been critiqued (e.g., Cummins, 2009), none of the opponents of bilingual education have argued that its conclusions regarding bilingual education lack credibility or that the panel was biased in any way. Any commentator who declares that "bilingual education doesn't work" without referencing the National Literacy Panel's conclusions has not done his or her homework and is demonstrating either willful blindness to the research or intentional dishonesty. Neither merits respect.

References

August, D., & Shanahan, T. (Eds.). (2006). *Developing literacy in second-language learners: Report of the National Literacy Panel on Language-Minority Children and Youth.* Mahwah, NJ: Erlbaum.

Baker, K. A., & de Kanter, A. A. (1981). *Effectiveness of bilingual education: A review of the literature.* Washington, DC: Office of Planning and Budget, U.S. Department of Education.

Bethell, T. (1979, February) Against bilingual education. *Harper's Magazine.*

Clines, F. X. (1981, March 3). Reagan defends cuts in budget and asks for help from mayors. *New York Times.* Available at www.nytimes.com/1981/03/03/us/reagan-defends-cuts-in-budget-and-asks-for-help-of-mayors.html

Crawford, J. (1995). *Bilingual education: History, politics, theory, and practice.* Third ed. Los Angeles: Bilingual Education Services.

Cummins, J. (1981). Age on arrival and immigrant second language learning in Canada: A reassessment. *Applied Linguistics, 2,* 132–149.

Cummins, J. (1999). The ethics of doublethink: Language rights and the bilingual education debate. *TESOL Journal, 8*(3), 13–17.

Cummins, J. (2001). *Negotiating identities: Education for empowerment in a diverse society.* Second ed. Los Angeles: California Association for Bilingual Education.

Cummins, J. (2009). Literacy and English-language learners: A shifting landscape for students, teachers, researchers, and policy makers. [Review of *Developing Reading and Writing in Second-Language Learners: Lessons from the Report of the National Literacy Panel on Language-Minority Children and Youth,* ed. D. August & T. Shanahan (New York: Routledge, 2008).] *Educational Researcher, 38,* 382–384.

Cummins, J., & Hornberger, N. H. (Eds.). (2008). *Encyclopedia of language and education.* Vol. 5: *Bilingual education.* New York: Springer.

Dressler, C., & Kamil, M. (2006). First- and second-language literacy. In D. August & T. Shanahan (Eds.), *Developing literacy in second-language learners: Report of the National Literacy Panel on Language-Minority Children and Youth* (pp. 197–238). Mahwah, NJ: Erlbaum.

Fishman, J. A. (1977). Letter to the editor in response to "Bilingual Danger" editorial. *TESOL Quarterly, 11*(1), 110–111.

Francis, D., Lesaux, N., & August, D. (2006). Language of instruction. In D. August & T. Shanahan (Eds.), *Developing literacy in second-language learners: Report of the National Literacy Panel on Language-Minority Children and Youth* (pp. 365–413). Mahwah, NJ: Erlbaum.

Genesee, F., Lindholm-Leary, K. J., Saunders, W., & Christian, D. (Eds.). (2006). *Educating English-language learners* (pp. 176–222). New York: Cambridge University Press.

Glazer, N., & Cummins, J. (1985). Viewpoints on bilingual education. *Equity and Choice, 2,* 47–52.

Hakuta, K., Butler, Y. G., & Witt, D. (2000). *How long does it take English learners to attain proficiency?* Santa Barbara: University of California Linguistic Minority Research Institute.

Heffernan, M. (2011). *Willful blindness: Why we ignore the obvious at our peril.* London: Walker.

Kozol, J. (2005). *The shame of the nation: The restoration of apartheid schooling in America.* New York: Crown.

Ladson-Billings, G. (1995). Toward a theory of culturally relevant pedagogy. *American Educational Research Journal, 32,* 465–491.

Lindholm-Leary, K. J., & Borsato, G. (2006). Academic achievement. In F. Genesee, K. J. Lindholm-Leary, W. Saunders, & D. Christian (Eds.), *Educating English-language learners* (pp. 176–222). New York: Cambridge University Press.

New York Times. (1977). Bilingual danger (editorial). *TESOL Quarterly, 11*(1), 109–110.

Orwell, G. 1949/1983. *Nineteen eighty-four.* In *The Penguin complete novels of George Orwell.* London: Penguin Books.

Parrish, T., Merickel, A., Perez, M., Linquanti, R., et al. (2006). *Effects of the implementation of Proposition 227 on the education of English learners, K-12: Findings from a five-year evaluation (final report).* Palo Alto and San Francisco: American Institutes for Research and WestEd.

Porter, R. P. (1990). *Forked tongue: The politics of bilingual education*. New York: Basic Books.

Rolstad, K., Mahoney, K., & Glass, G. V. (2005). The big picture: A meta-analysis of program effectiveness research on English-language learners. *Education Policy, 10,* 572–594.

Rossell, C. H., & Baker, K. (1996). The effectiveness of bilingual education. *Research in the Teaching of English, 30,* 7–74.

Schlesinger, A. J. (1991). *The disuniting of America*. New York: W. W. Norton.

TalkBack Live (2000, October 11). CNN. http://transcripts.cnn.com/TRANSCRIPTS/0010/11/tl.00.html

United States v. State of Texas (1981). Civil action #5281 (Bilingual Education), Memorandum Opinion.

6

THE TEST DOES NOT KNOW BEST

On Collecting Good Evidence for Student Learning

Deborah Meier

"It's lies, lies, and more lies," I mutter to myself as I read the media's usual account of the current school wars. At what point are we all witlessly drawn in by the winners of the war, the corporate interests, over how to tell the story? The problem is, the language of the winners becomes the language people use for responding to their lies. It begins to influence even me as I try to rebut increasingly familiar stories about "the decline of American public education" and how our public schools have aided and abetted the country's waning global economic competitiveness and standard of living.

So many lies fill the current "school reform" agenda, and they have a hold on the public. This has been true in some form or another for the past 60 years. I have two *Life* magazines, one from the 1950s and one from the 1970s, whose covers point to the "The Crisis of American Education." The first compares us with Russia, and the second focuses on the economy.

Once, when I challenged Al Shanker, former president of the American Federation of Teachers, for participating in the fabrication of these "crises," he agreed that it was nonsense. But after all, he argued, the more attention we pay to public schooling, the more funding we'll get, and that will be good for kids and teachers. Unfortunately, you reap what you sow, and what we're reaping now is one great big mess.

In contrast, my father used to say that if someone starts calling everything a "crisis," check your wallet and then check the other person's. And always follow the money.

One of the big lies misguiding today's conversations about strengthening public schools is that America's schools used to be really, really good, that they made it possible for the poor immigrants arriving on our shores or already living in our midst to join the great middle class or even the wealthier classes. Another big lie is that our economy's past and future rested and continues to rest on the work of our schools—that we "educated" ourselves into being the central world power. So, if our global dominance is being threatened, it must be because our schools no longer are effective, that our public school system no longer is successful. And even if this story isn't totally true, the argument goes, we're heading toward shaky times in the future, so we better fix our schools before it's too late. Sounds scary, right?

All of these lies are made to appear like reasonable concerns by a system of measuring success and effectiveness that is, itself, a big con. The worst thing about our increasing reliance on standardized testing to measure "achievement" is that so few people, including well-educated people, understand how the system of testing we've chosen operates and why it will not—why it *cannot*—work, especially if one of our goals is equal educational opportunity. It's a system for rank-ordering children that, as I used to say when I blew my whistle at the end of recess, always produces exactly the same number of children who were first, second, third, and last in line. And, lo and behold, it always produces a predictable lineup, with the most privileged students at the front of the line.

The Ease and Implications of Buying In

It might interest you to know that I, too, once was fond of standardized tests. It was hard for me to overcome that fondness, even though I did so under ideal circumstances, where few stakes were involved in my success or failure. Besides, if Diane Ravitch could change her mind about tests, it must be possible to "convert" just about anyone.

The problem has been trying to convert a lot of anyones. Part of the problem is that we reconfirm our beliefs in tests all the time, even if ostensibly we abhor them. I see it all the time: people using test scores as their evidence when making a case for some better, more equitable approach. Maybe it's because determining what *does work* when it comes to creating and sustaining schools in which all students can thrive can seem like an overwhelming task. Perhaps some of us think, in the face of that task, that it would be so much easier if only we had a clear and concise numerical system for keeping score.

So first I want to tackle, in a rather personal way, how tempting it can be to imagine standardized test scores as a euphemism for "achievement." This view has been prominent for the past half century (and probably longer), even back when schools used far fewer standardized tests. The search for a supposedly neutral, objective way of assessing who is and isn't intelligent and who is and isn't well educated (the two often are conflated, which is part of the problem) became a national obsession as soon as we rhetorically broke with our historical class/caste rhetoric. Few and far between were people in the Western world in the 19th century who didn't assume that poverty and skin color weren't either the same as or closely tied to intelligence, brain power, and even moral and ethnical understanding. Richard Herrnstein and Charles Murray, after all, wrote a persuasive and popular book, *The Bell Curve,* only 20 years ago in which they claimed to prove scientifically that race was causally related to intelligence—and that the reason white and wealthy people scored at one end of the normal curve was a simple fact of biology.

Today, amid demands that *all* children achieve at high levels alongside denials that racism or poverty affects achievement, we've placed schools in a paradoxical position, relying more than ever on a numerical tool and complex numerical equations for measuring the intelligence of students and the effectiveness of schools and teachers. In the process we have forsaken human judgment, such as that which would allow much more robust assessments of student learning and teacher effectiveness and that which would help us to recognize that, despite Herrnstein and Murray's claims, *race* does not explain the *achievement* gap; rather, *racism* explains the *opportunity* gap. It's hard to measure that on a multiple-choice test.

I actually grew up in a relatively testless setting, although apparently my parents once had my brother and me tested for IQ. I don't recall the results.

I didn't question the idea of measuring intelligence at the time. I viewed it as a scientific way of sorting test-takers' answers into rights and wrongs and in doing so finding the deeper and broader patterns could help rank us all with regard to our intelligence. To my mind, science was good; I was predisposed to it. Even the progressives of the time, including John Dewey, accepted most of the rhetoric on scientific standardized psychometrics. Most progressive educators were not even leery of tracking, separating schoolchildren by "intelligence" on the basis of early IQ testing. Achievement tests grew from these IQ tests and followed the same psychometric rules in the interest, at least ostensibly, of giving parents, educators, and the larger society information that would help us provide education and training that matched students' abilities and society's needs.

This was confirmed to my satisfaction when I took a standardized test in order to transfer into the graduate history department at the University of Chicago. It even covered topics that I never had studied or been particularly interested in. Still, I did well. I had a "knack," it seemed, for choosing "right" answers. That "knack," I assumed, was "native intelligence."

Coming to See the Trouble with Testing

I assumed the same would be true of my own three children. So I was amazed and unprepared when my older son's third-grade teacher informed me that he needed remedial reading help. He was a fluent and sophisticated reader, devouring books right and left, so I was dumbfounded. I didn't give in and was labeled in what were then secret cumulative records as a "troublemaker." Later I found an old copy of a third-grade test and administered it to my son. We discussed his answers and his approach to taking the test. He insisted that it was only fair to cover up reading passages before trying to answer the questions about them, which I explained he didn't need to do. He also wrote little notes next to some of his answers in which he explained why he chose what, he surmised, likely were not considered the "right" answer. Fortunately I convinced him not to do that on future tests, but not without a struggle over his own notion of what was morally right and wrong.

This experience coincided with my starting a new job teaching kindergarten in central Harlem. In my third year, a group of us, all viewing ourselves as "progressives," convinced the principal to let us transform the early-childhood wing of the school into a pre-K through second-grade cluster. Testing started at second grade at that time, so we were eager to see the results of our four years' worth of collaborative work. Oh, dear. They didn't match our expectations. Our students did not fare better or worse than other second graders. More startling, though, was our discovery that several youngsters we knew to be very good readers scored as nonreaders!

So we bought tape recorders and proceeded to interview students individually and in small groups. I wrote a pamphlet describing the results and began speaking everywhere about it. This was the late 1960s and early 1970s. I got a lot of applause and smiling faces, but New York City and the nation as a whole proceeded to require more testing, not less. It took a dozen or more years for my opinions about the ineffectiveness of these tests to be echoed widely by others. But by the 1980s, the anti-testing sentiment had become part of the educational mainstream. It wasn't the dominant part, but it was growing.

We even thought by 1990 that we had won! I remember Linda Darling-Hammond, one of our academic heroes, saying that Edward Thorndike—the early nineteenth-century educational psychologist and staunch advocate for quantifying, well, just about everything—had finally lost and that standardized testing was on its way out. Unfortunately, the reality is that we had blinded ourselves to another train of thought that was coming down the track. That train of thought was building steam and soon would bump us even further into the margins of the national conversation on what it means to be well educated.

The renewed and far more vigorous and rigorous use of standardized testing that returned during those years made some of us forget that the testing focus wasn't a new phenomenon. Its pernicious effects had been apparent for a long time. Of course, given the increasingly conservative political and economic climate in which we were living, we probably shouldn't have been so surprised by the renewed efforts to infect public schools with more and more testing regimens. Tests were being pitched as the free-market answer to the schools' and even the nation's woes.

Occasionally I wonder how it could have happened that the likes of Ted Sizer, Al Shanker, and me ended up preaching together to largely converted businesspeople and industrialists about what the new wave of schools would and should look like: schools that knew their students through their work, not their test scores. "Maybe," I'd say under my breath, "what's good for General Motors is good for progressive education."

Turns Out We Were Wrong, and I Should've Known Better

We slowly began to recognize the tenaciousness of the underlying assumptions that test scores confirmed. What was handy was that, generally speaking, students' test scores correlated with our expectations—the rank order looked more or less right. There were occasional kids, like my son, for whom this wasn't the case, but, the thinking went, these kinds of aberrations were rare and could be ignored as outliers in the vast piles of data.

Of course, expectations always are colored with bias. I soon learned from colleagues at Educational Testing Service, one of the companies often contracted to create and deliver standardized tests, that if the correlations didn't hold up—didn't closely match IQ scores, achievement test scores, and general expectations—there'd be trouble. It would be a sign that psychometric errors had been made. Sometimes this meant merely reconsidering particular misleading items and replacing them with others in the pool that "worked" properly. If the rank order was "off," it meant that either the scoring rubrics were off or that there was some irregularity in the test setting, like cheating.

If an item was answered correctly more often by low-income Black children than by upper-class White ones in the field tests, it would be struck from the test. It was clearly an outlier. Something must be wrong with it, they figured, even though nobody quite could say what.

I also learned that traditional psychometrics placed scores along a normal curve, so that the median score was at the top of the curve and labeled "grade level." In fact, later, when the idea that properly designed tests had to fit neatly onto that curve—that half of all test-takers would always score below and half would always score above grade level—seemed unacceptable, other ways of benchmarking the rank-ordered scores replaced the normal curve. "Norming" remained, but the percentile labels that accompanied the curve as a way of recording one's status changed. We invented many new names that lumped scores to fit new paradigms: not meeting expectations, meeting expectations, going beyond, and so on. I thought, at first, that these new paradigms would make a positive difference as they didn't pretend to be quite so precise. In many localities today the scores are divided into four groups, so we have 1s, 2s, 3s, and 4s. Which refers to the highest scores and which refers to the lowest is determined by local authorities or by the state. But kids in many districts commonly became known as "4s" or "2s," including in high schools that accept only the highest-ranked students, for example.

The scoring was confusing, too. Teachers and parents often had no idea what a score of 5.7, for example, meant under the old system. Even when told (it was the norm for the seventh month of fifth grade), few teachers could even pick out a book that they thought was 5.7 without external aids. The new system seemed easier, but it still used a formula that relied on field-tested norms to decide what "grade level" meant. Noting of substance changed.

As you might imagine, explaining to parents who thought their children were good readers that these same children had scored poorly on standardized tests produced many a peculiar discussion. It led me to develop new ways to describe a child as a reader to her or his parent or guardian, always with that parent and that child in mind. We began to tape-record children reading from various reading-level-appropriate texts at the beginning and near the end of each school year. We, the teachers, met and listened to tapes to try to decide the language we'd use to describe a child at this or that stage and to discuss how confident we were in our assessments. We even invented ways to assign numbers to the stages we identified and to graph our results. (Parents loved this sort of ongoing "hard data.") The important thing was that it was coming from a full understanding of the student and not a narrow measure from a narrow test.

Building and Rebuilding a Movement against Test-Centric Schools

This way of thinking spread widely to many other subjects; we found ourselves freed from what seemed more and more like the vicious cycle of narrow assessments that standardized testing had created. As part of the Coalition of Essential Schools, we developed, in collaboration with other schools, variations on this, ways to assess when students were ready to graduate from high school and into the big wide world.

Many educators liked our work, but they often thought it was either "utopian" or "flaky." To those who mattered in the policy world, including the media, we were seen at best as "interesting" and at worst as "the enemy." The media enthusiastically hyped schools whose scores had jumped three "years" from one school year to the next but rarely noted when the populations of these schools had changed. Nor did they note that, yes, of course, Stuyvesant High School's students did well on tests. After all, they were at Stuyvesant *because* they were at the very top of the test-score heap. Why couldn't all schools be like Stuyvesant, they asked. They pointed out that Stuyvesant had high-scoring students of every race, class, and ethnic background. They rarely got around to pointing out that those students had to pass a test just to be allowed to attend the school, that it didn't practice open enrollment. Despite all the "miracle" schools acclaimed by the mayor of New York or by the media, it never was disproved that tests were peculiarly sensitive to matters of race and class. These miracle test score gains rarely lasted for more than one year, and rarer still were those that were schoolwide, across race and class.

Many people who were reluctant to change how we measured success viewed what we were doing as a form of affirmative action, which itself was growing less popular. Particular scorn seemed to be pointed at immigrants, and especially English-language learners. We heard insistent claims from third- and fourth-generation Americans that their forebears in the United States had done well, enabling future generations to progress. Everybody seemed to forget that, in point of fact, until World War II most immigrants with low-income roots did not do well at school, most certainly didn't graduate, much less go to college. And they surely did not test well. Jews, for example, had lower-than-average IQ scores as a group when my parents immigrated, as did Asian immigrants. For most groups, economic improvement came first, and then, later, the children did better in school.

By the early 1990s we realized that our advocacy for a different approach had failed and that schools had become more committed to high-stakes standardized testing than ever—more so even than China, where standardized testing had been used for centuries. Scores came to determine a child's future in school, her opportunities to participate in certain prized activities, what school she could attend, whether she could graduate or attend college. Projecting all of this further in the future, one could argue that test scores helped determine somebody's ability to get a job that might pay enough to raise a family. More and more, everything came down to test scores.

Today the reach of these tests is even greater. We have school consolidation and closings based on test score data. Schools are being turned over to publicly funded, privately managed, and for-profit organizations because they did not meet Annual Yearly Progress criteria on test scores. Test scores are being used to justify the elimination of tenure and the firing of entire schools of teachers and administrators, almost exclusively from high-poverty schools with large percentages of students of color. The newer scapegoats include schools of education that prepare teachers for their futures in the classroom. Even in these institutions, filled with professional educators, a majority of whom are, at the very least, suspicious of the high-stakes testing craze, standardized tests are used to decide who should be admitted. Many teacher-education programs exist under the threat of decertification by state agencies if a certain percentage of their graduates do not perform well on the Praxis exams, assessments used to certify teachers.

The combination of these measures likely accounts at least in part for shifting teacher demographics. For example, Chicago's teaching population, which once was 44 percent Black and Hispanic, now is only 19 percent Black and Hispanic.

So Now What?

The future rests, however shakily, on us—"the people." It's not written in the stars how this will all turn out. I do not think we can assume, as I once naively did, that the interests of big business and stockholders are in sync with the interests of all children. In fact, I fear now that quite the opposite is true. I think, for example, that the civil rights advocates who originally bought into No Child Left Behind are gradually seeing more clearly where that paradigm and its obsession with testing lead us. Many have shifted their loyalties and advocacy. Certainly, a growing number of parents are actively opposing the effects this approach is having on the curriculum in their children's schools, the kind of work being rewarded in classrooms, and the increasing tendency to rank-order children and schools. Even students are beginning to object more noisily.

In a high school in Seattle, students refused to take one of the annual tests. By doing so, they made a clear statement about what was happening in and to their educational lives. Other schools followed. Diane Ravitch launched a nationwide organization, the Network for Public Education, to bring together the growing number of activists in local communities disturbed by how these assessments were being used to literally close schools in order to replace them with semiprivate charters or to push vouchers.

Perhaps the most exciting development, though, is that school boards, even in places like Texas and Florida, not known to be bastions of progressivism, are wary these days about who is deciding what when it comes to public schools. Business interests and billionaire foundations are spending millions of dollars to elect school board members who will enact business-friendly policies. You read that correctly. They are spending that money on local *school board elections*. But they are often being opposed and beaten by people with far less means.

In my view it's a little early for those of us who oppose this corporate-backed imposition of high-stakes testing on public schools to build a single coherent message, and maybe that's just as well. It's starting to come together, though. People are less cowed now when asked, "What's your alternative?"—which is good. But while we explore alternatives, we can stop the testing that is doing damage to students right now—tests on the basis of which high-stake decisions are made that affect individual people and institutions. We should not excuse the effects of a medicine that we know harms patients because the industry hasn't yet produced a better one that works (and is as cheap).

We are beginning to be able to point to counterexamples. Finland, for instance, did us a big favor by having high scores on international academic measures even though *it doesn't use standardized tests at all* between kindergarten and twelfth grade. Internationally normed tests, such as our one current national test (NAEP, the National Assessment of Educational Progress), do not test each and every child, nor do they report scores by individual students or schools. And there are alternatives for providing "scores" to individuals, and they are neither new nor untested. They involve the development of processes based upon the judgment of adults whom we collectively trust to decide whether Rosanna and Johnny can read. In these processes, the scores are the end result of collective decision making based on a wide range of evidence. We need these sorts of exhibitions of competence, as Ted Sizer called them, which we already use in most arenas of life. These exhibitions "show off" the skill, talent, and knowledge that demonstrate what we "mean" by being "ready to vote," "ready to serve on a jury," ready to take on complex adult tasks. They are like our "road test" for drivers, which I'm sure we'd all agree is more reliable and valid than a multiple-choice standardized test on driving. There is no lack of films, books, and articles describing these assessment approaches in detail—just visit FairTest.org for a reading list.

But just as important as reimagining assessment is joining together to discuss ways to defend public education itself—to work through why we're "incarcerating" our youth during their critical formative years in mandatory, overly standardized, testing-centered schools. We need clear language to describe what public education ought to be. We will disagree, of course, and when we do, *vive la différence*. But let's ask ourselves this: What values, beliefs, skills, habits of heart and mind, and aptitudes do we believe are essential to sustaining the most precious parts of who we are individually? Which equip us to inch closer and closer to a more authentic form of democracy?

Interestingly, most private and parochial schools of the past were built upon statements of commitment to these sorts of goals; many have mission statements to this effect that go back a century or more. Meanwhile, the mission of public education has been watered down to what we can measure cheaply on standardized tests, so that when somebody says "achievement" people automatically think "test scores." Everything else is made to seem soft and fuzzy. If our goal is to nurture citizens who are defined, at least in part, by their ability to exercise judgment in the town hall or the local voting booth, we cannot sit back and rely on some quaint practice of ye olden days to get us there. Nor will we nurture such citizens by handing them over for 12 or 13 years to adults who are forbidden to freely exercise their professional judgment about how to engage young people. As Ted Sizer has said, speaking as a parent, we want the right to look into the eyes of those who are making important decisions about our children.

Democracy flourishes when all of its institutions reward the exercise of judgment and when they all build their reputations on their past records of wise judgments. It remains an exciting and fragile idea to which to hold ourselves and our leaders accountable. Democracy will flourish only when we see it not only as an end goal or as the subject of a Sunday sermon but also as an essential means for carrying out the most important of all tasks: together raising the next generation.

PART III
Teachers and Teaching

7

LYING ABOUT TEACHERS AND THEIR TRAINING

Kristien Zenkov

Perhaps one of the greatest challenges our public schools face results from one of their most significant strengths: the fact that the vast majority of our nation's citizens have access to free public education and are able, at a minimum, to graduate from high school. Unfortunately, the fact that most of our nation's residents at one time—and for an extended period—attended some version of school (public, private, religious, independent, even home) has given rise to what have become increasingly dangerous assumptions that we *all* know what constitutes a "quality" school and that we *all* appreciate, almost by birthright, what effective teaching looks like. The positive outcomes of this near-universal schooling reality are that education is a topic that rarely leaves the public imagination and that we as a society seem to care enough about schools—at least in our *own* communities—to discuss and debate them ad nauseam. Even if most of these discussions about schools' and teachers' effectiveness are rooted in our narrow experiences, with pre-K–12 educators and our educational institutions critiqued by our untrained eyes, and the ways we manage and judge the teaching profession unapologetically shaped by our personal biases. I imagine the alternative—a nation that *never* engages in a conversation about its educational system—would be a likely indicator that schools and teaching were irrelevant afterthoughts, receiving considerably less attention but also likely less susceptible to manipulations and abuses. So the fact that our schools have such a ubiquitous presence in our national public dialogues is probably a very good sign.

This collective awareness and our unwitting confidence in our wisdom about all things related to education result in some peculiar version of anti-NIMBYism and a projective version of what the psychologist Gerhart Wiebe described in 1973 as a "well-informed futility." Guided by this "not in my back yard" ethic, we are almost militant about ensuring that *no one*—policymakers, reformers, educational entrepreneurs, or anyone else—from outside our communities exerts any control over *our* schools. Yet we have a peculiar propensity for expressing our opinions about and even voting for politicians who offer grand plans for *others'* educational institutions, children, and, increasingly, their teachers. And, while we might insist on the best, most responsive policies and practices in answer to complex educational, economic, and social concerns in our own cities, towns, and states, we have virtually no problem arguing for the simplest, most efficient, most sweeping, and least sensitive solutions to what we perceive as hopelessly knotty issues in others' communities—the very definition of Wiebe's "futility."

Scholars and politicians alike have highlighted for years how teachers are the single most important factor in a student's learning—that is, classroom teachers are the primary and some would argue the *only* element of our educational system that we can reasonably influence, manage, and control (Darling-Hammond, 2010). Recent U.S. census data estimate that across our public, private, and charter systems we now have approximately 130,000 schools, 80 million students, and 7.5 million teachers—with 200,000 new educators entering the profession each year. In a system this large and complex, it is not surprising—and it is perhaps even *responsible*—that our citizens increasingly focus their often-misguided attention on who these teachers are and how they are prepared.

But too often these policy and practical debates begin and end with the deceptive notion that teacher education programs are no longer necessary and that any individual with sufficient content knowledge can be an effective teacher. In this chapter, I detail the "faces" of these lies about the nature and necessity of teacher education programs and about the qualifications of teachers—including the forms they have taken, the motivations behind them, some of their impacts and implications, and several philosophical and practical alternatives to their assumptions. I begin with my own visage—my very personal history with and perspective on these "anyone can teach" and "teacher education is no longer necessary" topics.

The Imposter Syndrome

I have a particular sensitivity to the topics of teacher qualifications and preparation, not solely because I am a teacher and teacher educator. Rather, to this day I am self-conscious about my own teaching worthiness because I entered the profession through the equivalent of the "back door" that I now find so troubling. I began teaching in a publicly funded GED (General Equivalency Diploma) program in the late 1980s, working with two Franciscan sisters as my colleagues and school administrators in the small, economically depressed midwestern city of South Bend, Indiana, which was then being enveloped by the first wave of our postindustrial economy. We were attempting to serve displaced factory personnel who, when they had entered the world of work, had not needed even a high school diploma to find gainful, middle-class employment.

I started to teach then—while I was an undergraduate at the University of Notre Dame—because I had rather suddenly became aware of and uncomfortable with my own educational privilege. My parents were just high school graduates—my dad just barely accomplishing that—who struggled to make ends meet into their sixties and long after my four siblings and I had left home. But we were raised with a wealth of curiosity and an implicit message that education was perhaps the only means through which we might be able to attain more stable and comfortable lives than we had known growing up.

Throughout my elementary and high school years, I had been surrounded by classmates who did not appear to appreciate school in the same way that was quietly, yet almost religiously, being impressed upon me at home. Perhaps 10 percent of my high school peers attended college, with the majority taking factory and farming jobs upon their high school graduation that they explicitly named a bump in the road of life rather than viewing it as a foundation for other opportunities. At that stage I had longed only to escape, to be sure that I was not cursed with the same lack of prospects by which my dad had been tracked and that, I perceived, many of my contemporaries were consciously choosing—the result of their decisions not to pursue a formal post-secondary education.

I still share with my mostly future teacher students that during my first years as an education professional—unlicensed—in my city classrooms in South Bend, then Chicago, and eventually Madison, Wisconsin, I often felt as if I were nervously waiting for what I came to call the "Imposter Police" to appear. I feared that on a random school day I would hear a knock at my classroom door interrupting the activity in which my students and I were engaged. I would call out to the visitor to enter, only to see from across the room two very official-looking, likely uniformed men standing smugly near the corner of the blackboard. I would go quietly: I would scurry out of the classroom and out of the teaching profession, with maybe a brief, stumbling, rambling apology to my students through tears of embarrassment and relief and without even a thorough round of farewells to my colleagues up and down the hallway. I would be dramatically shackled to emphasize the horror of my criminal offense: having the audacity to pose as a competent teacher without sufficient training. All this professional existential angst in a time when almost no one in policy making or teacher education circles seemed interested in considering, questioning, or systematizing teachers' qualifications.

This is how conscious I was that while I loved teaching—mostly middle and high school English in urban contexts—I knew that I should not have been able to enter the profession so readily, on the basis, apparently, of my desire and my degree from a well-known university then respected as much for its football lore as its academics. Or the result, I thought, even then—perhaps somewhat cynically—of my Whiteness, my height, and my ability to talk a fairly charming game. But this is all it took in the 1990s for me to teach for nine years in public, independent, and Catholic schools in several diverse city contexts with young people who looked nothing like me and had known lives almost nothing like my own. It was more than a little bit incongruous that a few years hence I finally earned my first teaching license—simultaneously in two states, mind you—when I was also beginning my dissertation research for a PhD in—naturally—teacher education.

At that time, the "anyone can teach" and "teacher education is not necessary" lies were barely twinkles in politicians' and the general public's eyes, and both teacher licensure/assessment efforts and student evaluation systems were mixed bags and moving targets. States and schools had far fewer guidelines for judging both teachers' credentials and students' achievement, scant curricular objectives to guide teachers' practices or the measurement of students' learning, occasional and relatively low-stakes standardized tests for pre-K–12 children and youth, and just rudimentary sets of teacher licensing requirements. While I remain grateful to this day that I found a profession with which I have been able to engage with such passion and through which I have lived so intentionally, I remain clear that—back then in those variously sized cities in the Midwest—I simply was *not* qualified to teach children. Now, as a teacher, teacher educator, and citizen, I fear that my back-door story is quickly becoming the primary path through which new, temporary teachers find their way to serving our most vulnerable children.

Everyone Knows What a "Good" Teacher Is

Of course, when I work with the current students—virtually all of whom are future teachers—I do not conclude my tale of my entry into this teaching life and how I earned my qualifications as a teacher educator with this story. None of my colleagues or students would likely ever suggest that I am a traditional academic, but the fact is that, in terms of my professional aptitudes and pedigree, I am highly conventional. I spent more than 13 (again, mostly unlicensed) years as a classroom teacher, I continue to work with young people on at least a weekly basis, and I earned advanced degrees in education from some of the most reputable graduate programs in the United States. I have conducted dozens of studies of effective teaching practices in more than a decade as a professor, and my vita is filled with publications and presentations. While my penchant for personal and professional humility makes me shudder a bit as I write these words, I am, almost without dispute, now *qualified* not just to teach children, university students, and pre-service and veteran teachers, but also to have and express my critical, well-informed, professional opinions on the state and nature of teacher education policies and practices, including those "anyone can teach" and "teacher education is no longer necessary" untruths.

While the first "face" of these lies I introduced earlier was my own, the countenance that concerns me most now is that of an "everyman" or "everywoman" in the United States. One of the foundational—and most difficult to extract— aspects of this deception is the strangely ignorant assumption that simply by having lived in the United States, *every* one of us not only has a *right* to express an opinion about teacher quality and training but that each of us has intimate and more than sufficient *knowledge* of these subjects. Imagine projecting that assumed level of expertise to virtually any another field; you would be labeled ignorant, reckless, or negligent. For example, what if someone suggested that because we all drive on publicly funded roads, we are all, naturally, gifted with authoritative insights into road construction and repair. Or that because many of us have participated in some form of organized religion, we are, by default, fit to be preachers, prophets, or even gods. Or that as a result of the fact that many of us have been able to visit the doctor numerous times in our lives, we are now capable medical specialists or qualified to judge the expertise of surgeons.

This assumption of the general public's—or even many otherwise well-educated policymakers'—qualifications as arbiters of teachers' aptitudes and abilities is perhaps the most sinister and, one hopes, the most obviously indefensible position behind the "anyone can teach" and "teacher education programs are no longer necessary" lies that are proliferating in our nation—and with particular effectiveness in our most diverse and disenfranchised communities. Such an orientation is akin to giving someone credit for breathing: we do not deserve awards for the results of our involuntary reflexes or decorations for decisions we did not consciously make. When we conflate simple lived experience with expertise—when we confuse the right to have an opinion with the absolute expectation that this view should be the ultimate determinant in a policy discussion—we are in deep trouble indeed. Yet these are the sorts of inexpert views that are being given so much credence when communities consider the qualifications of their teachers (Darling-Hammond, 2010).

The History of the Content Knowledge Lie

Unfortunately—and, again, perhaps not surprisingly—ours is not the first era in which the "anyone can teach" deception has reigned or the first time in our nation's educational history that formal teacher training has come under such scrutiny or been challenged by fault-finding forces. Strangely, though, in previous generations, the primary critics of teacher education came from within the academy itself. The contemporary profiles behind this "anyone can teach" lie are actually shadows of these very different detractors from nearly a century ago—who argued a now very familiar theme.

The respected education scholars Ken Zeichner and Dan Liston have offered a number of histories of our teacher education traditions. They have detailed how in the 1930s many academics—most from outside the field of teacher education but who worked alongside education colleagues and scholars—argued that teacher preparation programs' fieldwork experiences in schools were superfluous. These same critics articulately contended that subject-matter knowledge was the most important element of a teacher's credentials and that courses in the teacher training curriculum were intellectually decrepit and even interfered with teachers' development.

A generation later—in the mid-twentieth century—teacher education opponents argued that considering only candidates' content knowledge would draw our nation's "best and brightest" into the teaching profession, appealing to individuals who would otherwise be driven away from teaching by the dubious value of the education curriculum. In 1953, Arthur Bestor summarized these critics' stances on a rigorous, appropriate teacher education program: "A new curriculum for the education of teachers, based firmly upon the liberal arts and sciences, rather than upon the mere vocational skills of pedagogy will do more to restore the repute of the public schools than any other step that can be taken." This position is eerily echoed by the words of numerous everyday citizens and policymakers today—and even sanctioned at state and federal levels by sweeping policies that offer "alternative" and "provisional" paths into the teaching profession for individuals with no qualifications other than undergraduate degrees and high grade-point averages, most often from elite and very frequently from Ivy League institutions (Maier, 2012). Yet it is instructive that these ideas from nearly a century ago were merely that—concepts and critiques that challenged and ultimately helped to develop a profession (Solomon, 2009). Even a few short decades ago, many of us might have *talked* about such a radical, irresponsible delimiting of the very nature of teachers' qualifications, but none of us would actually have *enacted* it.

The New Imposters and an *Anti*-Profession

It is impossible in any discussion of the state of the teaching profession and the "anyone can teach" and "teacher education is no longer necessary" lies not to consider the poster organization for this deceptive note: Teach for America (TFA). TFA is, in its own words, a "growing movement of leaders who work to ensure that kids growing up in poverty get an excellent education." In strictest terms, it is a teacher recruitment agency that enlists primarily recent college graduates to work in our nation's most diverse, impoverished communities for two-year stints, supported by a token five-week training regimen in the summer between "corps" members' university graduation and the following fall's new school year. While this chapter is not intended as a critique of TFA, it is impossible not to have a discussion of the "anyone can teach" and "teacher education is no longer necessary" lies—and the current teacher education policies and practices that support these notions—without exploring the nature of this phenomenon. The fact of this program's proliferation and the fact that one in five teachers now enters the profession through an "alternative" certification path (Sykes & Dibner, 2009) may be the ultimate sign of our nation's acceptance of these deceptions.

Today's TFA-influenced "anyone can teach" contract encompasses a constellation of real and symbolic "faces" and myriad motivations—three collections of which are most important to appreciate if we are to make sense of the duplicity of this lie. These include policymakers and education elites who have successfully convinced themselves, each other, and much of the U.S. public that the lie is, in fact, a self-evident truth rooted in some desperate attempt at schooling justice. We also cannot ignore the seemingly goodhearted and unquestionably well-educated individuals—the TFA "recruits"—who eventually serve as teachers in many of the most impoverished communities in our nation. And, perhaps most important, we simultaneously see and absolutely fail to recognize the economically disadvantaged, most often Black and brown students whom the "anyone can teach" TFA proponents and their intermediaries—the TFA "corps members"—purport to aid. But let us begin with something decidedly less metaphorical in this "anyone can teach" equation: some of the numbers.

TFA and Dollar Signs

Even a cursory examination of TFA gives us great insight into the motivations behind this sweeping deception. While the numbers of TFA alone would not appear to be significant—the program supplies less than 5 percent of our nation's new teachers (Donaldson & Johnson, 2010)—these percentages simply cannot help impacting the teaching profession far into the future. Since 1990, TFA has placed more than 25,000 individuals in public schools for planned two-year stints as teachers. In 2011, TFA was the top employer on 25 college campuses, including Dartmouth, Georgetown, Vanderbilt, and the University of Chicago, and fully 18 percent of the graduating class at Harvard applied for TFA in 2010.

While the sheer quantity of TFA recruits and others who have taken similar "alternative" routes into the teaching profession are significant and growing, other figures are perhaps more telling. TFA is essentially a professional recruitment program, with hiring districts required to pay a negotiated per-candidate fee—in addition to a standard starting teacher salary—that is typically between $2,000 and $5,000. And, before agreeing to send recruits into a community, TFA frequently acquires subsidies from local businesses, philanthropies, or state governments. Even more troubling is the fact that TFA frequently delivers these novices into districts that have recently laid off large numbers of considerably more expensive veteran teachers. Thus, one of the first "faces" of programs like TFA is—obviously, actually—the symbol of a dollar sign. As clichéd as it might seem, this character best represents the fact that the assumption that "anyone can teach" and that teacher education programs are not necessary is rooted in the fiscal concerns of economically challenged school districts and communities and in the privatizing orientation and profit motive of this lie's proponents, rather than in some theoretical stance or documented evidence of its verity.

Policymakers and Champions

While it is impossible to know with absolute certainty the motivations of the advocates of and participants in TFA and other programs that embody the "anyone can teach" lie, these financial incentives cannot be discounted. But these programs also unabashedly appeal to the notion of "service"—suggesting that working in these economically poor and decidedly diverse communities is akin to a great military or missionary duty to guide helpless citizens toward a rightful, democratic end. In terms of both political expediency and economic efficiency, policymakers simply cannot lose with such programs, as they are intentionally—proponents might argue *intelligently*—sending ("sacrificing"?) our "best and brightest" into these "war zones"—while saving the untold billions of dollars of shrinking but still significant public university subsidies that support traditional teacher education tracks and trading trained, experienced public school employee salaries for private corporations' recruitment fees.

"Good-Hearted"—and Yet Greedy—Recruits

The motivations of the TFA recruits are certainly just as complicated—if not as menacing—as those of the other players involved in the "anyone can teach" lie. Of course, working for two years in challenging communities in a profession for which you have no training is certainly a form of service. But it is also unquestionably self-serving, as one of TFA's expressed goals is to generate the next generation of education leaders—again, for privatized "public" schools that generate profits for education management organizations (EMOs) and that look little like the community institutions a democratic nation idealizes. This is an objective TFA and its "anyone can teach" kin have quite successfully achieved, as evidenced by the growing numbers of former TFA participants employed in school, district, state, federal, and corporate education administrative positions. It is difficult to imagine that the Wendy Kopps and education corporatists of the world did not recognize a grossly underregulated profession that serves the most disenfranchised—poor kids and communities—as a massive, untapped market and an opportunity for their own and their elite—if perhaps well-intentioned—peers' professional attainment and profits.

The explicit—and more often implicit—assumptions and motivations behind such programs are similarly disturbing. One does not have to look very deeply into our abyss of popular culture to recognize that, as a nation, we are addicted to naming and relying on "heroes" to solve "crisis" situations. Virtually every example of contemporary media—movies, television shows, even everyday news reports—unabashedly depicts teachers as either saviors or demons. "Natural born" may be the most common descriptor of anyone in the teaching profession whom we view as successful. In such a dichotomous equation—populated by redeemers or monsters—there is virtually no space for valuing teaching as a profession for which one is actually *trained* and in which one actually *develops* over the course of career (Berliner, 2000). And who among us would *not*—for a predetermined and relatively brief amount of time—want to be such a star? Particularly if we were promised that the rewards for this two-year sacrifice would be a lifetime of Purple Heart–quality public gratitude and enhanced employment opportunities?

Serving Only the "Other"

One of the most troubling—and, again, most duplicitous—of the TFA and the "anyone can teach" assumptions regards the faces of the children and communities such programs and this con are intended to serve. In its own literature—a 2010 report—TFA claimed to teach our nation's neediest children and youth, with 90 percent of students in the schools where the program places teachers African American or Hispanic and 80 percent receiving free or reduced lunch. Such programs may be the most blatantly racist of any in our nation's history, actually intending to consign untrained educators to the schools populated by our most disenfranchised young people.

When the irrational arguments that *no* training and an elite liberal arts education are de facto teacher qualifications fall away, proponents can still claim that these are crisis-context jobs that no one else will take—that desperate times call for desperate measures. The truth seems to be obvious, though: desperate privations call for substantial *investments* rather than Band-Aid policies and practices. Perhaps the real test of such a lie would be our nation's willingness to hire TFA recruits and unqualified do-gooders for the children of our Whitest and wealthiest citizens—a proposition that would likely strike even TFA proponents as an utter absurdity.

The Faces of the Truth

Retention, Research, and "Service"

While the racist, classist tendencies behind programs like TFA are troubling, it may be even more problematic that the "anyone can teach" and "teacher education programs are not necessary" lies have been built—and, with TFA's and similar programs' expansion, continue to be constructed—on an anti-intellectual, research-resistant, data-deprived, and anecdote-driven approach to teacher education, teacher performance, and student achievement policies. While TFA appears to be focusing on tracking and researching the impact of its recruits on student success, any education scholar is—and every policymaker and citizen *should* be—dubious if not outraged by even the prospect of a school or district hiring these teachers, given the random and occasional way in which such measures have been employed. While a nominal number of studies appear to suggest that TFA graduates are at least not doing students any damage during the typical two years they spend in these classrooms (Glazerman, Mayer, & Decker, 2006), these data have been collected in such an arbitrary manner that their reliability cannot be trusted (Schoeneberger, 2011). We are operating with and making decisions about *real* students' lives on the basis of the equivalent of a one-day snapshot of information, for a notion and a program that has been foisted upon the American people for more than two decades.

The element of this "anyone can teach" lie with which we should be most concerned—and that we can answer with existing teacher preparation programs—is the acceptance and even promotion of the short-term commitment to our children that this idea is inflicting upon the U.S. public. The "anyone can teach" lie is, more accurately, an "anyone can survive" ruse, rooted in the troubling, inaccurate assumption that our most challenged schools deserve and may be best served by untrained educators who, by design, remain in these classrooms for only two years. Published retention rates for TFA recruits in, for example, New York and Houston are only 10 to 15 percent by year four, and after five years only 27.8 percent of TFA "corps members" are still teaching—a number that is approximately half the retention rate of the overall teaching population (Donaldson & Johnson, 2010). Numerous studies have found that the positive impact of a teacher with three or more years of experience is much greater than the effect of any preparation program—TFA or similar options or even more traditional tracks—on student learning (Ronfeldt, Loeb, & Wyckoff, 2012).

If we are not swayed to reject the "anyone can teach" deception by any other arguments, the planned-obsolescence feature of such programs and the question of the teachers our students deserve intersect where the ideas behind and the science of *real* teacher preparation programs unequivocally offer our schools, communities, and young people the best option. We must be especially diligent to not be distracted by the reframing of the teacher education question upon which TFA-like programs and the "anyone can teach" lie are based.

When it comes to the teachers our students—*any* young people, but especially our most disenfranchised children and youth—merit, we should *never* begin *and* end with the historical challenges underresourced communities have faced in finding and retaining teachers. Such considerations have led us to fatalistic practices and policy responses, a cliff-like drop-off in our expectations for the professional preparation of teachers for these communities, and the tendency to be grateful that *anyone* is willing to work in these with "these" children in these contexts. A young teacher education colleague recently unwittingly summarized this framing best when, in a conversation about TFA-like programs, he asked, "If TFA-trained recruits are not going to serve these kids, then who will?" This query speaks to exactly the set of delimiting, unspoken assumptions and the deterministic, charity-driven, and antisocial justice stance upon which proponents of the "anyone can teach" lie are counting on us to continue to rely.

Full-Service Schools and Community Teachers

Of course, the mission of this chapter is not merely to intelligently disparage the "anyone can teach" and "teacher education programs are not necessary" lies. We do, in fact, already have the theory, practices, and data of alternative, *real* teacher education programs to answer any of these deceptions. And we have the hope proffered by numerous studies of both current and cutting-edge teacher education programs. These include the well-documented ideas behind, efforts of, and results of "full-service" schools, the concept of a "community" teacher, and teachers trained, retained, and operating successfully through Professional Development School and residency programs. While these require fundamental shifts in some of the assumptions behind and primary practices of schools, teaching, and teacher preparation, these are, in fact, already happening in numerous places around the United States. Let's briefly consider each of these ideas and options in turn—moving from our schools, to our teachers, and, finally, to the preparation programs that support these new professionals and institutions.

While schools have traditionally been considered merely sites where children go to learn the three R's (*sic*), a "full-service" school is one where the needs of the whole child—and, by extension, the well-being of the family and the community—are considered. Virtually every teacher—even of the TFA ilk—recognizes that students in every setting but particularly in underresourced communities have many more needs than teachers' professional training or daily class and school schedule allows them to meet. Teachers almost inevitably play part-time roles as therapists, nurses, job counselors, and even nutritionists.

But imagine if the school were a center where social service agencies, teachers, administrators, and community constituents partnered to identify this whole range of needs and then recognized that the school context and building was the ideal venue for addressing all of these objectives—in, around, and as part of an extended school day. Of course, the school's primary mission—to serve children's academic needs—would be enhanced, with students and teachers considerably less distracted by these unfortunate but unavoidable requirements for physical, emotional, and even economic sustenance. Numerous examples of such partnerships exist, with the most popular and successful of these models including the placement of health-care professionals in school settings, often operating on extended hours and able to access and serve children and their families (Garrett, 2012; Voyles, 2012).

Of course, the role of the teacher changes dramatically in these contexts, but, one could argue, if we are considering such a monumental change in the notion of what is an "education professional"—witness the TFA "anyone can teach" and "teacher education programs are not necessary" approach—why not consider *every* alternative? Particularly one that requires *additional,* rather than *diminished,* training and a more honest notion of the skills required by such education specialists? If we really are *that* desperate for alternative notions of a "teacher" in order to serve the needs of our most economically disadvantaged young people, then let's consider a model of a teacher that will both serve children well *and* remain in these settings. And, best of all, let's ensure that professionals are prepared to work in such contexts.

Perhaps the most comprehensive notion of the professional who is needed for these school contexts is that of a "community teacher." This concept has its roots in civil rights–era practices, where classroom teachers were expected not only to consider the academic needs of children but to be aware of—and even to contextualize their work and their daily curricula in—the relationship between education and larger social issues and movements. This is not to suggest that teachers need to be political activists but to appreciate, again, that our students arrive in schools with a wide range of needs. If we do not help to meet these needs, then children will be distracted from the academic objectives that are our primary focus; contextualizing their learning in these larger, authentic contexts can only help young people to appreciate, engage with, and remain in school.

Professional Development Schools and Teacher Residencies

Finally, we turn to the programs that are enacting these more expansive ideas and ideals of teachers and schools—including both Professional Development Schools and, more recently, teacher residency options (Darling-Hammond, 2008). It is hardly news among teacher educators and schools that many teacher education programs and university faculty are structurally isolated from the schools we are attempting to serve through the teachers we prepare. Constituents in both institutions involved in this teacher education equation—schools and universities—have long appreciated that most teacher preparation programs primarily aid the university partners, with veteran classroom teachers essentially volunteering their time to train pre-service teachers, primarily during their student teaching experiences, while university faculty offer introductory and, too often, *contradictory* information to novice teachers about the nature of their new work.

But, beginning in the 1980s, the Professional Development School model officially and honestly recognized the ineffective, inequitable, and unprofessional nature of this model. And the early proponents of this paradigm recognized that true partnerships of schools and universities could allow *both* institutions to be sites of learning and professional development for *all* of their constituents—children, pre-service teachers, veteran teachers, university faculty, and, by extension, family and community members (Henry, Tryjankowski, Bailey, & DiCamillo, 2010). These new teacher preparation models actually focused on a wider range of objectives, including pre-K–12 student learning, collaboratively conducted research, and the professional development of veteran teachers and university faculty—but did so through a model where school- and university-based personnel played formal roles in each others' institutions, where every element of the venture was considered a joint effort.

Arguably an extension of the Professional Development School approach, teacher residencies—which are most often designed for the urban contexts and the exact sets of K–12 student constituents and communities TFS-like programs purport to serve—prepare new educators in these intensified contexts. They do so with successful, veteran classroom teachers from these very settings playing the primary teacher educator roles and with residency recruits required to complete not just five weeks of "training"—à la TFA—but up to three *years* of fully mentored apprenticeships, only after which they are qualified as fully licensed classroom practitioners (Eckert, 2012). Perhaps most ironic of all is the fact that residency programs appreciate that becoming a teacher involves a dramatic personal and professional shift in identity—one that almost inevitably, again, lasts into the first decade of a new teacher's experience: most residency options require graduates to complete up to five years of induction, support, and development activities. Again, we have the models for the *best* teacher education programs—ones that train educators and help them remain in our neediest communities—if we can only muster the intelligence, honesty, and political wherewithal to enact them.

The One Bit of Truth in the Lie

I would be disingenuous if I did not acknowledge one bit of complexity—even a bit of truth—in the "anyone can teach" and "teacher education programs are not necessary" lies and the way that these have been interpreted and implemented over the past two decades in the United States. If we accept the fact that classroom teachers not only are the single most important and easily influenced element of the social contract that is universal K–12 education in the United States and if we can concede that schools are one of, if not, *the* most important institution in our society, then the simplest logic—perhaps the only real *common* sense—suggests that our best and brightest should be helping to mold the minds and hearts of our youngest and our most vulnerable, our children and our citizenry. TFA and similar programs *recruit* one narrow segment of the elite to play these teacher roles, and all teacher education programs should be ruthless about identifying the most capable among us to serve—long term—as classroom teachers.

We might be even more merciless when it comes to choosing and training those who will educate and support these classroom teachers. While I began this exploration of the "anyone can teach" and "teacher education programs are not necessary" lies with my own "face"—my own experience with this entire teacher education proposition—I will conclude with one last bit of candor: in a world where K–12 schools *really* mattered, where we judged our nation by how it served its most vulnerable—the children in its schools—maybe even I would no longer be qualified to do the work of teacher education that I so cherish. If another professional could be trained and retained to do it better, I would gladly step aside—no Imposter Police required.

References

Berliner, D.C. (2000). A personal response to those who bash teacher education. *Journal of Teacher Education, 51*(5), 358–371. doi:10.1177/0022487100051005004

Darling-Hammond, L. (2008). A future worthy of teaching for America. *Phi Delta Kappan, 89*(10), 730–733.

Darling-Hammond, L. (2010). Teacher education and the American future. *Journal of Teacher Education, 61*(1–2), 35–47. doi:10.1177/0022487109348024

Donaldson, M. L., & Johnson, S. M. (2010). The price of misassignment: The role of teaching assignments in Teach for America teachers' exit from low-income schools and the teaching profession. *Educational Evaluation and Policy Analysis, 32*(2), 299–323. doi:10.3102/0162373710367680

Eckert, S. A. (2012). What do teaching qualifications mean in urban schools? A mixed-methods study of teacher preparation and qualification. *Journal of Teacher Education, 64*(1), 75–89. doi:10.1177/0022487112460279

Garrett, K. (2012). Community schools: It takes a village. *The Education Digest, 78*(3), 14–20.

Glazerman, S., Mayer, D., & Decker, P. (2006). Alternative routes to teaching: The impacts of Teach for America on student achievement and other outcomes. *Journal of Personality and Social Psychology, 25*(1), 75–96. doi:10.1002/pam

Henry, J., Tryjankowski, A., Bailey, N., & DiCamillo, L. (Spring 2010). How Professional Development Schools can help to create friendly environments for teachers to integrate theory, research, and practice. *Childhood Education, 86*(5), 327–331.

Maier, A. (2012). Doing good and doing well: Credentialism and Teach for America. *Journal of Teacher Education, 63*(1), 10–22. doi:10.1177/0022487111422071

Ronfeldt, M., Loeb, S., & Wyckoff, J. (2012). How teacher turnover harms student achievement. *American Educational Research Journal, 50*(1), 4–36. doi:10.3102/0002831212463813

Schoeneberger, J. A. (2011, May 30). Evaluation of Teach for America in Charlotte-Mecklenburg schools. Retrieved from www.cms.k12.nc.us/cmsdepartments/account ability/cfre/Documents/TeachForAmerica_Evaluation_Report_2011.pdf

Solomon, J. (2009). The Boston teacher residency: District-based teacher education. *Journal of Teacher Education, 60*(5), 478–488. doi:10.1177/0022487109349915

Sykes, G., & Dibner, K. (2009). *Fifty years of federal teacher policy?: An appraisal.* Washington, DC: Center for Educational Policy.

Voyles, M. M. (2012). Perceived needs of at-risk families in a small town?: Implications for full-service community schools. *School Community Journal, 22*(2), 31–64.

8

TEACHERS' UNIONS ARE NOT BAD FOR KIDS

Katy Swalwell

The teachers unions have been basically running the system for decades now, and our kids are failing. Let's do what's right for the kids for a change instead of doing what's right for adults.

—Former Washington, D.C. Mayor Adrien Fenty
(September 12, 2012, on the *Diane Rehm Show*)

The big lie that teachers' unions are not doing "what's right for the kids" is based upon a fundamentally flawed logic about current school reform efforts. First, it assumes that two groups are fighting over the direction of public schools: those who want what is best for kids and those who want what is best for adults. It paints educational reformers as the heroes who are looking out for kids' interests and teachers' unions as the villains who get in the way by defending the status quo. In this logic, teachers' unions obstruct needed changes because the old ways provide them with undeserved benefits and keep them from being "accountable"—the buzziest of buzz words in the educational reform pantheon.

Within this logic, educational reformers take pains to distinguish between greedy, obstructionist teachers' unions and the noble, honorable individual teachers who (because they care about kids) embrace policies like standardized testing, merit pay, and school choice. For instance, Michelle Rhee claims to "believe in teachers and the power of teachers" but finds that "there are some problems that exist with teachers' union contracts, collective bargaining agreements, that have to be addressed because they're not good for kids" (Nnamdi, 2012). If you are a teacher who does not support her reforms (and instead critiques high-stakes tests, advocates for tenure, argues against the expansion of charter networks, and—gasp!—belongs to a union), then you must not care about kids.

This chapter debunks this lie's logic, posits why it persists despite evidence to the contrary, and articulates a path forward for a social justice unionism that might better fight against it. First, however, let's examine just how powerful this lie has become.

Spreading the Lie

According to a 2011 Phi Delta Kappa/Gallup poll on perceptions of public schools and teachers, 47 percent of respondents believe that the unionization of teachers has hurt the quality of public school education in the United States (Bushaw & Lopez, 2011). A poll conducted by researchers at Harvard's Program on Education Policy and Governance and the journal *Education Next* found that 51 percent of respondents believe unions have a negative impact on schools (Peterson, Howell, & West, 2012). The same poll found that only 22 percent of the general public supports teachers' unions, a decline of seven points from the year before.

This negative attitude toward teachers' unions is endemic in mainstream news and media accounts of why public schools are failing. For instance, a *Newsweek* cover story in March 2010 ("The Key to Saving American Education") had an image of a chalkboard covered with repetitions of the sentence "We must fire bad teachers"; inside, the article extolled Teach for America and nonunion charter schools. And the widely seen, heavily marketed, Oprah-promoted *Waiting for Superman* documentary used shoddy research to laud the same educational reform package and promote the idea that unions cannot be trusted (Swalwell and Apple, 2010).

This suspicion of teachers' unions has become a decidedly bipartisan affair; it is not just Republicans who are anti-union. Democrats like Mayor Rahm Emanuel of Chicago and Adrian Fenty, former mayor of Washington, DC, have not hesitated to fight teachers' unions. Democratic educational "reformers" like Michelle Rhee and Secretary of Education Arne Duncan have often been at odds with teachers' unions. And though President Obama won the endorsement of both major teachers' unions in 2008 and 2012, his educational policy initiatives, such as Race to the Top, have not garnered support from the American Federation of Teachers (AFT) or the National Education Association (NEA). Most notably, they recoiled at his and Secretary Duncan's applause for Rhode Island Central Falls High School's initial firing of *all* its teachers in 2010.

These attacks on unions in policy and popular culture have helped pave the way for the misleadingly named right-to-work laws. In recent years, these laws, which constrain unions by legislating against collective bargaining, have spread into traditional union stronghold states like Indiana, Michigan, and Wisconsin. Perhaps no other recent event better exposes the consequences of believing that teachers' unions are bad for public schools than the 2011 "Wisconsin Uprising," during which the state's teachers' union was stripped of its right to collectively bargain.

In February 2011, Wisconsin's newly elected Republican governor, Scott Walker, proposed the Budget Repair Bill, which, among many other objectives, aimed to strip public-sector unions (except those for police and firefighters) of their collective bargaining rights with the claim that this would save the state money. In response, hundreds of concerned citizens began sleeping in the rotunda of the capitol building, with tens of thousands more participating in weekend rallies that garnered international attention.

Amid this public uprising, the Budget Repair Bill was passed with the use of a neat procedural trick. Eight of the State Senate Democrats exiled themselves to Illinois to prevent a quorum and thus keep a vote on the bill from coming to the Senate floor. Because legislation with no fiscal implications could be passed without the Democrats in attendance, the Republicans simply separated the provision regarding public-sector unions' collective bargaining rights from the Budget Repair Bill, paradoxically declared it to be a nonfiscal provision despite having previously claimed that collective bargaining cost districts money, and passed it into law.

As a result, "Act 10" stripped public-sector unions of their collective bargaining power, denied their ability to automatically collect dues from teachers' paychecks, and demanded they reconstitute themselves every year. Given that any power a teachers' union may have is intimately linked to its ability to collect dues and collectively bargain (Winkler, Scull, & Zeehandelaar, 2012), this legislation dealt an enormous blow to the 98,000 members of the Wisconsin Education Association. With the teachers' union hobbled, there was little formal resistance to the governor's educational agenda: an increase in charter-school networks, an expansion of school vouchers, and movement toward performance pay for teachers.

In fall 2011, Governor Walker overcame a recall effort to win reelection. Though the Act 10 legislation was deemed unconstitutional by a state judge, a federal appeals court overturned the decision and ruled in favor of the governor. In the following months, districts developed handbooks (many modeled after a template from the Wisconsin Association of School Boards) that stipulated new employment conditions: the ability for administrators to fire teachers at will, higher employee contributions to health insurance, a reduction of postretirement benefits, fewer holidays and sick leave, a reduction in prep periods, an increase in duties, and the elimination of step-and-ladder pay scales that compensated teachers for graduate credits and years of service (Richards, 2011).

Though defended by a few journalists from progressive media outlets and with vague verbal support from President Obama, the teachers' unions during the "uprising" were largely framed in the public eye as outdated at best and obstructionist at worst. An examination of online comments posted in reference to news stories about the protests shows the degree to which the belief that unions are bad for kids had taken hold in Wisconsin, a state famed for its labor union history (Swalwell, 2012). Granted, online comments posted by angry or defensive readers tend not to be known for their measured eloquence, yet there is a rawness to these rants that reveals what people were thinking and what teachers (and their unions) were up against. For example, "Oldtime," a respondent to an editorial in the *Milwaukee Journal Sentinel,* articulated the belief that unions have no place in public education:

> Along with most everyone I talk to these days, I am filled with disgust by the teacher's union. Yes, there are plenty of good, honest teachers who actually do care about kids . . . but, almost all of them are still supporting the corrupt union that is about everything but kids. They support the same union that has helped to bankrupt this state, and bullies every single community into submission. The same union that protects the incompetent, the lazy, the crazy, and the truant. It is was [SIC] past time to open the doors of our schools to free the hostages.[1]

Let's examine Oldtime's arguments as representative of the "big lie" that unions are bad for children by addressing each point one by one: (1) unions cause fiscal crises ("bankrupt this state"); (2) unions protect bad teachers ("the incompetent, the lazy, the crazy, and the truant"); and (3) unions do not have kids' interests at heart ("about everything but kids").

Debunking the Lie

One important note before reviewing what existing research says with regards to whether teachers' unions are bad for public schools: this lie is most soundly debunked with the simple admission that we do not yet know enough to make a strong claim such as "unions are bad for kids." It is shocking what little research about teachers' unions exists, given their long-standing roles in public education, not to mention the antipathy they have inspired among the public and policymakers. Empirical studies examining the role of teachers' unions face many challenges: a lack of good long-term data sets with information about unionization, student achievement, and demographics that would make large representative samples possible; a constantly shifting political landscape impacting state and local laws that can render data irrelevant almost immediately; and a complex set of interrelated variables shaping student success and failure that are almost impossible to isolate (Hoxby, 1996; Winkler, Scull, & Zeehandelaar, 2012).

Regardless of whether their work is used to support policies that defend or disparage unions, scholars studying teachers' unions have noted and lamented this dearth of research (e.g., Goldhaber, 2006; Moe, 2001; Winkler, Scull, & Zeehandelaar, 2012). Because "even the simplest questions must often be answered through sketchy information that is patched together from various data sources (Moe, 2001, p. 155)," it is unwise to make any strong claims or policies based on the idea that teachers' unions are bad for kids.

In the foreword to a 2010 report about the strength of teachers' unions (funded in part by the conservative Thomas B. Fordham Institute and Education Reform Now, groups that are often at odds with the teachers' unions), Chester E. Finn and Michael J. Petrilli note that "no one on either side of the ed-reform divide should be glib about this topic" (Winkler, Scull, & Zeehandelaar, 2012, p. 6). This is absolutely right, and we would all be better served with more robust, objective research that tackles important questions about teachers' unions.

That said, there is some compelling evidence worth examining that helps to unpack why this particular lie is untrue or, at the very least, misleading.

Sub-Lie 1: Teachers' Unions Bankrupt States

First, unionized teachers do typically have higher salaries than nonunionized teachers (Baugh & Stone, 1982), and unionized districts do typically have increased costs (Eberts & Stone, 1986). To claim that these expenses have bankrupted states, however, is quite a leap. According to the Congressional Budget Office, states are experiencing fiscal stress due to "transitory economic shocks," including plummeting state revenues from income and sales tax due to the Great Recession in combination with long-term structural issues (Delisle, 2010, p. 2). Arrangements with public-sector unions in which mayors or councils have been unable to "control labor costs" are but one of many "structural budget imbalances" that "arise from a variety of sources and are difficult to disentangle" including paralysis caused by political infighting, demographic shifts, questionable accounting procedures, and unwise borrowing (Delisle, 2010, p. 3).

Harsh economic realities may mean that teachers temporarily lose some of their benefits or take a reduction in pay, but the blame for the financial crisis should not be laid solely at their feet—nor does it justify stripping unions of collective bargaining rights. Collective bargaining does not cost money. It simply ensures that budget decisions are based on input from multiple stakeholders. In Wisconsin, for example, the teachers' union made it clear that it was willing to accept pay cuts and higher contributions to teachers' insurance plans and retirement as long as its collective bargaining power remained intact. The governor, however, was unwilling to compromise (Woodruff, 2011). The "flexibility" that he and other opponents of unions argue for is really just a euphemism for unilateral decision making.

Next, we must consider that higher pay and fringe benefits, although they increase educational costs, may also increase the quality of education if they attract better teachers (Eberts, 2007). Rather than blame teachers' unions for what they have negotiated as a way to recruit and maintain good people in the field or to focus only on what these practices cost, we should also examine what is gained by these arrangements. How have contributions to the public fund been depleted? How have corporate tax breaks and funding formulas affected what resources are available to school districts? How should they be reallocated or restructured to provide schools with the resources they need? Though more empirical data would certainly help to make these decisions, questions about how resources ought to be collected and allocated also raise important normative issues that touch upon "competing budgetary priorities, views on intergenerational fairness, and the amount of risk that plans' sponsors are willing to take" (Russek, 2011, p. 2).

Sub-Lie 2: Teachers' Unions Protect Bad Teachers

The idea that teachers' unions protect bad teachers is especially seductive given that everyone has come into contact with at least one bad teacher while a student. When claiming that teachers' unions defend undesirable educators, critics most often point to tenure. We must remember, however, that tenure is not the same as a guaranteed job for life, as is commonly assumed. Rather, tenure simply guarantees an impartial hearing that ensures teachers' due process rights if there is evidence that they have failed their evaluations. In other words, under a collective bargaining agreement, a tenured teacher cannot be fired at will. Dismissal is a complex task, but certainly not an impossible one.

Historically, tenure has been an important facet of teachers' jobs to protect them from prejudiced treatment by an administrator, to prevent favoritism or nepotism, to guard themselves from parental pressures (e.g., to change course grades), to encourage professional development rather than dismissal, and to provide some safety net for those who speak out against school or district policies that harm students (Kersten, 2006). This is especially important as education reforms, often touted by those who claim to be putting "students first," have the potential to benefit markets more than children (Ravitch, 2010). In addition, some level of job security may help teachers to commit to a school community and invest in building up school programs and curricula.

Given these benefits, a more productive discussion about tenure ought to focus on why administrators may not gather appropriate evidence needed for dismissal or award tenure without proper evaluation. We must also question the criteria used to grant tenure in the first place (Goldhaber & Hansen, 2010). Examining the tenure procedures of a successful, highly unionized school system like Finland's could provide great insight in this debate (Ravitch, 2010).

Sub-Lie 3: Teachers' Unions Are at Odds with the Interests of Children

The fact that teachers' unions' primary purpose is to protect their members' rights as workers does not necessarily mean that children suffer. The most powerful data we could expect to find to document inflicted harm would be lower achievement data in unionized states—yet we find just the opposite (Ravitch, 2010). In fact, several studies have debunked Kurth's (1987) conclusion that declining SAT scores could be attributed to teachers' unions. As of 2008, twice as many studies showed a positive relationship between teachers' unions and student achievement as showed a negative relationship (Carini, 2008). When other factors are held constant, teacher unionization has been found to have a significant positive impact on student achievement as defined by a variety of learning measures (e.g., Eberts & Stone, 1987; Grimes & Register, 1990; Nelson & Gould, 1988; Register & Grimes, 1991).

For example, a 1996 report prepared for the Institute for Wisconsin's Future found that students in unionized states scored on average 43 points higher on national standardized tests (e.g., SAT and NAEP) than students in nonunionized states, and that poverty, race, large class size, student absenteeism, and higher rates of private school attendance were significantly related to poor performance when collective bargaining was removed from the analysis (Nelson & Rosen, 1996). According to the National Poverty Center, at least 20 percent of American children currently live in poverty (the highest proportion in any industrialized nation); given that alarming statistic, the report's executive summary sounds as relevant now as it did nearly twenty years ago:

> Public education faces serious problems but teachers organizing to secure decent wages and working conditions is not one of them. Growing poverty, social instability, high rates of mobility and household disorganization devastate children's lives. Governmental cuts in resources for school hiring, teacher training and educational resources have led to larger class size, inadequate educational materials and reduced programming in many schools.
>
> (p. 3)

Strategies to help mitigate some (though not all) effects of poverty include smaller classes, reduced duty schedules, expanded planning time, and meaningful professional development. These issues have long been important elements of collective bargaining agreements by which teachers have fought for better learning environments as well as for better working conditions (see Eberts & Stone, 1984; Johnson & Donaldson, 2006; Moe, 2009).

Only strong, politically active unions are able to negotiate contracts that demand attention to such details. Though this may place greater constraints on administrators (Strunk & Grissom, 2010), something that makes most corporate education reformers recoil, school principals' instructional leadership in unionized schools has been associated with significantly higher achievement scores than are found in nonorganized schools (Eberts & Stone, 1987).[2] In other words, ensuring that teachers' unions have a voice in school decisions does not threaten the well-being and success of students.

The interests of teachers' unions are thus not inherently at odds with the interests of children; in fact, they are often deeply aligned. And the assumption that principals, politicians, or education "reformers" are more concerned than unions with students' best interests is naïve. Given the immense pressures on administrators to boost test scores at all costs, the incentives for politicians to cut budgets regardless of whether or not programs are working, and the lucrative opportunities for profits that may benefit reformers' financial backers, these groups are not immune from acting in their own self interest even when it hurts kids.

Why This Lie?

If this lie is so easily debunked, why does it persist? Whose interests are served by perpetuating the lie that teachers' unions are bad for kids? Quite simply, whether current educational "reformers" earnestly believe in and/or profit from their policy agenda (e.g., charter school expansion, vouchers, merit pay based on out-comes of standardized testing, the proliferation of alternative teacher certification programs such as Teach for America), their vision is bolstered when unions are undermined or eliminated.

Getting rid of unions and their collective bargaining rights does not cure bud-get crises, eliminate bad educators, or raise student achievement. However, "it might just clear the way for budget-conscious governors to slash education spend-ing and privatize public schools without any organized opposition" (Ravitch, 2010, p. 256). Promoting the lie that teachers' unions bankrupt states, defend poor teaching, and are bad for kids becomes a strategy for removing the obstacle of teachers' unions—a strategy that is proving to be extremely successful.

At first glance, such a conclusion may seem conspiratorial at worst or cyni-cal at best. There are, no doubt, many well-intentioned reformers who sincerely believe in their ideas. It is unclear, however, why they ignore the ample evidence that their neoliberal policy solutions are bad for kids, teachers, schools, and even a robust democracy. Perhaps if they carefully considered the research, they, like Diane Ravitch, a noted educational scholar and former supporter of market reforms, would conclude that "most of the reform strategies that school dis-tricts, state officials, the Congress, and federal officials are pursuing, that mega-rich foundations are supporting, and that editorial boards are applauding are mistaken [and] . . . corrupting educational values" (Ravitch, 2010, p. 14).

Though some reform advocates may want what is best for kids and simply have not yet stumbled across existing research that would redirect their energies, emerg-ing information about the inner workings of well-funded reform foundations sheds some light about other possible intentions. These are the "new philanthro-pists" (Scott, 2009) and include the leaders of hedge funds, charter school net-works, management organizations, real estate development groups, and alternative leadership/teacher education programs that greatly influence the leaders of school districts and departments of education. These groups are "bastions of unaccount-able power" (Ravitch, 2010, p. 201) in that there is no way for citizens to vote them out of office or even to have a voice about the ways in which they spend millions of dollars. Even if they are well intentioned (i.e., with their decisions not driven by the profit motive), this unchecked power is troubling (Hess, 2012).

One of the best examples of this "new philanthropy" is Students First, Michelle Rhee's organization, founded in 2010. The group is attempting to raise $1 billion specifically to compete with unions under the belief that "there is no big organized interest group that defends and promotes the interests of children (Turque & Anderson, 2010, p. 1)." In 2012, the group (supported by the American Legislative Exchange Council (ALEC)[3] and funded in part by Michael Bloomberg, the Laura and John Arnold Foundation, the Charles and Helen Schwab Foundation, the Broad Foundation, the Walton Foundation, and the Bill and Melinda Gates Foundation) spent more than a million dollars to support anti-union state ballot measures and local school board candidates as a way to promote its market-based reform agenda (Denvir, 2012; Simon, 2012).[4]

This kind of influence in policymaking is especially worrisome when it becomes clear that at least some of those dollars are being spent to open up markets in public schools as a strategy of crony capitalism. As the educational policy scholar Patricia Burch (2009) notes, "ideologies of neoliberalism are remaking education policy to fit the needs of the market. The ideas are pushed as helping public education although the arguments have little empirical basis (p. 136)." Recently, for example, e-mails between Jeb Bush's Foundation in Excellence for Education and state education officials in Florida, Louisiana, Rhode Island, Oklahoma, and New Mexico have shown that the group is producing ALEC-like legislation to promote the interests of its corporate funders' priorities rather than the interest of students (*In the Public Interest,* 2013). Not surprisingly, these legislative templates include weakening unions.

Dismantling teachers' unions with right-to-work legislation like Act 10 in Wisconsin or promoting the expansion of nonunion charter school networks is an important strategy in what Apple (2006) has called the commodification of education, a process that transforms public services for the common good into a site of profit-making for owners and investors with risk underwritten by the state. In other words, there is growing evidence that these "new philanthropists" are focused on doing what is best for the market while arguing that what they are doing is best for kids. And unions get in the way.

What Now?

It is not enough to simply debunk the big lie that teachers' unions are bad for schools and to understand who benefits from the perpetuation of this myth. We must also ask what kinds of unions are best for teachers, students, and their school communities.

First, in order to find out what they might look like and how they might act, the research community needs to more thoroughly investigate how and why teachers' unions impact public schools. This is especially important in view of the few studies that point to negative effects. Take Hoxby's (1996) study, which found that higher student dropout rates are linked to the unionization of schools. Though she mistakenly uses dropout rates as a proxy for student achievement, her thorough research raises questions about how unionization may be impacting students' decisions to leave school. Another example is Eberts & Stone's (1987) study, which found that, despite an overall gain for student achievement in unionized districts, students with special needs scored lower than their general education peers in those same districts.

In addition to supporting research investigating their impact, teachers' unions must also repair relationships with families and community members who have come to believe this big lie. One way to do this is to engage in a social justice unionism linking traditional models of industrial and professional unions with collaborative parental relationships to focus on reforms that serve all children and help to build a more robust, socially just democratic society. "If teacher unions are to survive," notes Bob Peterson in *Transforming Teacher Unions: Fighting for Better Schools and Social Justice* (Peterson, 1999), "they must take responsibility for building better and more equitable schools" (p. 12). A recent example of social justice unionism in which teachers' unions allied with parents and community members to stand up against a neoliberal reform agenda is the Chicago teachers' strike in 2012.

Starting in 2008, the Caucus of Rank-and-File Educators (CORE) began to organize against the reforms of Renaissance 2010 (a series of neoliberal policies put into place by Arne Duncan, at the time the CEO of the Chicago public schools). Though the leadership of the Chicago Teachers Union (CTU) initially avoided aggressive resistance to these policies, CORE members rose through the ranks. They organized with parents and community members as partners in the struggle for community justice and put forth research-based proposals offering alternatives to school leaders. Though still working on reducing class size and increasing compensation for teachers, union members won the ability to write their own lesson plans, access textbooks and materials, create better facilities for clinicians, reduce paperwork, and institute an anti-bullying clause (Sokolower, 2012). The example set by CORE leadership of CTU provides one template for how justice-oriented teachers' unions can use their professional and political strength to stand up against reforms they know to be bad for kids.

Conclusion

Though teachers' unions are not perfect institutions, we can answer the following questions with some degree of confidence: Are teachers' unions bankrupting states? No. Is tenure to blame for bad teaching? No. Are teachers' unions bad for children? No. A better question is how unions can support both their members' interests and the interests of students and their families. This may mean going against the administration, engaging in internal reforms, and/or standing up against policies that have been shown to damage students and limit learning. As Deborah Meier (2004) reminds us, "Healthy resistance is sometimes what we most need, side by side with thoughtful proposals for change—and this is what we will sorely miss if teachers' unions are defeated by the relentless hostility of their many opponents" (p. 55). Rather than dismantling teachers' unions, then, policy and research efforts should focus on understanding and improving them. Not only will this be better for teachers; it will be better for kids and the schools that serve them.

Notes

1. This post responded to an editorial titled "The Budget Showdown: Teachers Set Wrong Example," by Brian Brehmer (2011), published on February 17.
2. This study defined instructional leadership as the time spent on curriculum and program development, monitoring, and evaluation.
3. Founded in 1973, ALEC is a group that writes "model bills" for conservative representatives to introduce in state legislatures across the United States. For more information about this group's purpose and functions, see the noted historian William Cronin's blog, "Scholar as Citizen": http://scholarcitizen.williamcronon.net/2011/03/15/alec/
4. In addition to this financial influence, Rhee has spoken out in support of Governor Scott Walker's anti-union policies in Wisconsin and worked with Republican governor Rick Scott's team to develop anti-union educational policies in Florida.

References

Apple, M. W. (2006). *Educating the "right" way: Markets, standards, God, and inequality.* 2nd ed. New York: Routledge.

Baugh, W. H., & Stone, J. A. (1982). Teachers, unions and wages in the 1970s: Unionism now pays. *Industrial and Labor Relations Review, 35*(3), 368–376.

Brehmer, B. (2011, February 17). The budget showdown: Teachers set wrong example. *Milwaukee Journal Sentinel.* Retrieved from www.jsonline.com/news/opinion/116433734.html

Burch, P. (2009). *Hidden markets: The new education privatization.* New York: Routledge.

Bushaw, W. J., & Lopez, S. J. (2011). Betting on teachers: The 43rd annual Phi Delta Kappa/Gallup poll of the public's attitudes toward the public schools. *Kappan, 93*(1), 8–26.

Carini, R. M. (2008). Is collective bargaining detrimental to student achievement?: Evidence from a national study. *Journal of Collective Negotiations, 32*(3), 215–35.

Delisle, E. C. (2010). *Economic and budget issue brief: Fiscal stress faced by local governments.* Washington, DC: Congressional Budget Office. Retrieved from www.cbo.gov/sites/default/files/cbofiles/ftpdocs/120xx/doc12005/12–09-municipalities_brief.pdf

Denvir, D. (2012, November 17). Michelle Rhee's right turn. *Salon.* Retrieved from www.salon.com/2012/11/17/michele_rhees_right_turn/

Eberts, R. W. (1984). Union effects on teacher productivity. *Industrial and Labor Relations Review, 37*(3), 346–348.

Eberts, R. W. (2007). The future of children. *Excellence in the Classroom, 17*(1), 175–200.

Eberts, R. W., & Stone, J. A. (1984). *Unions and the public schools: The effect of collective bargaining on American education.* Lexington, MA: Lexington Books.

Eberts, R. W., & Stone, J. A. (1986). Teacher unions and the cost of public education. *Economic Inquiry, 24*(4), 631–644.

Eberts, R. W. & Stone, J. A. (1987). Teacher unions and the productivity of public schools. *Industrial and Labor Relations Review, 40*(3), 354–363.

Goldhaber, D. (2006). Are teachers unions good for students? In J. Hannaway & A. J. Rotherham (Eds.), *Collective bargaining in education: Negotiating change in today's schools* (pp. 141–157). Cambridge, MA: Harvard University Press.

Goldhaber, D., & Hansen, M. (2010). Using performance on the job to inform teacher tenure decisions. *American Economic Review, 100*(2), 250–255.

Grimes, P. W., & Register, C. A. (1990). Teachers' unions and student achievement in high school economics. *Journal of Economic Education, 21*(3), 297–306.

Hess, F. M. (2012). Philanthropy gets in the ring: Ed-funders get serious about education policy, *Kappan, 93*(8), 17–21.

Hoxby, C. M. (1996). How teachers' unions affect education production. *Quarterly Journal of Economics, 111*(3), 671–718.

In the Public Interest (2013). Corporate interests pay to play to shape education policy, reap profits. Retrieved from www.inthepublicinterest.org/node/2747

Johnson, S., & Donaldson, M. L. (2006). The effects of collective bargaining on teacher quality. In J. Hannaway & A. J. Rotherham (Eds.), *Collective bargaining in education: Negotiating change in today's schools* (pp. 111–140). Cambridge, MA: Harvard Education Press.

Kersten, T. A. (2006). Teacher tenure: Illinois school board presidents' perspectives and suggestions for improvement. *Planning and Changing, 37*(3&4), 234–257.

Kurth, M. M. (1987). Teachers' unions and excellence in education: An analysis of the decline of SAT scores. *Journal of Labor Research, 8*(4), 351–367.

Meier, D. (2004). On unions and education. *Dissent* (Winter), 51–55.

Moe, T. (2001). Teachers unions and the public schools. In T. Moe (Ed.), *A primer on America's schools* (pp. 151–183). United States: Hoover Institution Press Publication No. 486.

Moe, T. (2009). Collective bargaining and the performance of the public schools. *American Journal of Political Science, 53*(1), 156–174.

Nelson, H., & Gould, J. C. (1988). Teachers' unions and excellence in education: Comment. *Journal of Labor Research, 9*(4), 379–387.

Nelson, F. H., & Rosen, M. (1996). *Are teachers' unions hurting public education? A state-by-state analysis of the impact of collective bargaining among teachers on student performance.* Milwaukee, WI: Institute for Wisconsin's Future.

Nnamdi, K. (2012, August 30). The politics of education with Michelle Rhee [interview]. *The Kojo Nnamdi Show.* Retrieved from http://thekojonnamdishow.org/shows/2012–08–30/politics-education-michelle-rhee/transcript

Peterson, B. (1999). Survival and justice: Rethinking teacher union strategy. In B. Peterson & M. Charney (Eds.), *Transforming teacher unions: Fighting for better schools and social justice* (pp. 11–19). Milwaukee, WI: Rethinking Schools.

Peterson, P. E., Howell, W., & West, M. (2012, June 4). Teachers unions have a popularity problem. *Wall Street Journal.* Retrieved from http://online.wsj.com/article/SB10001424052702303640104577440390966357830.html

Ravitch, D. (2010). *The death and life of the great American school system.* New York: Basic Books.

Register, C. A., & Grimes, P. W. (1991). Collective bargaining, teachers, and student achievement. *Journal of Labor Research, 9*(2), 99–109.

Rehm, D. (2012, September 12). Chicago teacher's strike [interview]. *The Diane Rehm Show.* Retrieved from http://thedianerehmshow.org/shows/2012–09–12/chicago-teachers-strike/transcript

Richards, E. (2011, August 13). Handbooks replace union contracts in Wisconsin schools. *Milwaukee Journal Sentinel.* Retrieved from www.jsonline.com/news/education/127669538.html

Russek, F. (2011). *Economic and budget issue brief: The underfunding of state and local pension plans.* Washington, DC: Congressional Budget Office. Retrieved from www.cbo.gov/sites/default/files/cbofiles/ftpdocs/120xx/ doc12084/05–04-pensions.pdf

Scott, J. O. (2009). The politics of venture philanthropy in charter school policy and advocacy. *Educational Policy, 23*(1), 106–136.

Simon, S. (2012, May 15). Activist targeting U.S. schools, backed by big bucks. *Chicago Tribune.* Retrieved from http://articles.chicagotribune.com/2012–05–15/news/sns-rt-us-usa-education-rheebre84e1oa-20120515_1_michelle-rhee-studentsfirst-grade-level

Strunk, K. O., & Grissom, J. A. (2010). Do strong unions shape district policies? Collective bargaining, teacher contract restrictiveness, and the political power of teachers' unions. *Educational Evaluation and Policy Analysis, 32*(3), 389–406.

Sokolower, J. (2012). Lessons in social justice unionism: An interview with Chicago Teachers Union president Karen Lewis. *Rethinking Schools* (Winter), 11–17.

Swalwell, K. (2012, April 15). "See you on the square": The contested nature of teachers' public activism. Paper presented at the American Educational Research Association (AERA) Annual Conference, Vancouver, British Columbia, Canada.

Swalwell, K., & Apple, M. (2010). Starting the wrong conversation: The public school crisis and *Waiting for Superman. Educational Policy, 25*(2), 368–382.

Turque, B., & Anderson, N. (2010, December 6). Former DC schools chancellor Michelle Rhee starts student advocacy group. *Washington Post.* Retrieved from www.washingtonpost.com/wpdyn/content/article/2010/12/06/AR2010120602718.html

Winkler, A. M., Scull, J., & Zeehandelaar, D. (2012). *How strong are U.S. teacher unions? A state-by-state comparison.* Fordham Institute & Education Reform Now. Retrieved from www.edexcellencemedia.net/publications/2012/20121029-How-Strong-Are-US-Teacher-Unions/20121029-Union-Strength-Full-Report.pdf

Woodruff, J. (2011, February 21). Gov. Walker rejects compromise as Wisconsin protests continue. *PBS News Hour.* Retrieved from www.pbs.org/newshour/bb/politics/jan-june11/wisconsin_02–21.html

PART IV

Schools and Policy

9

THE TRUTH ABOUT TRACKING

Lauren Anderson and Jeannie Oakes

Tracking practices—labeling students according to their perceived competencies and deficits and placing them in classes and programs accordingly—are among the most entrenched in American education. People rarely question them and often assume that they represent the most effective, efficient, and equitable methods for organizing students, delivering instruction, and ensuring that youth achieve to their highest capabilities. In reality, however, tracking does far more harm than good.

In this chapter, we debunk some of the key myths about tracking's effectiveness, efficiency, and relationship to equity, and we present some alternative approaches for ensuring that students' needs are met. We begin by addressing how and why schools track students and the implications for students' opportunities to learn. We then review some of the evidence showing that tracking practices often do as much to *create* differences and *perpetuate* inequities as they do to support students in reaching their full potential. Finally, we briefly address the efforts of those who are avoiding or striving to undo tracking and implementing in its place more multidimensional, developmental, and socially just practices.

The Foundation on Which Tracking Rests: Labeling, Sorting, and Grouping

For as long as schools have existed in the United States, educators have used assessment and evaluation strategies to compare, rank, and assign relative value to students' abilities and achievements. Students have been labeled slow, incompetent, gifted, high achieving, below average, learning disabled, limited English proficient, and more. Such labels have long shaped how students are sorted into instructional groups, classes, and programs (Fass, 1991; Lucas, 1999; Oakes, 2005; Spring, 2007; Tyack, 1974).

Today, "ability level," previous achievement, postsecondary aspirations, English-language proficiency, and disability status have become almost taken-for-granted or "common-sense" criteria used for grouping students. Other loaded criteria— "individual effort," "talent," "motivation," and completion of various prerequisites, among others—are also used when placing students in "appropriate" groups, classes, and programs. While specifics vary from school to school, ultimately nearly all grouping assignments are made and justified by schools' predictions about students' (relative) *capacity* to succeed in any given group. While stated intentions emphasize placing students in or encouraging students to take the most demanding courses in which the school thinks they can succeed, these predictions have always been fraught with inconsistency and are often just plain wrong (Burris, Heubert, & Levin, 2006; Oakes, 2005). The experience of Kimberly Aragon, an eighth-grade humanities teacher, for example, is telling.

> Grouping pervades almost every area of my K–8 school. Some students enter a "VISTA" (gifted according to various intelligences) program as early as second grade, and, as those students progress, there will be at least one VISTA class in every grade. Every grade, 2 to 8, also has what is called a "SHARP" class. SHARP is an acronym for "Students with High Achievement in Reading Program." Students are placed in a SHARP class based on their previous years' test scores and their grades in English. Although the rest of the students at my school are not labeled as "DULL," the implication of the "SHARP" name is obvious. . . . Moreover, some grades are divided further by placing the Limited English Proficient (LEP) students in one class and all of the rest of the students in another class. . . . The school [has also] instituted a middle-school reading elective, which requires 10 students who scored in the bottom quartile on the previous year's standardized test to receive extra reading instruction. . . . Those students are then not able to participate in the other electives offered, such as drama, Spanish, communications, art, and computers.[1]

Of course, there's nothing inherently wrong with teachers grouping students in order to provide targeted instruction or tailored scaffolding so that students can access the content they are expected to learn. The problem comes, as Kimberly describes, when grouping determinations are made using narrow indicators of students' "ability" and when the actions based on those determinations separate students, restrict access to the curriculum, and create public and enduring hierarchies that classify some as having more or less ability and potential than others.

What Is Tracking, and What Does It Involve?

Tracking refers to the routine sorting of students into so-called homogeneous groups and classes of "high," "average," and "low" ability, achievement, or potential (or any of the creative euphemisms in vogue, such as "advanced," "accelerated," "opportunity," "basic," "SHARP," or "VISTA"). Such sorting typically begins early in elementary school—sometimes even in kindergarten—and it continues throughout the gradespan.[2]

Many elementary schools provide separate classes so that students spend the entire day with peers judged to be at the same "ability level." Others group students by "ability" for specific parts of the day or for specific subjects such as reading and math; still others offer evidently leveled instruction to small groups within individual classrooms. For example, schools often maintain programs that group the highest-achieving students for enrichment or accelerated instruction in separate classes, in pull-out programs, or in "gifted" clusters within regular classrooms.

Nearly all middle schools and high schools group students for at least some academic subjects (typically English, mathematics, and science and less commonly social studies) on the basis of "ability" as determined by past grades, test scores, and teacher recommendations (Oakes, 2005; Yonezawa, Wells & Serna, 2002). Analyses of national surveys suggest, for example, that for the past two decades roughly three-fourths of eighth graders have been assigned to math classes on the basis of "ability" (Loveless, 2013).

Traditionally, and not unrelated to judgments of "ability" and placement decisions made in elementary and middle grades, high schools have also prescribed different course sequences for students assumed to have different futures. For example, those expected to attend college and those expected to enter the workforce after high school have historically been placed into different tracks. In some secondary schools, this has meant assigning students to whole blocks of classes all at the same "ability level" or enrolling them in a pre-set program of study—whether college preparatory, general (noncollege), or vocational—that dictates their entire array of courses. While some schools are striving to elevate the rigor and status of general and vocational offerings by reimagining them as pathways to career *and* college preparation (Oakes & Saunders, 2008), traditional general or vocational tracks usually coincide with lower levels of academic challenge and include courses that don't satisfy college entrance requirements or promote a college-going culture. Thus, students' expected futures shape their track placements, which in turn shape the actual futures to which they gain access.

Even *within* college-prep tracks, different course sequences emerge—some designed to prepare students for highly competitive universities, some for less competitive ones, and some for two-year community colleges. Most high schools, for example, offer advanced placement (AP) classes for high-achieving eleventh and twelfth graders. These courses open up opportunities for students to pursue college-level content and accrue college credits; many high schools also weight AP courses more heavily than others when calculating grade-point averages, thus further distinguishing students already privileged by the education system.

Policies affecting ability grouping and tracking have ebbed and flowed over the years, especially since the mid-1980s, when research began in earnest to document their ill effects and inequalities. Since then, many schools and scholars have distinguished between ability grouping and tracking—defining the latter narrowly as a permanent, block assignment of students into courses that prepare them for different futures, such as entry into two- or four-year colleges, direct entry into the workforce, and so on. Because of the well-established problems—described in greater detail later—caused by placing students in different tracks, today's schools typically try to avoid tracking (even if only rhetorically) often while still favoring ability grouping. Again, while grouping students for instruction can be useful, even essential to ensuring that students' learning needs are met, this holds only if groups are flexible, temporary, and done within classes for particular assignments or lessons and do not attach status labels to students such as "fast," "remedial," and so forth. Unfortunately, what some schools call ability grouping often amounts to tracking under a more acceptable name.

There is some evidence that worrisome practices and the perspectives and policies that support them are on the rise. In the early part of 2013, a flurry of columns (e.g., Garelick, 2013; Welner, 2013) and news features (e.g., Garland, 2013; Sparks, 2013; Yee, 2013) addressed the topic, some coming in response to reports that teachers in recent years were relying more on grouping students by "ability" than they had a decade or two ago (Loveless, 2013). Around the same time, Texas passed a bill establishing a new tiered diploma system that involves enrolling some ninth graders in a track leading to a "distinguished" diploma, while others prepare for a "foundational" diploma (Texas H.B. 5, 2013, Welner & Burris, 2013a)—an approach that echoes those implemented and under consideration in other states. While it remains to be seen what these resurgent practices and new systems will yield, decades of research indicate the strong potential for such approaches to further imperil equity and opportunity (Welner, 2013; Welner & Burris, 2013b).

What Makes Tracking Inefficient, Ineffective, and Inequitable?

The conventional explanation for labeling and sorting students into separate classes and programs is that, once a school identifies educationally relevant differences, teachers can teach groups of students with meaningful similarities, and students will benefit from instruction in these groups. However, below this superficially sensible explanation are troubling cultural and historical patterns that connect school-level labeling and sorting to the social construction of race, class, and ability and the maintenance of competitive advantage for members of the dominant group.

Current policies demand, at least rhetorically, that schools educate every student to high academic standards, regardless of presumed intellectual ability, disability, social status, gender, or race, and that they prepare all high school graduates for both college and careers. It follows that today's tracking practices must be judged by whether they are helping teachers reach these goals. As we explain later, while today's tracking practices may enable success for a privileged few, they are not efficient or effective or equitable.

Tracking Relies on Faulty Assumptions of Homogeneity

The very idea of homogeneous grouping assumes that students in a given class are similar in notable ways. But even those assumed to be similar differ from one another in important ways and do not benefit from a learning environment that ignores those differences. Indeed, ample scholarship suggests that learning suffers when learners are presumed to be the same (e.g., Crawford, 2004; Engeström, 1999; Gutiérrez & Rogoff, 2003; Lee, 2007; Nieto & Bode, 2011; Rogoff, 2003). Classes designed for specific ability, disability, and language "levels" are filled with students who display noteworthy differences in the readiness, interest, effort, and aptitude they bring to various tasks. Tracked schools—by virtue of their structure and the messages that structure sends—may draw attention away from such diversity, potentially discouraging teachers from attending to students' inevitable differences and/or from developing multidimensional lessons or instruction tailored to individual students' needs.

Furthermore, substantial evidence demonstrates that schools often disregard their own criteria—allowing, for example, parent preferences or student behavior to influence students' placements. In such situations especially, tracking practices—given their underlying assumptions and projected veneer of homogeneity—do more than mask difference; they actually miseducate teachers about the students who are assigned to their classes. As one ninth-grade mathematics teacher, Marilyn Cortez, discovered firsthand, many school systems designate classes for students of a particular ability or language level but then enroll students erroneously, even by their own standards (Burris, 2003; Mehan, Mercer, & Rueda, 2002; Welner, 2001; Yonezawa, Wells, & Serna, 2002).

> Placing students in the correct math class was something I assumed was done. . . . I found out over the course of the year that many students had been misplaced and were not aware of it. They knew the course name and number, but they did not know the type of content that would be covered. They just assumed that counselors placed them correctly. Misplaced students are also plentiful in my "sheltered" [English] class [designated for native Spanish speakers]. . . . I asked students individually whether they spoke Spanish fluently, and if so, whether they considered it their primary language. Three students! Only three students in my entire sheltered course considered Spanish their primary language, and only four others spoke it fluently.

Still other factors, some discussed later—including testing, parent activism, the school's master schedule, and more—make such assignments prone to error and unfairness.

Tracking Relies on Flawed Tests and Arbitrary Cutoffs

Schools risk enormous unfairness when they use test scores to sort students across courses and tracks. And yet they often rely on standardized testing, school performance, or both to determine students' designated achievement levels. Depending on the situation—particularly in instances of exemplary or lagging achievement—IQ scores specifically factor into grouping determinations. For example, "gifted" students are generally identified as those meeting specific criteria, sometimes including IQ scores or other standardized measures.

Developed in the early twentieth century, IQ tests were considered by their advocates to be scientific, accurate, and impartial. In reality, as explained in Chapter 6, they were anything but; for example, questions selected for inclusion in the tests were those that socioeconomically privileged, White test takers would be much more likely to answer "correctly." As a result, IQ scores mostly served to legitimize preexisting ways of sorting, producing groups composed of students of similar family background, wealth, and race.

While today's schools rarely rely on IQ alone, these early practices established enduring placement patterns. Standardized achievement test scores often influence students' placement into "ability" groups, classes, and compensatory education programs. Standardized language-proficiency tests often determine placements for English learners. Both can be problematic, leading to seemingly arbitrary placements.

As well, states, districts, and schools differ widely in how they use test scores to define "high," "average," and "low" ability (Rubin, 2008); a student identified as belonging in any one category in one community might wind up in a different category somewhere else. Our own research found wide disparities in cut-off scores used by high schools to decide which students should be admitted to honors, regular, and lower-level classes (Oakes, 2005; Oakes & Guiton, 1995). For example, a student in a lower-performing high school may require a lower score on a standardized test to get into an honors class than a student in a higher-performing school. In addition, the same schools might apply different criteria in different years. These inconsistencies further exacerbate the arbitrary and unfair nature of tracking (Welner, 2001).

Tracking, by Definition, Means Separate and Unequal Tracks and Outcomes

Of course, the issue with tracking isn't just that placement occurs problematically but that also it tends to confer upon students significantly different learning opportunities, depending on their track assignments, and these differences accumulate over years spent in school to the extreme advantage of some and the extreme detriment of others. Some of the well-documented differences between high- and low-level classes are listed in table 9.1 (Oakes, 2005; Watanabe, 2008; Welner, 2001).

Simply put, in every aspect of what makes for a quality education, kids in lower tracks typically get less than those in higher tracks and gifted programs.[3] As a result, research shows that students placed at lower levels consistently achieve less than classmates with the same abilities who were placed at higher levels and

TABLE 9.1 Grouping-Related Differences in Learning Opportunities

Higher-Group Advantages	*Lower-Group Disadvantages*
Curriculum emphasizing concepts, inquiry, and problem-solving	Curriculum emphasizing low-level facts and skills
Emphasis on students developing as autonomous thinkers	Emphasis on teaching students to follow rules and procedures
More time spent on instruction	More time spent on discipline and socializing
More active and interactive learning activities	More worksheets and seatwork
Computers used as learning tools	Computers used as tutors or for worksheet completion and other low-level "busywork"
More qualified and experienced teachers	More uncertified and inexperienced teachers
Extra enrichment activities and resources	Few enrichment opportunities
More engaging and friendly classroom atmosphere	More alienating and hostile classroom atmosphere
"Hard work" a likely classroom norm	"Not working" a likely classroom norm

that students with both high *and* low test scores do better when they are in higher-level courses (Boaler, 2006; Burris et al., 2006; Hallinan, 2000; Oakes, 1995; Welner, 2001; Watanabe, 2008). In fact, the very conditions, resources, and instructional approaches typically prescribed (and reserved) for "gifted" students—including "thematic, broad-based, and integrative content," "concept-based instruction," and "open-ended questions that stimulate inquiry, active exploration, and discovery" (Berger, 1996)—are the same conditions, resources, and instructional approaches that have been shown to contribute to the success of *all* students, regardless of their so-called ability levels, when grouped together in heterogeneous classes (e.g., Boaler, 2006; Tomlinson, 1995, 2001; Watanabe, 2011). Interestingly enough, a commitment to heterogeneous grouping is also among the conditions characterizing Finland's education system and that of other countries so often lauded for high overall achievement levels and narrow achievement gaps (Oakes, 2008).

Tracking Restricts Access and Undermines Achievement

Most students placed in low-ability or even average groups in elementary school continue in these tracks in middle school. Senior high schools usually place these students in non-college-preparatory tracks or "lower-level" college-prep tracks that offer access to less-competitive colleges or majors, to two-year colleges, or to remedial classes as college freshmen. For example, national survey data from the 1980s indicated that 60 to 70 percent of tenth graders in honors math were also enrolled in honors English; a similar degree of overlap existed between enrollment in remedial math and remedial or low-level English (Gamoran, 1988). And, in large part, these patterns endure (Oakes, 2005; Welner, 2001).

Since some subjects, such as math, follow a set sequence, students' assignments in earlier grades determine how far they can progress before graduation (Garet & DeLany, 1988; DeLany, 1991; Oakes, 2005). Students who end up in top math classes during high school are often identified by the sixth grade or before. Those not placed in top-track math classes by sixth grade often stand only the slimmest chance of completing calculus in high school. Because students' track placements rarely change, differences among students accumulate over time—in terms of what students experience, what they learn, how they see themselves and school, and what they expect for their futures—and become most obvious in high school, by which point they often seem natural, inevitable, and irreparable to students and educators alike. For example, by the time many students learn about colleges' expectations—the role of AP courses in gaining admission and course credit, the costs associated with having to enroll in remedial math, and so on—it often feels, and in many cases *is,* "too late" to adjust.

Certainly, there are exceptions. Many teachers know students who become inspired and transcend the labels assigned to them and/or the tracks to which they are assigned. Some manage, despite odds, to pull themselves out of low-track classes and into higher-track ones. However, exceptions occur in spite of tracking, not because of it, and those who do succeed against the odds often carry bitter memories of their struggle.

Tracking Miseducates Students about Their Own and One Another's Potential

Being in a low-level class or lower track most often fosters lower achievement, lower esteem (particularly concerning one's academic ability), lowered aspirations, negative attitudes toward self and/or school, and even dropping out (Fine, 1991; Oakes, Gamoran, & Page, 1992; Orfield, 2004; Werblow, Urick, & Duesbery, 2013). Consider, for example, the account shared by Michael Alvarez, a first-year ninth-grade English teacher:

> My students believe they are in classes for stupid people. They say things such as, "We can't do this. We're only '103' [low-ability class] students." . . .
> Many teachers [at my school] believe not only that low-track students will not do the work but that they cannot do the work. Any readings I assign for them to do at home I have to photocopy since they are not allowed their own books. There is only a class set because someone has decided that they will not do any homework anyway, and they will probably just lose the books. . . . Many of them tell me I am the only teacher that gives homework.

During my first semester, I taught my English classes in the print shop. My next room turned out not to be a classroom at all. My students had nowhere to sit, and one of the kids said, "Mr. Alvarez, they always give you the cheap classrooms." She sure was right. Finally, with 10 weeks to go in the year, I moved into a [third] room . . . with one window that does not open, no air conditioner, and only one door to let in air. It has been close to 90 degrees every day.

The students are being cheated out of a quality education. . . . I look at all the classes that have to endure this environment, and I see they all have one thing in common: they are lower-track classes. The four teachers who were in the print shop and now in the windowless bungalows for the most part have "103" students. . . . The school decided that the kids who need the most attention, the most help, should get the worst environment in which to learn. There is no way that the school would put honors kids in these rooms.

Accounts like these reveal how the distribution of resources and curricular differentiation can systematically shortchange students who are not in the uppermost track. And if the school and teachers "buy into" the idea that these students are "less able," then it's likely students will as well. The result is that not all students are seen as warranting similarly engaging learning experiences and opportunities—including access to teachers with reputations for being the most experienced and highly skilled (Oakes, 2005; Welner, 2001).

The labels that accompany grouping and tracking (even if masked in local codes such as "VISTA" or "103") often translate into lowered self-confidence and lowered expectations for all students not graced with the highest status label. Placement in a low, middle, or almost-but-not-quite-top class often becomes a self-fulfilling prophecy—a cycle of lower expectations, fewer opportunities, and academic performance that usually matches (but does not exceed) expected performance levels (Darling-Hammond, 2004; Oakes, 2005). Though arguably not as detrimental to their development and academic self-concept, tracking also miseducates those placed into higher tracks, where they experience less diversity than they would in untracked classes, where they sometimes face counterproductive competiveness, and where they come to misunderstand their own success as merely reflecting merit (rather than being a by-product, at least in part, of structural privilege) (Yonezawa & Jones, 2006).

These labels and track assignments don't just impact students. Their effects permeate the cultures of our schools and communities. Thus, we hear references to "gifted parents." Teachers talk about "my low kids." Parents and educators alike confer greater status on teachers of higher-level classes. For example, at public meetings, a teacher may identify herself as an AP calculus teacher rather than a teacher of basic math, even if she teaches both. While teachers of low-track classes may be admired for how "tough" their job is, they are often judged to be less accomplished in their content areas. Even highly qualified special education and bilingual teachers are not typically thought of as having the background and training needed to work with highly able students. These tendencies reflect deeply problematic (often racist and classist) assumptions and reinforce the idea that tracks represent "real" differences in one's value and potential.

Tracking Is Highly Subject to Bias

In U.S. schools, labeling and sorting have always had strong statistical overlaps with students' race, ethnicity, language status, and social class. White, wealthy, native English-speaking students are far more likely to be labeled as high ability or gifted and placed in high-level classes and in programs for those assumed to be college-bound. Meanwhile, low-income students, African Americans, Latinos, and English learners are disproportionately identified as less able and placed in low-ability, remedial, and special education classes and programs (Villegas, 1988). In New York City, for example, Black and Latino youth make up 70 percent of the student population but only 30 percent of those identified as gifted and talented (Garland, 2013). A recent *New York Times* article profiled one representative elementary school, where White students represented 27 percent of the overall population but 47 percent of students in the school's gifted program (Baker, 2013).

Our own research found that African American and Latino students were much less likely than White or Asian students *with the same test scores* to be placed in high-ability classes. In one school system, White and Asian students with average scores on standardized tests were more than twice as likely to be placed in "accelerated" classes than Latino students with *the same scores*. The discrimination was even more striking among the highest-scoring students. Whereas only 56 percent of very high-scoring Latinos were in accelerated classes, 93 percent of Whites and 97 percent of Asians with *comparable* test scores were. In three additional school systems, we found similar discrepancies between African American and White students (Lareau, 1989; Oakes, 1990; Oakes & Guiton, 1995; Yonezawa, 1997).

One history teacher, Matthew Flanders, described the outcome of these dynamics and discrepancies:

> This high school contains "two schools." . . . First, there is the advanced placement division. Highly motivated, adequately supported and taught, most of the students are White and are expected to go to college. Then there is the second "school" that is not expected to go on to higher education. These students are not motivated or engaged by school, are not given the best resources or teachers, and are overwhelmingly Latino and African American. This school's dropout rate is significantly higher than the first school's . . . [its] students have lost faith in themselves, in school, in peers.

More often than not this "two-schools" phenomenon—and the bias that contributes to its construction—reappears in some form wherever tracking occurs nationwide (Oakes, 1995, 2005; Welner, 2001).

While educators play a powerful role in how students are labeled and grouped, parents and students themselves may also acquire by their own actions certain advantages that an unbiased system would otherwise prevent (Lareau, 1989; Roda & Wells, 2013; Useem, 1991; Welner, 2001; Yonezawa & Oakes, 2004). For example, high-achieving, affluent, White students and parents are often more knowledgeable about grouping practices and more willing to "push the system" if they are displeased with the way they or their children are labeled or assigned to courses or if they see opportunities to secure a comparative advantage. Parents of lower-achieving students, low-income parents, those who are not native English speakers, and/or those who are cautious when interacting with public institutions, meanwhile, are frequently less comfortable challenging the system, and, given these parents' trepidation and/or limited "clout," some officials feel safe dismissing or ignoring their concerns. Indeed, underrepresented students themselves may opt out of higher-track classes if they feel those spaces are ones where students like themselves will be few in number, singled out, misunderstood, socially isolated, and so on (Rubin, 2008; Yonezawa, Wells & Serna, 2002). For these reasons among others, relying on "choice" mechanisms to place students into ability groups and tracks holds little promise for ameliorating problematic dynamics and outcomes.

Defenders of ability grouping and tracking sometimes claim that assignments are "objective" or "color-blind," and they attribute the disproportionate assignment of some students into college-prep or remedial classes to unfortunate differences in students' backgrounds and abilities. But these claims of scientific and bias-free objectivity are not supported when viewed in the context of historical and contemporary tracking practices and their results.

Tracking Privileges Organizational Needs over Student Needs

Ultimately, tracking practices are organizationally centered, rather than student centered. In other words, they privilege organizational imperatives—assigning teachers, managing students, distributing resources, coordinating schedules, and so on—over students' academic well-being. In secondary schools, administrators juggle many factors that may influence placements. For example, they must make sure that each student has a class every hour. Those who want football, beginning string class, or second-year computer drafting often get those classes, even if that means students wind up in low- rather than high-level content area courses, or vice versa. In addition, since each class must have approximately the same number of students, schools may place borderline students or students who enroll last in higher- or lower-level classes more out of convenience than anything else. As scholars have observed, "If there are 30 slots for learning disabled students in a school, then there will be 30 kids to fill those slots" (Mehan, Mercer & Rueda, 2002, p. 623). In other words, course distinctions, sequences, and tracks generally predate the students assigned to them; students are plugged and programmed into structures more often than structures are designed to "fit" students and their needs.

These structures, in turn, send powerful and legitimizing messages about students' needs and potentials. Consider the recent comments of a local school board committee member in Rhode Island who, when presenting more inclusive alternatives to an exclusive program for "accelerated" students, noted that part of the program's flaw was that "The kids that were left over in the [regular] classroom, a lot of them were labeled as 'dumb kids' and they weren't *necessarily* dumb" (Rodrigues, 2013, our italics). Even as such comments call out existing structures for their damaging impact on how students see themselves and one another, they also reveal deeper-seated tendencies among adults to categorize students in simplistic ways and to place some degree of faith in those categories and in the organizational structures that have long been built up around them.

Indeed, despite all the evidence to the contrary, tracking still appears efficient on its surface to some—particularly those who believe in bell-curve-like distributions of intelligence and talent. But these claims to efficiency hold only if one's ideas about efficiency have more to do with creating and perpetuating stratification by race and class than with meeting all students' needs and ensuring that students reach their full potential. One need only look at the track record (pun intended) of so many comprehensive (tracked) high schools and their tendency to produce outcomes that largely reflect racist, classist, and curve-like assumptions—relatively few students will excel, some young people will fare well enough, and many youth will underachieve and/or leave school before graduation—that undergird the structural design of the tracks into which students are placed and the distribution of resources across them.

What Are the Alternatives?

Taken together, the preceding sections of this chapter make it clear why, over years of schooling, students who are initially similar in background and skills become increasingly different in achievement when schools place them into separate, ability-grouped, tracked classes. Yet, in many ways, tracking remains a taken-for-granted, "common-sense" feature of many public schools and most secondary schools. Recognizing that this prevailing "common sense" hasn't helped to produce desired outcomes, many observers have recommended that schools begin dismantling structures that privilege so-called homogeneous grouping. They include many eminent scholars, policymakers, community leaders, and organizations: the directors of the Third International Mathematics and Science Study, who concluded that tracking "fails to provide satisfactory achievement for either average or advanced students" (Schmidt, 1998, 4); the Carnegie Corporation's (1989) *Turning Points* initiative, which took aim at homogeneous grouping in middle schools specifically; the National Governors' Association (1993), whose members proposed eliminating most ability grouping and tracking; the College Board (2000), which argued that grouping practices erect barriers to minority students' achievement and called for eliminating mathematics tracking in racially diverse high schools; the National Research Council (2003), which has argued that "both formal and informal tracking by ability be eliminated" (p. 6); and even most publishers of standardized achievement tests, who caution about using their assessments to group students. In addition, the NAACP Legal Defense Fund, the Children's Defense Fund, the ACLU, the federal Government Accounting Office, and numerous community-based and advocacy organizations have all identified ability grouping, gifted education, and special education as second-generation segregation issues.

Even deeply problematic policies, such as No Child Left Behind, render tracking practices obsolete, for nothing in schools leaves children behind more systematically than tracking. Nevertheless, the usual response to well-supported charges that current grouping practices don't work and aren't fair is to fix, adjust, or modify them so that they better meet educators' intended goals. These are not the most promising ways forward for a various reasons.

The argument that educators can fix the technology of homogeneous grouping underestimates the cultural and political pressure to resist such modification and the consequent difficulty in making modifications stick. What we need instead are new ways of thinking about the relationship among students, curriculum, and the structures of schooling—guiding philosophies that aren't based on deterministic assumptions about some students' inevitable success and other students' inevitable failure. We also need new ways of teaching—ambitious pedagogies that maximize the potential of heterogeneous grouping and leverage diversity for deeper and more expansive learning.

To be fair, in an effort to eliminate discriminatory grouping practices and ensure that all students have access to high-quality curriculum, teachers, and learning experiences, schools around the country have been working—some now for decades—to alter their practices by moving away from tracking and providing rigorous college- and career-preparatory learning experiences for all students. We offer one sidebar example to demonstrate that sustained school-level detracking efforts *are* yielding transformative outcomes and doing so in open defiance of those who would argue that such efforts are futile or unlikely to generate desired improvements (Burris, Heubert, & Levin, 2006; Burris, Wiley, Welner, & Murphy, 2008; Oakes, 2005). Such efforts have a body of literature on which to draw to help make detracked classrooms work (e.g., Boaler & Staples, 2008; Cohen & Lotan, 1995; Lotan, 2006; Rubin, 2006; Watanabe, 2011; Welner & Burris, 2006). At the same time, more can and should be done, with an eye toward radical revisioning beyond what any existing example might represent.

What Else Will It Take?

Whatever the method or model, with any effort to reverse or resist ability grouping and tracking, the pedagogical challenges are significant and the political challenges even more daunting. Success will require that those who may now see themselves as being in *competition*—such as advocates for the gifted, for students with disabilities, for students of color, and so on—make *common cause* around serving all students well. Educators have a critical role to play in building coalitions among these divergent constituencies and helping to disrupt forces that would seek to drive wedges between them in order to preserve the status quo. Educators must be prepared to guarantee—and also demonstrate—that new and different proposed practices will provide all students with opportunities that are at least as rich and rigorous as those students previously enjoyed. Few parents or advocates would agree to less. That said, some will object to *any* changes that take away the *comparative* advantages that privileged children enjoy—no matter how promising the new approaches might be. Confronting these challenges will require astute political leadership on educators' part—leadership that we should be wise and purposeful in cultivating.

Ending tracking will require changes similar in magnitude to social shifts such as the slow erosion of legal racial segregation and gender discrimination and the changes in norms regarding cigarette smoking. As with all deeply embedded social practices, knowledge, research, and righteous arguments alone will not be enough to bring about rapid transformation. But coalitions of people who see the harm in these practices *are* forming and making important headway in challenging the status quo. Those with much-needed professional knowledge and credible moral standing in the community are joining in the chorus of criticism *against* ability grouping and tracking and *for* inclusive, democratic, and socially just approaches that leverage student diversity for learning. While progress has been made, we have a long way to go and worthy trails to blaze.

DETRACKING IN ROCKVILLE CENTER

In 1990, Rockville Centre School District, a diverse suburban school district located on Long Island, New York, began replacing tracked classes with mixed-ability classes and teaching everyone the curriculum formerly reserved for the district's highest-track students. Previously, the high school had three tracks and the middle school had two or more tracks in each subject. African American and Latino students were enrolled disproportionately in the lowest tracks. The superintendent and the local Board of Education set ambitious goals: having 75 percent of graduates earn New York State Regents diplomas and closing racial and social-class gaps.

Realizing that tracking stood in the way of achieving those goals, the district decided that all students would study the accelerated middle-school math curriculum, since the Regents math test posed the greatest challenge. So the middle school enrolled mixed-ability groups in math classes formerly reserved for the district's highest achievers, and it provided support classes and after-school tutoring to those who needed it. The following year, more than 90 percent of incoming freshman, excluding special education students, entered the district's South Side High School having passed the first Regents math examination. The percentages of African American and Latino students passing the algebra-based Regents exam in the eighth grade also increased dramatically—from 54 percent to 98 percent. Inspired but not satisfied, the district pushed further. The following year, special education students were included as well; detracking expanded to other subjects; and in 1999 detracking followed students into the ninth and tenth grades. Enrollment in South Side's advanced placement (AP) and International Baccalaureate classes was opened up to everyone who wanted to enroll.

During the first decade of detracking reform, the school became a U.S. Department of Education Blue Ribbon School of Excellence, and one of *Newsweek*'s "100 Best High Schools in the United States." By 2003, the gap among Rockville Centre graduates had diminished significantly. Eighty-two percent of all African American or Latino and 97 percent of all white or Asian American graduates earned a Regents diploma. In 2004, the overall Regents diploma rate increased to a remarkable 94 percent.

Research on students' pathways through and beyond South Side High School further debunks the myth that detracking compromises the learning of high-track students. To the contrary, researchers offer South Side's case as evidence that "a well-executed detracking reform can help increasing numbers of students reach state and worldclass standards without adversely affecting high-achieving students" (Burris, Wiley, Welner, and Murphy (2008), p. 601). In Rockville Centre, detracking raised the bar for all students. Every group improved at the same time that the achievement gap narrowed dramatically.

Carol Burris the principal of South Side High School, now spends a great deal of her time helping other schools create heterogeneous classrooms with rigorous college preparatory curriculum. She has become widely known for her research, advocacy, and expertise in creating high-quality "detracked" schools. She was named 2013 High School Principal of the Year by the School Administrators Association of New York State.

Notes

1. The block quotations in this chapter are adapted from the text of an earlier chapter published in *Teaching to Change the World* (Oakes, Lipton, Anderson, & Stillman, 2013). The excerpts have been used with permission from the writing of former University of California, Los Angeles teacher education students.

2. Although labels don't always convey it explicitly, everyone tends to know the so-called ability level of various groups.
3. This is not to say that *particular* classes for lower-ability students are not given wonderful facilities, a solid curriculum, and well-qualified teachers, but such situations are generally exceptions to the rule.

References

Baker, A. L. (2013, January 1). Gifted, talented and separated. *New York Times*. Available at www.nytimes.com/2013/01/13/education/in-one-school-students-are-divided-by-gifted-label-and-race.html?pagewanted=all

Berger, S. L. (1996). *Differentiating curriculum for gifted students. ERIC Digest #E510*. Reston, VA: Council for Exceptional Children.

Boaler, J. (2006). "Opening our ideas": How a detracked mathematics approach promoted respect, responsibility, and high achievement. *Theory Into Practice, 45*(1), 40–46.

Boaler, J., & Staples, M. (2008). Creating mathematical futures through an equitable teaching approach: The case of Railside School. *Teachers College Record, 110*(3), 608–645.

Burris, C. C. (2003). Providing accelerated mathematics to heterogeneously grouped middle school students. *Dissertations Abstracts International, 64*(5), 1570.

Burris, C. C., Heubert, J. P., & Levin, H. M. (2006). Accelerating mathematics achievement using heterogeneous grouping. *American Educational Research Journal, 43*(1), 105–136.

Burris, C. C., Wiley, E., Welner, K. G., & Murphy, J. (2008). Accountability, rigor, and detracking: Achievement effects of embracing a challenging curriculum as a universal good for all students. *Teachers College Record, 110*(3), 571–608.

Carnegie Council on Adolescent Development. (1989). *Turning points: Preparing youth for the 21st Century*. New York: Carnegie Corporation of New York.

Cohen, E., & Lotan, R. (1995). Producing equal-status interaction in the heterogeneous classroom. *American Educational Research Journal, 32*(1), 99–120.

Crawford, J. (2004). *Educating bilingual students: Language diversity in the classroom*. Fifth ed. Los Angeles, CA: Bilingual Education Services.

Darling-Hammond, L. (2004). The color line in American education: Race, resources, and student achievement. *W.E.B. DuBois Review: Social Science Research on Race, 1*(2), 213–246.

DeLany, B. (1991). Allocation, choice, and stratification within high schools: How the sorting machine copes. *American Journal of Education, 99*(3), 191–207.

Engeström, Y. (1999). Innovative learning in work teams: Analyzing cycles of knowledge creation in practice. In Y. Engeström, R. Miettinen, & R. Punamäki (Eds.), *Perspectives on activity theory* (pp. 377–406). Cambridge: Cambridge University Press.

Fass, P. (1991). *Outside in: Minorities and the transformation of American education*. New York: Oxford University Press.

Fine, M. (1991). *Framing dropouts: Notes on the politics of an urban high school*. Albany, NY: State University of New York Press.

Gamoran, A. (1988, August). *A multi-level analysis of the effects of tracking*. Paper presented at the Annual Meeting of the American Sociological Association, Atlanta, GA.

Garelick, B. (2013, March 26). Let's go back to grouping students by ability. *The Atlantic Monthly*. Available at www.theatlantic.com/national/archive/2013/03/lets-go-back-to-grouping-students-by-ability/274362/

Garet, M., & DeLany, B. (1988). Students, courses, and stratification. *Sociology of Education, 61*(2), 61–77.

Garland, S. (2013). Who should be in the gifted program? *Slate*. Available at www.slate.com/articles/health_and_science/science/2013/03/gifted_and_talented_education_cities_try_to_make_programs_more_inclusive.html

Gutiérrez, K., & Rogoff, B. (2003). Cultural ways of learning: Individual traits or repertoires of practice? *Educational Researcher, 32*(5), 19–25.

Hallinan, M. (2000, August 15). *Ability group effects on high school learning outcomes*. Paper presented at the Annual Meeting of the American Sociological Association, Washington, DC.

Lareau, A. (1989). *Home advantage: Social class and parental intervention in elementary education*. London: Falmer.

Lee, C. (2007). *The role of culture in academic literacies: Conducting our blooming in the midst of the whirlwind*. New York: Teachers College Press.

Lotan, R. (2006). Teaching teachers to build equitable classrooms. *Theory into Practice, 45*(1), 32–39.

Loveless, T. (2013). The resurgence of ability grouping and the persistence of tracking. *The 2013 Brown Center Report on American Education: How well are American students learning?* (pp. 13–20). Washington, DC: The Brookings Institution.

Lucas, S. (1999). *Tracking inequality: Stratification and mobility in American high schools*. New York: Teachers College Press.

Mehan, H., Mercer, J., & Rueda, R. (2002) Special education. In D. L. Levinson, P. W. Cookson, & A. R. Sadovnik (Eds.), *Education and sociology: An encyclopedia of education and sociology*, pp. 619–624. New York: Routledge Falmer.

National Governors' Association. (1993). *Ability grouping and tracking: Current issues and concerns*. Washington, D.C.: Authors.

National Research Council. (2003). *Engaging schools: Fostering high school students' motivation to learn*. Washington, DC: The National Academies Press.

Nieto, S., & Bode, P. (2011). *Affirming diversity: The sociopolitical context of multicultural education*. Sixth ed. New York: Pearson.

Oakes, J. (1990). *Multiplying inequalities*. Santa Monica, CA: RAND.

Oakes, J. (1995). Two cities' tracking and within-school segregation. *Teachers College Press, 96*(4), 681–690.

Oakes, J. (2005). *Keeping track: How schools structure inequality*. Second ed. New Haven, CT: Yale University Press.

Oakes, J. (2008). Keeping track: Structuring equality and inequality in an era of accountability. *Teachers College Press, 11*(3), 700–712.

Oakes, J., Gamoran, A., & Page, R. (1992). Curriculum differentiation. In P. Jackson (Ed.), *Handbook of research on curriculum* (pp. 570–608). New York: Macmillan.

Oakes, J., & Guiton, G. (1995). Matchmaking: The dynamics of high school tracking decisions, *American Educational Research Journal, 32*(1), 3–33.

Oakes, J., Lipton, M., Anderson, L., & Stillman, J. (2013). *Teaching to change the world*. Fourth ed. Boulder, CO: Paradigm Publishers.

Oakes, J., & Saunders, M. (2008). *Beyond tracking: Multiple pathways to college, career, and civic participation*. Cambridge, MA: Harvard Education Press.

Orfield, G. (2004). *Dropouts in America: Confronting the graduation crisis*. Cambridge, MA: Harvard Education Press.

Roda, A., & Wells, A. S. (2013) School choice policies and racial segregation: Where white parents' good intentions, anxiety, and privilege collide. *American Journal of Education, 119*(2), 261–293.

Rodrigues, J. (2013, August 15). Parents say new programs can't replace Accelerated Learning Activities Program (ALAP). *Warwick Beacon*. Available at www.warwickonline.com/stories/Parents-say-new-programs-cant-replace-ALAP,84641

Rogoff, B. (2003). *The cultural nature of human development.* New York: Oxford University Press.

Rubin, B. C. (2006). Tracking and detracking: Debates, evidence, and best practices for a heterogeneous world. *Theory into Practice, 45*(1), 4–14.

Rubin, B. C. (2008). Detracking in context: How local constructions of ability complicate equity-geared reform. *Teachers College Record, 110*(3), 647–700.

Schmidt, W. (1998). Are there surprises in the TIMSS twelfth grade results? *TIMSS United States,* Report No. 8. East Lansing, MI: Trends in International Mathematics and Science Study (TIMSS), U.S. National Research Center, Michigan State University.

Sparks, S. (2013, March 26). More teachers group students by ability. *Education Week.* Available at www.edweek.org/ew/articles/2013/03/27/26tracking.h32.html

Spring, J. (2007). *The American school: From the Puritans to No Child Left Behind.* New York: McGraw-Hill.

Texas H.B. 5 (2013). An Act relating to public school accountability, including assessment, and curriculum requirements; providing a criminal penalty. Available at www.capitol.state.tx.us/tlodocs/83R/billtext/pdf/HB00005F.pdf#navpanes=0

The College Board. (2000). EQUITY 2000: A systemic education reform model. A summary report. Washington, DC: Author.

Tomlinson, C. (1995). *How to differentiate instruction for mixed-ability classrooms.* Alexandria, VA: ASCD.

Tomlinson, C. (2001). Differentiated instruction in the regular classroom: What does it mean? How does it look? *Understanding Our Gifted, 14*(1), 3–6.

Tyack, D. (1974). *The one best system: A history of American urban education.* Cambridge, MA: Harvard University Press.

Useem, E. (1991). Student selection into course sequences in mathematics: The impact of parental involvement and school policies. *Journal of Research on Adolescence, 1*(3), 231–250.

Villegas, A. M. (1988). School failure and cultural mismatch: Another view. *The Urban Review, 20*(4), 253–265.

Watanabe, M. (2008). Tracking in the era of high-stakes state accountability reform: Case studies of classroom instruction in North Carolina. *Teachers College Record, 110*(3), 489–534.

Watanabe, M. (2011). *"Heterogenius" classrooms behind the scenes: Detracking math and science—a look at groupwork in action.* New York: Teachers College Press.

Welner, K. (2001). *Legal rights, local wrongs: When community control collides with educational equity.* Buffalo: State University of New York Press.

Welner, K. (2013, March 20). The answer sheet: The bottom line on student tracking. *Washington Post.* Available at www.washingtonpost.com/blogs/answer-sheet/wp/2013/06/10/the-bottom-line-on-student-tracking/

Welner, K., & Burris, C. (2006). Alternative approaches to the politics of detracking. *Theory into Practice, 45*(1), 90–99.

Welner, K., & Burris, C. (2013a, June 7). *Is American education on a bad track?* Available at www.timesunion.com/opinion/article/Is-American-education-on-a-bad-track-4586828.phpv

Welner, K., & Burris, C. (2013b, June 29). Texas must avoid a return to the vocational track. *Star-Telegram.* Available at www.star-telegram.com/2013/06/29/4971293/texas-must-avoid-a-return-to-the.html

Werblow, J., Urick, A., & Duesbery, L. (2013). On the wrong track: How tracking is associated with becoming a high school dropout. *Equity and Excellence in Education, 46*(2), 270–284.

Yee, V. (2013, June 9). Grouping students by ability regains favor in the classroom. *New York Times.* Available at www.nytimes.com/2013/06/10/education/grouping-students-by-ability-regains-favor-with-educators.html?pagewanted=all

Yonezawa, S. (1997). *Making decisions about students' lives: A dissertation.* Los Angeles: University of California at Los Angeles.

Yonezawa, S., & Jones, M. (2006). Students' perspectives on tracking and detracking. *Theory into Practice, 45*(1), 15–23.

Yonezawa, S., & Oakes, J. (2004). Making all parents partners in the placement process. *Education Leadership, 56*(7), 33-36.

Yonezawa, S., Wells, A. S., & Serna, I. (2002). Choosing tracks: "Freedom of choice" in detracked schools. *American Educational Research Journal, 39*(1), 37–67.

10

POVERTY, ECONOMIC INEQUALITY, AND THE IMPOSSIBLE PROMISE OF SCHOOL REFORM

Paul C. Gorski

I have thought and written much the past several years about deficit ideology—about how we, as educators, often spurn and endorse it simultaneously. Deficit ideology refers to a set of beliefs (or ideology) that pegs people in poverty as morally, intellectually, and even spiritually deficient. Equally sinister, it attributes outcome inequalities, such as those related to high school graduation rates or standardized test scores, to that deficiency. In fact, the deficit ideologue generally believes that poverty itself is an outcome of an individual's deficiencies. *Everybody has an equal opportunity to succeed,* the thinking goes, *if people just work hard enough.* So people who get good grades, graduate from college, or earn loads of money are assumed to have put in the effort and earned it. And those who don't? Well, they just didn't work hard enough.

In order to embrace a deficit ideology, the deficit ideologue has to ignore many, many factors that have little to do with students' or families' effort or commitment. Take, for example, what Jonathan Kozol (1992) has called the "savage inequalities" of public schools. We send the most privileged youth, on average, to the most well-funded schools with the smallest class sizes, smallest teacher-to-student ratios, best-equipped labs and gyms and music rooms and libraries, and most experienced teachers. Meanwhile, we send the most economically disadvantaged youth to, well, pretty much the opposite of that. Suffice it to say, for now, that although many of us in the United States like to think of education as the great equalizer and although many of us use some version of this myth to motivate youth, society's grossest inequalities are reproduced with impressive precision in our schools. We will explore some of these inequalities momentarily.

The trouble is, the trouble doesn't end there. Take a step or two back and an even bleaker picture emerges. Poor and working-class youth and their families are subject to a whole host of inequalities that oughtn't exist in the wealthiest country in the world, ranging from unequal access to health care to unequal access to recreational opportunities. Although they might be seen as outside-school issues, these inequalities, which we also will discuss in more detail momentarily, have a considerable impact on learning. Education, we are told, is the key to overcoming these barriers, as though teachers and schools are equipped to undo an entire network of structured disadvantage.

I do not mean to argue, by pointing out these realities, that low-income youth are incapable of learning. Low-income youth have the same potentials and capabilities as their wealthier peers, but they are cheated out of some of the opportunities other youth have to nurture these potentials and capabilities, which means we all lose. Nor am I making "excuses" for teachers or administrators in high-poverty schools, as the no-excuses rhetoric of the modern school reform movement might suggest. I am arguing, instead, that the presumption that schools are equipped to make up for gross wealth inequality and all of its implications, including unequal access to health care, quality child care, and nutritious food is, in the end, less about equality than about squelching a much more fundamental conversation about democracy and opportunity. I'm arguing, in fact, that the national discourse on poverty and education in the United States happens, in almost every case, backward, starting with the assumption that education itself is the cure for poverty and ignoring the fact that even as high school and college graduation rates increase in the United States today, so increase income and wealth inequality and the number of people in poverty.

Consider an example. There is much chatter these days about the "economic achievement gap"—a term that harkens to a deficit view, which is why many equity-minded educators choose to focus instead on the "opportunity gap" or "education debt" (Ladson-Billings, 2006). A good portion of this chatter is driven, I'm afraid, not by a deep understanding of poverty and its toll on youth and their learning but by a series of deflections, like the education-as-the-great-equalizer mythology. The sources of these deflections—most often neoliberal education reformers who sell deficit ideology along with their corporate-friendly reforms—have, during the most recent wave of school reform, pointed the blaming finger at low-income parents for not being involved enough in their children's education, at teachers and administrators in high-poverty schools for not adequately boosting students' test scores, at teachers' unions, and at just about everybody and everything other than the underlying cause of outcome inequalities: poverty itself.

By doing so they propagate what I consider to be the mother of all lies in today's school reform discourse: that we can equalize educational opportunity and outcomes without addressing fundamental economic inequalities in the United States and its schools. In this chapter I peel apart the layers of this lie and its implications. I begin by exploring what makes this lie a lie, challenging the notion of school as the "great equalizer." Then, by detailing some of the disadvantages low-income families face in and out of schools, I describe the diversionary tactic of blaming schools and educators for not doing something that is more or less impossible to do: making up gross societal inequalities. I end by calling on educators and policymakers to shift reform efforts to focus on addressing the structural conditions that ensure the persistence of disparities in educational outcomes—to recognize income inequality, wealth inequality, and poverty as the biggest barriers to school success for low-income families.

School, the Great Un-Equalizer

There is no denying this point: on average, by virtually any outcome measure, students from families in poverty do not fare as well in school as their wealthier peers. They score lower on the most narrow measures of achievement, such as standardized test scores, and drop out (or are pushed out) of school at four times the rate of children who are not in poverty. If you want to know what sort of ideology somebody brings to a conversation about education and student performance, listen carefully to her or his characterization of these gaps and explanation for why they exist. Then consider this: if I hope to achieve something that resembles educational equity, my first task is to determine, beyond the rhetoric, why the inequalities exist.

Let's begin in the public school system itself. In order to concede, if only for the sake of argument, the widely accepted notion that education can undo the effects of existing income and wealth inequality—that education has a mitigating effect on poverty—we would need to assume that the school system itself is a level playing field. But it's not—not by a long shot.

In every imaginable way, and in some unimaginable ways, the odds are stacked against poor and working-class youth even within the system we call the "great equalizer." Many of the disadvantages in this stack of odds are well known, which, I admit, renders me puzzled when I think that so many people still buy into the great-equalizer mythology. Even at the basest level of basic funding, schools in low-income districts are funded, on average, at lower rates than schools in wealthier districts. Kozol detailed this issue in 1992. His book was a best seller; these funding disparities are no big secret. And yet, two decades later, they persist (Baker & Corcoran, 2012).

Other inequalities, just as widely acknowledged, abound. Low-income students have considerably less access to quality preschool programs than their wealthier peers (Freeman, 2010). Once they get to elementary school, they are steered disproportionately into less rigorous academic tracks even when their academic performance doesn't warrant it (Futrell & Gomez, 2008). They are more likely than their wealthier peers to have teachers who are inexperienced or uncertified in the subjects they are teaching (Orfield, Frankenberg, & Siegel-Hawley, 2010). They are subject more consistently than their wealthier peers to rote, skills-and-drills instruction, despite the fact that research clearly shows that all students, including low-income students, learn better when they are engaged by student-centered, higher-order pedagogies. Additionally, class sizes in high-poverty schools, and particularly high-poverty urban schools, are larger on average than those in low-poverty schools

(Barton, 2004). I suspect none of this is revelatory to people with even a rudimentary knowledge of U.S. public schools.

But there's more. Youth from families in poverty are more likely than their wealthier peers to attend schools that do not employ full-time school nurses. Their school libraries are less well stocked on average than those at low-poverty schools. And, perhaps most illogical of all, whether they attend high-poverty schools or mixed-class schools (where they are likely to be segregated into lower tracks, anyway), poor youth are more likely than wealthier peers to have reduced access, if any at all, to physical education and the arts. This, despite the fact that research consistently has shown that access to exercise and the arts at school improves engagement and performance for all students, especially low-income students, whose parents are less likely to be able to enroll them in sports leagues, arts camps, or music lessons.

What I find most fascinating, in a disturbing sort of way, is that, as with school funding disparities, nobody is pretending that these inequalities *don't* exist. Nobody—not the Heritage Foundation, the Hoover Institution, or any other think tank or school reform apologist bent on diverting every possible penny from public schools and pumping them into private enterprise—is attempting to convince us that schools *are* funded equally or that the class sizes in schools located in wealthy suburban neighborhoods *are* just as big as those in high-poverty urban neighborhoods. No, the data are far too clear for that. Astoundingly, they tend to insist, instead, that these inequalities don't matter—that class size doesn't matter, that "throwing more money" at low-income schools won't solve anything. Of course, these are lies, as well. Who would pay $40,000 to send their children to a boarding school with small class sizes, experienced teachers with advanced degrees, designated school nurses, and every other advantage if they believed a school's financial resources didn't matter?

If the funders and drivers of the current school reform movement—Bill Gates and Jeff Bezos and other people and organizations putting millions of dollars behind movements for charter schools and school vouchers and hyperaccountability through high-stakes tests and workarounds to teacher certification—really were interested in improving schools for low-income families, they'd be fighting, at the very least, to make sure those families had access to the kind of educational opportunity their own children receive. Last time I checked, the administration at Sidwell Friends School, where the Obamas send their daughters, hadn't discontinued the arts program or doubled class sizes or eliminated engaging pedagogies in favor of high-stakes, test-driven direct instruction after realizing such things cost too much and have no impact on learning. That's because they *do* have an impact on learning.

Out-of-School Inequities That Affect School Performance

But if we really want to put into perspective the lie that we can equalize educational opportunity while failing to eliminate gross economic inequalities, we need to take a broader view. We can begin by considering the bigger social and political context of class inequality and how it affects school engagement and outcomes. Understand, first of all, that perhaps the most profound lie sold to U.S. citizens is the myth of meritocracy: the idea that we can achieve whatever we want if we just work hard enough, that success, however measured, is fully earned rather than rendered on the basis of, say, the wealth of one's parents or the tone of one's skin. If that were true, then wouldn't we expect to see decreases in wealth and income inequality as, for example, more and more people in the United States earn college and graduate degrees? What sense can we make out of the fact that, even as poverty rates have increased over the past several years, corporate profits have reached record highs?

In fact, since 1980 income inequality has been on the rise in the United States. Currently it stands at its highest level since the 1970s (McCall & Percheski, 2010). In 2011, for example, the incomes of middle- and working-class people—those who occupy the middle 60 percent of the income pyramid in the United States— *fell* on average between 1.6 and 1.9 percent. In the meantime, the incomes of the wealthiest 20 percent of people *grew* an average of 1.6 percent. The wealthiest 1 percent must not have noticed there was a recession. Their incomes grew by an average of 6 percent (Luhby, 2012b)—not too shabby for a year of supposed economic crisis, when many people in the bottom half of the economic pyramid were losing their jobs. What might be even more surprising is that such a situation is not unique in the United States, which, among Western industrialized countries, has the most unequal distribution of income (Reid, 2006).

In more direct terms, about 47 million people in the United States live in poverty, roughly 15 percent of the population (U.S. Census Bureau, 2012). That figure is based on the government-defined poverty-line income, $22,400 for a family of four (Kaufman, 2011). Using the same standard, another 30 million people live barely above the poverty line (Luhby, 2012a).

Complicating matters, poverty is not equally distributed. It is tied to a whole range of other forms of inequality, including racism, sexism, and even ableism (Gorski, 2013). Women are more likely than men to be in poverty even though they are more likely to have college degrees, including graduate degrees (Wang & Parker, 2011). African American, Latina/o, and American Indian people are more likely than White or Asian American people to be poor (Kochlar, Fry, & Taylor, 2011). Poverty rates among people with two or more disabilities are among the highest for any identity group in the United States (Palmer, 2011). Complicating matters even further, there are differences of rates in poverty within identity groups. For example, Hmong people and others of Asian ancestry whose forebears came to the United States as refugees and were likely poor when they arrived are more likely to be in poverty now than people of Asian ancestry whose families moved to the United States to attend college or work at a diplomatic post (Southeast Asia Resource Action Center, 2011).

Now you still might be thinking, as the notion of meritocracy easily leads us to do, that, despite this mess of inequality, any individual who is born into a low-income family but who works her or his buns off in school has access to every opportunity afforded people who are born wealthy. This can be an easy assumption given the many stereotypes about poor people being lazy or not valuing education and given the popularity of school reform discourses that play off these stereotypes, such as by targeting bad parenting or ineffective teaching, rather than awful levels of economic inequality, as the primary culprit of unequal educational outcomes. The assumption shatters when we realize that this description of low-income parents as, for example, uninterested in school contradicts decades of research showing that they have the same attitudes about the value of education and exert the same amount of energy on their children's education as their wealthier peers (e.g., Li, 2010).

What I find most *instructive* about the "poor people don't value education" stereotype is that it appears to result primarily from educators' observations that some parents and guardians are less likely than others to participate in on-site school involvement activities, like Back to School Nights and parent-teacher conferences. Of course, the way these events are scheduled is, itself, riddled with inequalities. Do schools, an average, schedule these events in ways that are equally accessible to a wealthy parent and a low-income parent when the latter is more likely to work multiple jobs, including evening jobs, without paid leave, more likely to struggle to afford child care, more likely to rely primarily on public transportation to get from place to place, more likely to have experienced school her- or himself as a hostile environment?

What I find most *destructive* about the mindset that labels poor parents or other caregivers as the problem is that it is a classic case of blaming the victim, a perfect example of deficit ideology. Not only does it add yet another layer of repression and subtle hostility to the shoulders of low-income families and students, but it all but ensures that we ignore the bigger picture of inequality—that we continue to feed the "great-equalizer" lie. As we're busy trying to fix imagined defects in the most vulnerable families, we all too often forget to consider the role poverty and economic inequality play in determining the distribution of access and opportunity.

Before I get into the specifics of this distribution, it bears repeating that despite the "no excuses" rhetoric, to acknowledge gross life *opportunity* gaps among youth with different levels of access to financial resources is not excuse making. Rather, it is a reality check. It is an attempt to understand how the educational outcome inequalities we all bemoan are not the result of uninterested parents or a lack of school choice or bad teaching or too little curricular standardization or any of the myriad other "problems" driving the bulk of corporate-style school reform initiatives today. No, the inequalities are logical, unjust, results that will persist so long as we pretend we can equalize educational access and outcomes despite overwhelming societal disparities, particularly wealth inequality and poverty. These include disparities in access to health care, healthy living and working conditions, social and public services, exercise and recreation opportunities, and many, many other resources and opportunities that have a direct impact on school performance.

Access to Health Care

It comes as no surprise, I'm sure, that children from families in poverty are considerably more likely than their wealthier peers to lack health insurance. They also are considerably less likely to have access to preventive health care and regular checkups (Pampel, Krueger, & Denney, 2010), rendering them more susceptible to serious illness. These disparities begin even before childbirth when we consider how unequal access to prenatal care partially explains the fact that children born into economically disadvantaged families are more likely than those born into wealthier families to be born prematurely and with lower than normal birth weights (Temple, Reynolds, & Arteaga, 2010). This, in turn, helps explain increased rates of ailments such as asthma and respiratory diseases among poor children, just the sort of challenge that can disrupt school attendance and academic focus. Economically disadvantaged youth also are more likely to have unmet mental health needs (Fulda et al., 2009).

The effects of disparities in access to health care, like most other disparities, compound over the course of low-income students' school lives. They affect cognitive development, school attendance, and many other factors that predict school performance. Unfortunately, the disappearance of dedicated nursing positions at high-poverty schools exacerbates these disparities. Imagine how educational outcomes might be different if every family had access to regular, preventive health care.

Access to Healthy Living Conditions

Making disparities in access to health care all the more devastating, people in poverty are more likely than their wealthier counterparts to live in poorly built and structurally unsafe housing (Whiteside-Mansell et al., 2010). They are more likely to live near environmental waste sites, contributing to their higher rates of asthma, respiratory infections, and other diseases (Walker et al., 2005). Meanwhile, they are less likely to have access to adequate or healthy food and, as a result, suffer disproportionately from hunger, food insecurity, and nutritional deficits (Coles, 2008). This results, in part, from the absence of grocery stores in poor communities, which often means that low-income families are forced into purchasing highly processed food at convenience stores, which, in turn, means they actually *pay more* for groceries than folks who liver near Trader Joe's or Costco (Brown, 2009).

Hunger and nutritional deficits, along with other dangerous and destructive living and working conditions that disproportionately affect youth in poverty, impact cognitive development, energy, and focus. They also contribute to the sorts of health challenges described earlier. Imagine how educational outcomes might be different if all youth grew up breathing clean air and eating an adequate amount of healthy food.

Access to Social and Public Services

Almost invariably, the quality of social and municipal services—including the most basic services, such as water, electricity, and road maintenance—in high-poverty neighborhoods is considerably lower than that in wealthier neighborhoods (National Commission on Teaching and America's Future, 2004). This is a result, in large part, of the fact that state and local governments fund these services at lower levels in high-poverty areas than in wealthier areas, especially in rural neighborhoods. To use an example most immediately relevant to education, libraries in high-poverty areas, if they exist at all, tend to be more poorly stocked, have shorter hours, and face a more consistent threat of closure than libraries in wealthier communities. (Libraries in high-poverty schools also tend to be under-resourced when compared with those in low-poverty schools.)

We know that access to books is related directly to literacy, especially to reading proficiency. We also know, on the basis of a recent multinational study (Krashen, Lee, & McQuillan, 2010), that libraries can play a mitigating role when it comes to gaps in access to reading materials between poor and more well-to-do youth. Imagine how educational outcomes might be different if, in addition to receiving equitable services across the board, all communities were provided with well-stocked neighborhood libraries with long hours and access to other social and municipal services now reserved only for the most privileged communities.

Access to Exercise and Recreation Opportunities

Low-income families are not able to pay as much as wealthier families for participation in organized sports leagues, athletic equipment, gym memberships, and other fitness and recreational "goods," giving them less access to physically enriching activities (Swartz, 2008). Recreation centers, including playgrounds, in poor communities are more likely than those in wealthier areas to be in disrepair, and green spaces, such as ball fields, are far less common in high-poverty neighborhoods, especially those in urban areas (Macpherson et al., 2010). Poor and working-class youth also are more likely than their middle-class or wealthier counterparts to care for younger siblings after school, adding another barrier to their engagement in regular fitness activities (Fahlman et al., 2006). As with libraries, the effects of these disparities are exacerbated as high-poverty schools continue to cut physical education and recess.

Charles Basch (2011), who reviewed two decades of research on the relationship between fitness and academic achievement, found that students who are fit and who regularly exercise fare better in school. Seems obvious, right? They have longer attention spans, more energy, more self-confidence, and more intellectual endurance. Imagine how educational outcomes might be different if all families could afford to provide their children with fitness and recreational opportunities.

Rethinking the Problems and Solutions of Unequal Educational Outcomes

What strikes me most forcefully as I consider these and the many other inequalities with which youth in poverty contend is that none of them—not a single one—has anything to do with students' desires to learn, their intellectual capacities, or their value systems. These conditions do not result from low-income parents disregarding the importance of education, from lackluster efforts on the parts of teachers, or from school administrators' failures to lead effectively, as much of today's school reform rhetoric might have us believe. They are symptoms of wealth and income inequality, symptoms of poverty, symptoms of a lack of commitment in the wealthiest country in the world to be what it claims to the rest of the world and its own citizens to be: a place where everybody gets a fair shake.

So imagine, now, how educational outcomes might be different if every child had high-quality consistent health care, including preventive care; clean air to breathe and adequate, healthy food to eat; access to books and computers at local libraries and the protection provided by the level of other social and municipal services enjoyed by their wealthier peers; and opportunities to exercise and stay fit. Throw in the well-funded schools, smaller class sizes, fully certified teaching force, and higher-order pedagogies currently reserved, for the most part, for wealthier youth, and we finally might begin to see the gaps fade away.

Finally imagine this: How might the solutions we devise for eradicating disparities in educational outcomes change if we consider the reality of these inequalities? How might we think differently about wave after wave of school reform movements and initiatives that ignore them? How might we understand the challenges facing teachers and administrators at high-poverty schools differently? How might we reallocate our own efforts toward creating equitable educational opportunity?

As I reflect upon these questions and the ways I spend my own efforts toward educational justice, I see a continuum of opportunities to address the disparities largely ignored in today's school reform conversations. On one end of the continuum are initiatives that *mitigate* the inequalities—that acknowledge the impact of poverty and attempt to lighten its influence in the immediate term. On the other end are initiatives meant to *eradicate* the inequalities by addressing their root: poverty. Recognizing that each of us has a unique sphere of influence, I find it useful to imagine a path toward equal educational opportunity that incorporates actions and initiatives that span this continuum, all of which acknowledge *poverty,* rather than *poor people and their families and teachers,* as the problem to be resolved.

Mitigating the Effects of Poverty

There are many things we can do *right now* to begin mitigating the effects of poverty: actions and initiatives that have proved to bolster but not equalize educational outcomes for low-income youth (Gorski, 2013). They are commonly practiced in classrooms and schools full of wealthier students. For example, we can:

- incorporate movement pedagogies and other opportunities for exercise across the curriculum;
- adopt higher-order, learner-centered, inquiry-driven, rigorous pedagogies—this is the most important way to demonstrate high expectations;
- incorporate the arts, including both visual and performing arts, into the curriculum;
- make curricula relevant to the lives of students in poverty;
- analyze and encourage students to analyze learning materials for bias;
- make opportunities for on-site school involvement accessible to parents and guardians who are most likely to work evenings, to not have paid leave, and to struggle to pay for child care, and so on; and
- fight to protect dedicated school nurse positions.

If every school adopted these strategies, freed from the weight of high-stakes standardized testing and the threat of shutdown—that is, if every school simply offered what we already know is the best possible education for every student and family—progress would be inevitable. Unfortunately, many contemporary school reform initiatives—most notably, the imposition of high-stakes testing regimens—have left low-income students, on average, with less of just about every sort of school practice that has proven to be effective for engaging and retaining them. This, of course, raises another question that is addressed at length in several other chapters in this book: who, then, benefits—or perhaps the right word is *profits*—from these "reform" initiatives? What would motivate us to do *less* of what we know works?

Eradicating the Effects of Poverty

Of course, despite the mitigating potential of these and other strategies, the only real way to eliminate class-based educational outcome disparities, in my opinion, is to eliminate poverty—to work at the roots of the problem rather than fall ultimately into the same trap as the people and organizations pushing *more* testing, *more* voucher systems, *more* merit pay, *more* of anything that ignores the persisting impact of income and wealth inequality.

But as we move through the center of the continuum, we come across strategies that, while not eradicating poverty, at least equip low-income communities with access to critical services and opportunities that may eradicate some of the effects of poverty. We can, for example:

- forge cross-sector relationships between schools and community agencies and organizations, giving low-income students access to goods and services their families cannot afford, such as medical attention, healthy food, and recreational opportunities;

- extend school health screenings and services; and
- advocate against redistricting measures that result in increased levels of class- or race-based school segregation.

Taking a few more steps along the continuum, we might begin to help eliminate some of the structural barriers that both deny basic rights to low-income people and all but ensure the persistence of poverty. If we are committed to educational equity, then we have a stake in many parallel movements for equity and justice. We might advocate, for example, for:

- universal food justice, helping to ensure that all people have access to ample, nutritious, food that is not highly processed;
- universal health care with special attention to preventive medicine;
- universal access to safe and affordable housing; and
- universal access to clean water and air.

I don't mean to suggest we all need to be waist-deep in each of these movements. Even if we see our purview as education specifically, understanding how these basic rights relate to educational opportunity and how the denial of any of them is tied to the denial of all of them, we will better understand how we might team with people from other movements to secure for students in poverty some measure of economic justice. However we place ourselves in these or other movements, though, the most important thing we can do is to collaborate with local communities—to fight *alongside* them rather than *in place of* them.

As we move toward the far end of the continuum, it becomes harder and harder to avoid this difficult question: Can there be any real movement, any real reform initiative, with the goal of eliminating class-based disparities in school that is not also a movement to eradicate poverty? After spending the bulk of the past ten years considering this question through the lenses of activist, educator, and scholar, the only sensible answer I can come up with is, *absolutely not*. Again, I'm not saying here that everybody who cares about educational equity should refocus all of her or his energies on eradicating poverty. We need people working all along this continuum. The trouble, as I see it, is that so few of us are working on *this* end of the continuum. As a result, a goal like eradicating poverty is so overwhelming that the big lies behind initiatives like voucher programs or more testing can start to sound a bit alluring. Even in my own life I have, until recently, thought of my work in the realm of educational equity as oddly separate from my work in the realm of economic justice.

But now I see no alternative to an intersectional, cross-issue effort on the parts of people and organizations working in various spheres for the rights of economically disadvantaged youth and families. After all, in the end, we all are after the same thing. We all want what's best for all youth, whether we're fighting for living-wage laws, fighting against growing wealth inequality, fighting for universal health care, fighting against growing corporate influence on supposedly public schools, fighting for food justice, fighting against the school-to-prison pipeline, fighting for racial equity. All of these issues are intermingled, and so the movements attached to them must be intermingled. All of these issues are related directly or indirectly to educational access and opportunity, so education people belong in the conversations. But, in order for this intersectional approach to work and to push back against the idea that schools themselves are capable of eliminating the effects of poverty, those of us who see education as our primary work almost must expand our own understandings of how these inequalities fit together. When we fail to do so, we make it too easy for ourselves and others to slide into a deficit view that ignores the web of inequality and continues the cycle of school reforms that fail to address the fundamental causes of educational disparities and outcome gaps.

References

Baker, B., & Corcoran, S. (2012). *Stealth inequities of school funding.* Washington, DC: Center for American Progress.

Barton, P. E. (2004). Why does the gap persist? *Educational Leadership, 62*(3), 8–13.

Basch, C. (2011). Physical activity and the achievement gap among urban minority youth. *Journal of School Health, 81*(10), 626–634.

Brown, D. L. (2009, May 18). The high cost of poverty: Why the poor pay more. *Washington Post.* Retrieved August 4, 2011, from www.washingtonpost.com/wp-dyn/content/article/2009/05/17/AR2009051702053.html?sid=ST2009051801162

Coles, G. (2008). Hunger, academic success, and the hard bigotry of indifference. *Rethinking Schools, 23*(2). Retrieved May 30, 2011, from www.rethinkingschools.org/ProdDetails.asp?ID=RTSVOL23N2&d=etoc

Fahlman, M. M., Hall, H. L., & Lock, R. (2006). Ethnic and socioeconomic comparisons of fitness, activity levels, and barriers to exercise in high school females. *Journal of School Health, 76*(1), 12–17.

Freeman, E. (2010). The shifting geography of urban education. *Education and Urban Society, 42*(6), 674–704.

Fulda, K. G., Lykens, K. K., Bae, S., & Singh, K. P. (2009). Unmet health care needs for children with special health care needs stratified by socioeconomic status. *Child and Adolescent Mental Health, 14*(4), 190–199.

Futrell, M., & Gomez, J. (2008). How tracking creates a poverty of learning. *Educational Leadership, 65*(8), 74–78.

Gorski, P. C. (2013). *Reaching and teaching students in poverty: Strategies for erasing the opportunity gap.* New York: Teachers College Press.

Kaufman, G. (2011, March 22). U.S. poverty: Past, present, and future. *The Nation.* Retrieved June 11, 2011, from www.thenation.com

Kochlar, R., Fry, R., & Taylor, P. (2011). *Wealth gaps rise to record highs between Whites, Blacks and Hispanics.* Washington, DC: Pew Social & Demographic Trends.

Kozol, J. (1992). *Savage inequalities: Children in America's schools.* New York: Harper Perennial.

Krashen, S., Lee, S., & McQuillan, J. (2010). An analysis of the PIRLS (2006) data: Can the school library reduce the effect of poverty on reaching achievement? *CSLA Journal, 34*(1), 26–28.

Ladson-Billings, G. (2006). From the achievement gap to the education debt: Understanding achievement in U.S. schools. *Educational Researcher, 35*(7), 3–12.

Li, G. (2010). Race, class, and schooling: Multicultural families doing the hard work of home literacy in America's inner city. *Reading & Writing Quarterly, 26,* 140–165.

Luhby, T. (2012a). American's near poor: 30 million and struggling. *CNNMoney.* Retrieved December 31, 2012, from http://money.cnn.com/2012/10/24/news/economy/americans-poverty/index.html

Luhby, T. (2012b). Median income falls, but so does poverty. *CNNMoney.* Retrieved December 31, 2012, from http://money.cnn.com/2012/09/12/news/economy/median-income-poverty/index.html?iid=EL

Macpherson, A. K., Jones, J., Rothman, L., Macarthur, C., & Howard, A. W. (2010). Safety standards and socioeconomic disparities in school playground injuries: A retrospective cohort study. *BMC Public Health, 10,* 542–547.

McCall, L., & Percheski, C. (2010). Income inequality: New trends and research directions. *Annual Review of Sociology, 16,* 329–347.

National Commission on Teaching and America's Future. (2004). *2004 summit on high quality teacher preparation.* Retrieved April 2, 2011, from www.nctaf.org/resoruces/events/2004_summit-1

Orfield, G., Frankenberg, E., & Siegel-Hawley, G. (2010). Integrated schools: Finding a new path. *Educational Leadership, 68*(3), 22–27.

Palmer, M. (2011). Disability and poverty: A conceptual overview. *Journal of Disability Policy Studies, 21*(4), 210–218.

Pampel, F. C., Krueger, P. M., & Denney, J. T. (2010). Socioeconomic disparities in health behaviors. *Annual Review of Sociology, 36,* 349–370.

Reid, J. (2006). *New census data shows 1.3 million children have fallen into poverty since 2000.* Available at http://cdf.childrensdefense.org/site/News2?page=NewsArticle&id=7887

Southeast Asia Resource Action Center. (2011). *Southeast Asian Americans at a glance.* Washington, DC: Author.

Swartz, T. T. (2008). Family capital and the invisible transfer of privilege: Intergenerational support and social class in early adulthood. *New Directions in Child Adolescent Development, 119,* 11–24.

Temple, J. A., Reynolds, A. J., & Arteaga, I. (2010). Low birth weight, preschool education, and school remediation. *Education & Urban Society, 42*(6), 705–729.

U.S. Census Bureau. (2012). Current population survey: Annual social and economic supplements. Washington, DC: Author.

Walker, G. P., Mitchell, G., Fairburn, J., & Smith, G. (2005). Industrial pollution and social deprivation: Evidence and complexity in evaluating and responding to environmental inequality. *Local Environment, 10*(4), 361–377.

Wang, W., & Parker, K. (2011). *Women see value and benefits of college; men lag on both fronts.* Washington, DC: Pew Social and Demographic Trends.

Whiteside-Mansell, L., Johnson, D., Aitken, M., Bokony, P., Conners-Burrow, N., and McKelvey, L. (2010). Head Start and unintended injury: The use of the family map interview to document risk. *Early Childhood Education Journal, 38*(1), 33–41.

11

SEEING STUDENTS AS HUMANS, NOT PRODUCTS

Why Public Schools Should Not Be Run Like Private Businesses

Wayne Au

One of the centerpieces of corporate, neoliberal education reform in the United States is the idea that public schools should be viewed and run like private businesses, operating within the competition of the capitalist "free" market. We see this most clearly within the structures of current education reform policies being implemented in across the United States. Whether it is the idea of schools competing against one another such that those with low test scores close and new ones open, the promotion of entrepreneurial management organizations opening "innovative" charter schools, or teachers competing through merit pay structures that reward or penalize individuals for student test scores, the business-like logic of free-market competition abounds in current education policy. Consistent with neoliberalism, this model advances the removal of any perceived obstacles to competition (e.g., state regulation and unions) in favor of allowing the market to determine success or failure (Apple, 2006). The problem is that at every point, the neoliberal logic of running schools as if they were businesses is a lie.

History of the Lie

The idea that public schools in the United States should be viewed, organized, and run like private businesses has a history as old as public education itself. The turn of the twentieth century in the United States was a pinnacle of industrial capitalism for the country and saw a rise of factory production on a mass scale. This was the time of the establishment of public education in the United States, as well. In essence, mass schooling came about at the same time as mass factory production, and in this context schools were envisioned as factory production lines (Au, 2009). As Stanford University professor Ellwood Cubberly (1916) put it,

> Our schools are, in a sense, factories in which the raw products (children) are to be shaped and fashioned into products to meet the various demands of life. The specifications for manufacturing come from the demands of twentieth-century civilization, and it is the business of school to build its pupils according to specifications laid down.
>
> (p. 338)

In this vision, students are to be shaped into finished products, teachers are the workers who employ the most efficient methods to get students to meet the pre-determined standards and objectives, administrators are the managers who determine and dictate to teachers the most efficient methods in the production process, and the school is the factory assembly line where this process takes place. We see this now in the general structures of our high schools, where students accumulate credits by moving from class to class at timed intervals (periods), while a different teacher adds something at each stop. The students are considered "finished" when they've passed inspection at the end and receive their diplomas, an inspection that increasingly is based on a high-stakes standardized test score (Au, 2009).

This turn-of-the-twentieth-century model of education-as-production provides some foundational logics for viewing education as a business:

1. Students are viewed as products.
2. Schools are the businesses that make products (students).
3. Teachers are the workers who, through their labor (teaching), "build" products (students) by imparting knowledge.
4. Administrators are the managers who facilitate, oversee, and ensure the functioning of the process.
5. In addition to credits or grades, high-stakes standardized tests are used for inspection of the products (students), the workers (teachers), the management (administrators), and the business (the schools).

The Lie Now

The United States economy does not have the same focus on industrial capitalism that it once had, particularly with the steady evolution toward production that is reliant on global connections (Greider, 1997). This evolution has paralleled a shift in ideology toward "neoliberalism," where the emphasis is increasingly on deregulating the economy, shrinking state and national governments, and "freeing" markets from policies and structures seen as obstacles to competition (Apple, 2006). In education, this shift has meant the ubiquity of high-stakes testing as the sole metric for judging productivity in the educational "marketplace," where tests are used to determine all aspects of student, teacher, administrator, and school performance within the context of competition among educational providers (Au, 2009). By extension, such test-based productivity and competition has also become the basis for charter school advocacy and for challenging the protections provided by teachers' unions (Fabricant & Fine, 2012). As such, the neoliberal model for education reform has included the principles already mentioned for viewing education as a business and added a few more layers:

6. Businesses (schools) operate in direct competition with one another, and the best businesses (schools) are identified by having a higher rate of products (students) pass inspection (high-stakes testing) than do competing bad businesses.
7. Presumably the quality of product (student test scores) is a result of the business (school) being run by the best managers (administrators) with the best labor (teaching) provided by the best workers (teachers).
8. The contribution of each individual worker (teacher) to each individual product (student) can be isolated and measured in order to judge individual worker (teacher) effectiveness through the statistical analysis of the inspection results (high-stakes test scores). This is called Value-Added Measurement.
9. Bad businesses (schools) will go out of business (be closed) because their products (students) do not pass inspection (high-stakes testing) at a greater rate.
10. To replace bad businesses (closed schools), entrepreneurs (charter management organizations) will be encouraged to open new businesses (charter schools) free of most regulation and public oversight.
11. Parents are the consumers who choose which businesses (schools) will produce the best products (students with the highest test scores). If consumers (parents) don't like how a business (school) is building its products (teaching their students), then they can choose to invest their money (state education funding) in another business (school) to build their product (teach their student).
12. As an extension of these propositions, the use of private industry is always preferable to that of public services due to increased "choice" and the efficiency supposedly generated through market choice.

The problem, of course, is that this entire chain of logic is a lie. The foundation of the lie is in the view of students-as-products, and layers of the lie then pile up and amplify throughout the chain.

Exposing the Lie

Fundamentally, the view of students-as-products is incorrect. Students are human beings, not "things" to be produced or products to be made. Instead, what we know from research in human development is that humans are in a state of perpetual growth, movement, and transformation—a constantly unfolding interplay between their own biological development and their relationships with the physical and social worlds around them (Siegel, 2012; Vygotsky, 1978). Similarly, learning doesn't happen in a simply additive manner. Instead of proceeding along an even and straight line of progress, learning often happens in fits and starts, going through times of chaos and order and following a path that is more U-shaped than straight (Calucci & Case, 2013). Viewing students as "things," as part of a process of production, simply cuts against what we know about learning and human development.

Understanding human development and learning also challenges how teachers and teaching are viewed within the neoliberal lie of running public education like private business. As discussed earlier, in the neoliberal model, students-as-products move from teacher to teacher, and educational value is simply added to the products along the way. Once we recognize that learning and human development do not operate this in this simplistic manner, then we have to further recognize the reality that teaching is not simply a technical operation of putting the next piece of information into students' brains. Rather, teaching is in fact a profession that requires expertise, the ability to handle complex tasks, and high levels of cognitive processing (Darling-Hammond, 2005). Similarly, the act of teaching is as dynamic and fluid as human development itself and thus requires pedagogy that promotes interaction and engagement of students (Shor & Freire, 1987).

Additionally, once we recognize that students are not products being constructed in the assembly line of education and that teaching is more than a simple act of adding the next part to that product, the use of high-stakes standardized tests to measure learning, teaching, and school performance is indefensible (Au, 2009). High-stakes standardized testing essentially reduces students, learning, and teaching to a single number (test score) in order to make competitive comparisons between individuals. Doing so requires that we ignore all of the subjective conditions associated with students' lives, their cultures, classroom resources, and teachers (Lipman, 2004)—for if we acknowledged all of that subjectivity, then we would have to further acknowledge that a test score represents only a very small sliver of teaching and learning and would therefore have no grounds to make any high-stakes decisions purely on the basis of a score. Evidence of subjectivity in test scores abounds. For instance, Kane and Staiger (2002) found that one-time, randomly occurring factors (e.g., whether or not a child ate breakfast on test day, whether a window was open and a distracting dog was barking outside during the test, variations among teachers who happened to be administering the test) account for 50–80 percent of any gains or losses on a given student's standardized test score (see also Au, 2010–11).

Historically, we also know that high-stakes standardized tests descend directly from the racist, classist, and sexist eugenics movement in the United States (a movement that believed that human characteristics such as intelligence and morality were based upon genetics) and that standardized tests from more than 100 years ago essentially produced the same kinds of test-score achievement gaps that we see today: low-income students, students of color, and/or immigrants don't perform as well as affluent, white, U.S.-born students on standardized tests (Au, 2009). This history should raise serious questions about what it exactly is that standardized tests measure, and it jibes with what we know from research: scores on high-stakes standardized tests correlate more strongly with out-of-school factors than anything else (Berliner, 2009).

Under neoliberalism, the lie that public schools should be treated like private businesses is extended beyond the education-as-production metaphor into the idea that public education, like the capitalist marketplace, needs to be deregulated—that is, obstacles to competition, such as state regulations and protections provided by unions, need to be removed in order to let failure and success happen more freely (Apple, 2006). Indeed, neoliberal deregulation is at the heart of the arguments for charter schools in the United States, where charter school advocates regularly cite the need to be free from the rules and regulations imposed by districts, states, and unions in order to develop more flexible or "innovative" schools (Fabricant & Fine, 2012). Charter schools, however, also illustrate the problems with the neoliberal deregulation of public education. For instance, without state rules regarding free and open enrollment to hold them accountable and despite their claims to serve all children, charter schools have been found to consistently exclude English-language learners and students who need special education services from their schools through selective enrollment practices (Frankenberg, Siegel-Hawley, & Wang, 2011; Simon, 2013). Additionally, some charter school operators around the country have taken advantage of the lack of regulation and oversight, which has led to numerous scandals involving embezzlement, cheating, and other illegal practices (Higgins, 2013).

From the foundational misconception of students-as-products, to the inaccuracy and subjectivity of high-stakes standardized tests, to the issues raised by the use of private companies for test scoring, to the deregulation of charter schools, the neoliberal idea that public schools are best run like private businesses, competing in the capitalist free market, is a lie.

Humanizing Public Education

The current crop of education reformers in the United States regularly assert that their neoliberal business model of student production, deregulation, and market competition will be the cure for educational inequality, despite the lack of a solid research base to support their claims (Fabricant & Fine, 2012; National Research Council, 2011). What the leaders of today's education reform movement ignore is that there are several examples of ways to structure public education that do promote educational equality, and these have nothing to do with the logics of the neoliberal, business model of education reform.

Public Schools in Finland

Finland is often cited by education reformers as an example of a country that turned itself around in terms of educational achievement, advancing from being a poorly performing country to a very high-performing country in a very short amount of time (according to typical measures). The irony is that Finland's educational restructuring is almost the exact opposite of what we have in the United States. Early grades focus on creative play. Teachers must have master's degrees, are paid well, and are unionized, and the profession is highly respected. Principals are mainly responsible for teacher evaluation. There are no high-stakes standardized tests—just a single test given toward the end of their equiva-lent to high school. Students are assessed and graded individually by teachers. Public schools and social services are very well funded, and there are no private schools. There are no lists comparing schools and teachers, and the driving rela-tionship between educators is cooperation, not competition. Further still, the Finnish education system doesn't bother engaging with private-sector businesses at all (Darling-Hammond, 2010; Partanen, 2011). At the root of the Finnish model for education reform is this: "Since the 1980s, the main driver of Finnish education policy has been the idea that every child should have exactly the same opportunity to learn, regardless of family background, income, or geographic location" (Partanen, 2011, n.p.). Contrary to U.S. education policy, Finnish pol-icy actually tries to make sure that issues like poverty and health care are taken care of as part of equalizing student opportunity to learn. Educational needs are seen as human needs.

The Ethnic/Mexican American Studies Program, Tucson, Arizona

Another example of a successful program that promotes educational equality and that has little to do with treating public education like a private business can be found in the Mexican American Studies (MAS) program in the Tucson Unified School District, Arizona. Instructors in this program developed a curriculum and pedagogy to support the identities and cultures of Mexican American students, one that made use of indigenous concepts to help students understand how their lives and communities have been impacted by forces of racism and colonization. As a team of researchers and MAS teachers explain:

> Through *Tezcatlipoca,* a Chicano Indigenous epistemology/concept/principle that speaks to a critical reflection of self, family, and community that calls for the liberation of the mind and spirit, we help our students create their counter-stories. These counter-stories help us understand that the experi-ences of . . . our students are a reality.
>
> (Romero, Arce, & Cammarota, 2009)

In addressing the reality of their students' experiences through a Mexican American lens, teachers in the MAS program are effectively taking up what

Ladson-Billings (1995) calls "culturally relevant pedagogy." Indeed, such a culturally relevant approach challenges the view of students-as-products that underpins the lie of treating schools as businesses and pushes back against the idea of standardization in how we teach children from different communities by fundamentally suggesting that students are cultural beings, not "things." And this approach has worked. Two different studies have found that the MAS program in Tucson has increased graduation rates as well as raised achievement by other typical measures such as test scores (Cabrera, Milem, & Marx, 2012; Cappellucci et al., 2011). Sadly, despite the empirical evidence, conservative politicians in Arizona have been working steadily to either shut the program down or gut it of its sharpest, culturally relevant curriculum (Rethinking Schools, 2012; Sleeter, 2012).

Democratic Schools

There are, of course, other examples of schools and programs that challenge the lie that schools should be run along the lines of private business, many of which are included in the collection *Democratic Schools* (Apple & Beane, 2007). One such historic example was found at Central Park East High School in New York City. Central Park East was notable for its humanistic approach to working with young people, and, instead of a high-stakes standardized graduation exam, its exit assessment consisted of a substantial portfolio in each of five major subject areas that students were required to defend orally to a committee consisting of teachers, community members, and their peers (Meier & Schwarz, 2007). Another such example is La Escuela Fratney, located in Milwaukee, Wisconsin. This elementary school was created through community activism; it not only was founded with principles of social justice and collaboration at its core but also was developed as a two-way bilingual Spanish/English school, in part to meet the needs of Milwaukee's Spanish-speaking student population (Peterson, 2007).

Union City Schools, New Jersey

As a final example, the public schools in Union City, New Jersey, have also seen a dramatic turnaround in student performance. As a part of this turnaround, schools there explicitly focused on the link between students' emotional and intellectual needs and are making use of an influx of state resources for education (Kirp, 2013). Further, as Kirp (2013) explains, in Union City:

> The district's best educators were asked to design a curriculum based on evidence, not hunch. Learning by doing replaced learning by rote. Kids who came to school speaking only Spanish became truly bilingual, taught how to read and write in their native tongue before tackling English. . . . Teachers were urged to work together, the superstars mentoring the stragglers

and coaches recruited to add expertise. Principals were expected to become educational leaders, not just disciplinarians and paper-shufflers.

(n.p.)

What is notable is that, in making this transformation, Union City schools have eschewed the neoliberal, business-like logic driving education reform in the United States today. There has been no union busting, no reliance on charter schools, and no mass of school closures. Cooperation, not competition, is paramount to success, as is the idea that students' needs as learners are critical.

The one big idea that connects these effective examples that counter the big lie that schools should be run like private businesses is that they understand that students and teachers are humans. Instead of seeing students as products (or as things to be produced), learning/teaching as simply adding the next piece to the product, and teachers as assembly-line workers performing easy, mechanical tasks, these models, whether through bilingual education, culturally relevant pedagogy, or increased resources, recognize that the entirety of students' lives and backgrounds cannot and should not be separated from student learning. Further, these models generally place a high value on cooperation and collaboration, not competition, and they tend to value assessments that are closely grounded in the classroom practices of teachers and closely tied to students' experiences in those classrooms and that measure students more holistically than a high-stakes standardized test. Sadly, some of these examples (i.e., Central Park East) no longer exist, and others (i.e., La Escuela Fratney) are struggling to hold onto their principles in the face of increased high-stakes standardized testing and budget cuts. And all exist as anomalies within the context neoliberal, corporate models of education reform.

References

Apple, M. W. (2006). *Educating the "right" way: Markets, standards, god, and inequality.* Second ed. New York: Routledge.

Apple, M. W., & Beane, J. A. (Eds.). (2007). *Democratic schools.* Second ed. Portsmouth, NH: Heinemann.

Au, W. (2009). *Unequal by design: High-stakes testing and the standardization of inequality.* New York: Routledge.

Au, W. (2010–11). Neither fair nor accurate: Research-based reasons why high-stakes tests should not be used to evaluate teachers. *Rethinking Schools, 25*(2), 34–38.

Berliner, D. C. (2009). Poverty and potential: Out-of-school factors and school success. Education and the Public Interest Center & Educational Policy Research Unit, Boulder, CO, & Tempe, AZ. Retrieved from http://epicpolicy.org/publication/poverty-and-potential

Cabrera, N. L., Milem, J. F., & Marx, R. W. (2012). An empirical analysis of the effects of Mexican American Studies participation on student achievement within Tucson Unified School District. Report to Special Master Dr. Willis D. Hawley on the Tucson Unified School District Desegregation Case., Tucson, AZ. Retrieved from http://works.bepress. com/nolan_l_cabrera/17/

Calucci, L., & Case, J. (2013). On the necessity of u-shaped learning. *Topics in cognitive science, 5*(1), 56–88. doi: 10.1111/tops.12002

Cappellucci, D. F., Williams, C., Hernandez, J. J., Nelson, L. P., Casteel, T., Gilzean, G., & Faulkner, G. (2011). Curriculum audit of the Mexican American studies department Tucson Unified School District Tucson, Arizona. Cambium Learning, Inc.; National Academic Educational Partners, Miami Lakes, FL. Retrieved from www.tucsonweekly.com/images/blogimages/2011/06/16/1308282079-az_masd_audit_final_1_.pdf

Cubberley, E. P. (1916). *Public school administration.* Boston: Houghton Mifflin.

Darling-Hammond, L. (2005). Teaching as a profession: Lessons in teacher preparation and professional development. *Phi Delta Kappan, 87*(3), 237–240.

Darling-Hammond, L. (2010). Steady work: Finland builds a strong teaching and learning system. *Rethinking Schools, 24*(4). Retrieved from www.rethinkingschools.org/archive/24_04/24_04_finland.shtml

Fabricant, M., & Fine, M. (2012). *Charter schools and the corporate makeover of public education.* New York: Teachers College Press.

Frankenberg, E., Siegel-Hawley, G., & Wang, J. (2011). Choice without equity: Charter school segregation. *Educational Policy Analysis Archives, 19*(1). Retrieved from http://epaa.asu.edu/ojs/article/view/779

Greider, W. (1997). *One world, ready or not: The manic logic of global capitalism.* New York: Simon & Schuster.

Higgins, S. (2013). Charter school scandals. Retrieved from http://charterschoolscandals.blogspot.com/

Kane, T. J., & Staiger, D. O. (2002). Volatility in school test scores: Implications for test-based accountability systems. In D. Ravitch (Ed.), *Brookings papers on education policy 2002* (pp. 235–284). Washington, DC: The Brookings Institution.

Kirp, D. J. (2013). The secret to fixing bad schools. *New York Times.* Retrieved from www.nytimes.com/2013/02/10/opinion/sunday/the-secret-to-fixing-bad-schools.html?pagewanted=all

Ladson-Billings, G. (1995). Toward a theory of culturally relevant pedagogy. *American Educational Research Journal, 32*(3), 465–491.

Lipman, P. (2004). *High stakes education: Inequality, globalization, and urban school reform.* New York: RoutledgeFalmer.

Meier, D., & Schwarz, P. (2007). Central Park East secondary school: The hard part is making it happen. In M. W. Apple & J. A. Beane (Eds.), *Democratic schools* (pp. 130–149). Portsmouth, NH: Heinemann.

National Research Council. (2011). *Incentives and test-based accountability in education.* Washington, DC: The National Academies Press.

Partanen, A. (2011). What Americans keep ignoring about Finland's school success. *The Atlantic.* Retrieved from www.theatlantic.com/national/archive/2011/12/what-americans-keep-ignoring-about-finlands-school-success/250564/

Peterson, B. (2007). La Escuela Fratney: A journey towards democracy. In M. W. Apple & J. A. Beane (Eds.), *Democratic schools: Lessons in powerful education* (pp. 30–61). Portsmouth, NH: Heinemann.

Rethinking Schools. (2012). Outlawing solidarity in Tucson. Retrieved from http://rethinkingschoolsblog.wordpress.com/2012/02/23/outlawing-solidarity-in-tucson/

Romero, A., Arce, S., & Cammarota, J. (2009). A barrio pedagogy: Identity, intellectualism, activism, and academic achievement through the evolution of critically compassionate intellectualism. *Race, Ethnicity and Education, 12*(2), 217–233.

Shor, I., & Freire, P. (1987). *A pedagogy for liberation: Dialogues on transforming education*. South Hadley, MA: Bergin & Garvey.

Siegel, D. J. (2012). *The developing mind: How relationships and the brain interact to shape who we are.* New York: Guilford.

Simon, S. (2013). Special report: Class struggle—how charter schools get the students they want. *Reuters.* Retrieved from www.reuters.com/article/2013/02/15/us-usa-charters-admissions-idUSBRE91E0HF20130215

Sleeter, C. (2012). Ethnic studies and the struggle in Tucson. *Education Week, 31*(21). Retrieved from www.edweek.org/ew/articles/2012/02/15/21sleeter.h31.html?tkn= VRMFRGuUcYPvsaR7iQ0tSO0BuBkBdu8hRyIN&cmp=clp-edweek

Vygotsky, L. S. (1978). Internalization of higher psychological functions. In M. Cole, V. John-Steiner, S. Scribner, & E. Souberman (Eds.), *Mind in society: The development of higher psychological processes* (pp. 52–57). Cambridge, MA: Harvard University Press.

12

THE TROUBLE WITH FEDERAL TURNAROUND POLICIES AND THEIR IMPACT ON LOW-SCORING SCHOOLS

Michelle Renée and Tina Trujillo

The federal School Improvement Grant (SIG) program aims to increase educational equity and improve the economy by transforming the nation's lowest performing schools into high-performing learning environments. Early press releases and speeches from President Obama and Education Secretary Duncan about the SIG program reinforced the oft-heard notion that a subset of the public school system is failing to adequately educate children, thereby squelching America's economic hopes (U.S. DOE, 2013). In his 2010 State of the Union address, President Obama nested the SIG policy in his overall economic recovery plan:

> Instead of funding the status quo, we [will] only invest in reform—reform that raises student achievement . . . and turns around failing schools that steal the future of too many young Americans. . . . In the 21st century, one of the best anti-poverty programs is a world-class education.
>
> (Obama, 2011)

His message was unambiguous: strengthening the economy requires the federal government to fix the schools at the bottom of the system. The policy itself has honorable aims, but it will likely never reach them because it is based on erroneous assumptions about what is needed to drastically improve persistent low school performance. Specifically, the federal SIG program is based on the faulty, contradictory notion that federal turnaround policies, which bank largely on mass layoffs and financial incentives, are the best way to improve low-scoring schools. This is a big lie. It assumes that schools can and should behave the same way as private corporations and that turning around a persistently low-performing school simply requires personnel restructuring and a short-term infusion of funding, overseen by a rigid accountability system. From this perspective, market-based principles

of competition, performance measurement, monitoring, and high-stakes accountability for results are assumed to produce more effective and efficient schools.

The SIG program is not the first government initiative to be based on flawed
market-based logic; the No Child Left Behind Act's sanctions for low-test scores,
state and mayoral takeovers, and outsourcing schools to external educational management organizations are all rooted in the same falsehood (Mintrop & Trujillo,
2005; Shipps, 2006; Trujillo, 2012). As we will show, many of the emerging reports
on the implementation of the SIG program echo findings that are already well
documented in the research on school improvement. At the same time, this small
but rapidly growing literature looks a lot like the school and district effectiveness
research from the 1970s, '80s, and '90s (Trujillo, 2013). It suffers from several of
the methodological errors of the earlier studies, and it continues to rely narrowly
on standardized test scores as the primary measure of success.

The SIG program and its early research focus almost exclusively on within-
school factors that shape student outcomes; it is virtually silent on the pervasive effects of contextual factors, such as poverty, racism, and systemic funding
disparities—factors that research has repeatedly proved to have enormous effects
on student achievement (Ladson–Billings, 2006; Oakes et al., 2012; Rothstein, 2004).
The guiding assumption in the earlier effectiveness research and now the new
turnaround literature is that schools, given the right mix of talented personnel and
short-term increases in funding, can overcome the structural, systemic constraints
that led to their situations in the first place. Thus, punitive sanctions are justified.
Yet the research evidence on such managerial quick fixes suggests that the current
federal SIG program is destined to fail unless the policies' details are aligned with
more equitable, democratic goals for public schools.

Background: The Federal School Improvement Grant Program

The SIG program works like this: each state engages in its own process (following loosely defined federal guidelines) of identifying the bottom 5 percent
of its schools. Identified schools can then apply for a competitive federal grant
of up to $2 million per year for three years.[1] For impoverished schools already
struggling to meet students' needs amid local and state fiscal crises, the amount
of money is significant. However, SIG-funded schools revert to their original
funding levels after the three-year federal commitment expires. Along with the
money comes a heavy mandate: adopt one of four prescribed interventions (each
derived from private-sector practices): turnaround, transformation, restart, or closure (U.S. Congress, 2010). Each of these models requires massive administrative
and teacher replacement. As of March 2011, states had granted 820 schools federal SIG funding. Transformation is the most common model, accounting for
74 percent of SIG schools. Turnarounds account for another 20 percent (Hurlburt
et al., 2011).

Deconstructing the Lie

In the public debate about the SIG program, reforms like these have been described as new and innovative. In reality, the nation has significant experience with these models, particularly over the past 40 years. Generations of research show that SIG reforms are based on faulty, unwarranted claims (Trujillo, 2012). In our review of the emergent literature on turnarounds (Trujillo & Renée, 2012), we identified three books on schools or districts with "turned around" student performance scores (Duke, 2008; Pappano, 2010; Zavadsky, 2012), ten journal articles on turnaround policies and their effectiveness (Berkeley, 2012; Duke, 2012; Hansen, 2012; Herman, 2012; Hochbein, 2012; McGuinn, 2012; Meyers et al., 2012; Shaffer et al., 2012; Stuit, 2012; Stuit & Stringfield, 2012), and twenty-seven non-peer-reviewed reports from think tanks, research centers, or advocacy organizations on the subject of school turnaround.[2] The bulk of the sources speculate about the characteristics and behaviors of schools or districts that may lead to an effective turnaround.

On the basis of our analysis of current and historical research, we believe that the most prominent error in these analyses is the claim that these corporate-based models yield transformative results. The second most prominent error is the assumption that the drastic reconstitution of school staff will prove beneficial. Neither claim is supported by research. Third, fairly identifying schools "in need of turnaround" and schools that have successfully turned around poses significant challenges. Finally, SIG policies focus schools' sights almost exclusively on the results of invalid standardized tests as measures of performance, rather than on tools for strengthening teaching and learning. In the following section we examine each of these errors.

The Lie, Part 1: Corporate-Based Models Can Yield Transformative Results

The majority of the literature on school turnarounds urges schools and districts to pattern their efforts after corporate management and turnaround strategies (Stewart, 2009).[3] It encourages schools to avail themselves of the lessons gleaned in the corporate sector on the basis of an assumption that businesses have experienced success with these types of interventions (Murphy & Meyers, 2007; Rhim et al., 2007). However, researchers learned long ago that corporate turnarounds and related management strategies rarely yield the positive results that reformers expect (Altman, 1968; Nystrom & Starbuck, 1984). One analysis linked only a quarter of business turnaround efforts with certain improvements (David, 2010). Other analyses of popular turnaround-style management found that such efforts are linked with greater outsider appeal and perceptions of innovation but not with improved company performance over either short- or long-term periods (Staw & Epstein, 2000).

Scholars of critical policy studies call attention to the broader political economy within which corporate school turnaround efforts take place. They point to the school improvement industry (Rowan, 2002), also referred to as the education management industry (Gunter, 1997), which is flourishing as a result of such federal education policies. The SIG program and other high-stakes accountability policies either mandate that schools contract with external organizations as a condition of their funding or create situations in which schools must search for outside help to meet the policies' demands around testing, data management, and training (Burch, 2009; Trujillo, in press, a; in press, b). For outside consultants, school reform agencies, for-profit companies, postsecondary institutions, and other self-styled "turnaround specialists," the SIG program has been a windfall (Klein, 2012b). Yet the effectiveness of these private providers of technical assistance is not tracked, and accountability for their results is not written into the policies (Klein, 2012b).

In Colorado, for example, these private providers received 35 percent of the state's SIG money—$9.4 million—over two years (Klein, 2012a). The dollars paid for data analysts, principal and teacher coaches, and professional development, but the effectiveness of these analysts has been called into question. One of the more expensive contractors, Global Partnership Schools, received $7.4 million to support five SIG-funded schools in Pueblo whose performance declined during their partnership. Some scholars caution that relying on these untested agencies risks narrowing the types of teaching and learning that are promoted in SIG schools to only standardized test-based content and activities (Burch, 2009; Trujillo, in press, a). They tend to promote reforms centered on simple measurable outcomes, standardized processes, and observable indicators of test-based effectiveness, rather than broader, democratic aims around social justice (Trujillo, in press, b). These theorists also interrogate the ways in which such policy arrangements can thwart more democratic schooling, particularly for schools in racially and socioeconomically isolated neighborhoods (Lipman, 2011; Saltman, 2007). They articulate a neoliberal policy framework that frames education as a private good over which private contractors can compete, rather than a public good that contributes to the broader society.

The Lie, Part 2: The Drastic Reconstitution of School Staff Can Prove Beneficial

In the educational literature, a sizable body of rigorous, systematic research on early reconstitution reforms shows that firing and replacing school staff nearly always fails to achieve the intended effects. One meta-analysis revealed that reconstituted schools in San Francisco continued to appear on lists of low-performing schools (Mintrop & Trujillo, 2005). In Chicago, longitudinal research on reconstitution showed that staff replacements were no higher in quality than their predecessors and that teacher morale deteriorated under these reforms (Hess, 2003). And a comprehensive, long-term study in Maryland demonstrated that reconstitution inadvertently reduced the social stability and climate of schools and was never associated with organizational improvements or heightened student performance (Malen et al., 2002).

Also implicit in this notion about the efficacy of reconstitution is the assumption that the benefits accrued from replacing the bulk of a school's staff outweigh the unintended consequences. Yet, retrospective analyses of such dramatic interventions conclude that the resulting logistical challenges, political fallout, and loss of organizational culture make such interventions ill advised (Dowdall, 2011; Mathis, 2009). Finding enough qualified personnel to fill newly vacant slots in reconstituted or turnaround schools has proved difficult. In some cities, for example, districts found themselves swapping principals from one SIG-funded school to another. In other places, more than 40 percent of the teachers hired to work in turnaround schools were completely new to teaching (Klein, 2012a). Another study showed how hiring difficulties forced many reconstituted schools to begin the school year with high numbers of substitutes (Center on Education Policy, 2008).

The Lie, Part 3: Schools in Need of Turnaround and Successful Turnaround Cases Can Be Simply and Accurately Identified

In addition to the lessons found in the previous research, the emerging research on recent school and district turnarounds offers other important takeaways for policymakers and practitioners. Another of the key findings from our review is that there are significant challenges in identifying schools in need of turnaround and in identifying successful turnarounds. As mentioned earlier, the federal guidelines to states for identifying the bottom 5 percent of schools are purposefully vague. States are instructed to identify the consistently lowest-achieving Title 1 schools on the basis of the schools' absolute performance on state language arts and math assessments and their lack of test-score growth over a period of time. High schools with low graduation rates are also eligible (U.S. Congress, 2010; U.S. DOE, 2012). This means that only two to three data sources are used to define SIG eligibility: the presence of poverty, low-test scores, and/or low graduation rates. Yet huge variation and other problems exist within this limited list of criteria. States select which assessments they use, determine how much weight one factor receives over another (absolute test scores or lack of test-score progress over time), and decide how to prioritize schools. Such loosely defined criteria yield lists of schools that can vary widely on the basis of which measures states use, how those measures are calculated, and how accurate the data are in the first place.

Another problem is that the federal guidelines use Title 1 eligibility to identify schools with high concentrations of poverty. However, Title 1 eligibility tends to be underreported. In addition, the federal guidelines do not account for schools serving high concentrations of English learners or students with special needs. The result is a federal program that is based on inconsistent definitions of successful turnarounds, that relies on faulty, test-based measures of effectiveness, and that continues to subject schools to high-stakes decisions based on these invalid measures.

Although researchers have begun to put forward various proposals for systematically identifying successful turnarounds (Hansen, 2012; Hansen and Choi, 2011; Huberman et al., 2011; Meyers et al., 2012), no single agreed-upon definition exists for the amount of growth that is required, the length of time in which this growth should occur, or the requisite sustainability of the results. Techniques for tracking growth in single cohorts of students, rather than comparing different groups of students, have not been devised. As a result, many of the initial studies of successful turnaround cases resemble the earlier studies of effective schools and districts—they are selected on the basis of anecdotal evidence or reputation, and they ignore counterexamples in which turnaround efforts are associated with decreased test scores. Furthermore, given that a turnaround is, by definition, a case of swift, dramatic gains in test performance, identifying effective turnaround schools requires researchers to rely on single- or two-year fluctuations in test scores—patterns that tend not to hold up from one year to the next (Bowers, 2010).

Unlike measuring the absolute number of widgets produced in a factory, measuring the number of students who are successfully educated by a school or the overall quality of teaching and learning in a school is no simple task. The challenge is a fundamental one. How we measure success depends on what we believe the ultimate purposes of schooling to be. Whether policymakers judge the purposes of schooling to be economic in nature—preparation for a competitive, differentiated labor force—or more democratic—development of skills and attitudes for civic engagement and social or political awareness—leads to the use of quite different measures of success. Even if broad agreement about these purposes of education existed, developing valid, reliable metrics of success would still pose considerable measurement obstacles. By reducing our gauge of a good school to the number of students who pass a standardized test, juxtaposed with inaccurate measures of poverty and high school graduation rates, the SIG program not only perpetuates schools' reliance on invalid measures of a reform's effects but also relies on narrowly economic goals for schooling to the detriment of broader, democratic aims that many practitioners and policymakers see as the ultimate purpose behind school improvement efforts.

The Lie, Part 4: Focusing on Testing (Rather Than Teaching and Learning) Is the Most Effective Way to Turn Around a Persistently Low-Performing School

Given that the criteria for defining SIG eligibility and measuring success are based largely on test scores, it is not surprising that the prescribed SIG reforms center so heavily on techniques for rapidly boosting test scores as their primary strategy. This test-based focus is already being documented both in the early investigations of SIG implementation efforts and in SIG schools themselves. In this way, the school turnaround literature extends the earlier school and district effectiveness studies' emphasis on test-based notions of success (Trujillo, 2013). In fact, all but one of the analyses that we reviewed measured school effects in terms of student scores on a standardized assessment. The exception was a case study of one school in which the author found that non-test-based indicators of quality, such as classroom learning climate, the level of intellectually challenging academic work, and family and community involvement, did not correlate with the schools' test scores from year to year (Berkeley, 2012). Only a handful of analyses also considered graduation or attendance rates (Luppescu et al., 2011). This pattern shows that a narrow focus on standardized test scores still predominates in this field. It also shows how rarely studies consider multiple forms of effectiveness to either triangulate findings or explore potential areas of contradictions between test performance and other indicators of quality.

Summarizing Our Critique

Lessons derived from the empirical research on educational effectiveness and high-stakes accountability suggest that the current SIG policies will require different foci, guidelines, and measures of success if they are to promote more equitable, democratic turnarounds. Indeed, SIG policies' overwhelming reliance on market-based strategies to improve the nation's persistently low-scoring schools shows how the administration is erroneously banking on tools like competition, standardization, and test-based accountability to improve performance, despite what research tells us about their consistent lack of success in both the business and the education sectors.

Moreover, because the early literature on turnarounds repeats many of the methodological and conceptual errors that characterized previous "effectiveness" studies, its recommendations end up perpetuating the very inequalities in conditions and resources that turnaround proponents claim they want to interrupt. These policies also mistakenly rely on limited, often flawed test-based indicators of success. Thus, turnarounds carry on a long policy tradition that promotes narrowly economic purposes of schooling. In so doing, the policies edge out schools' attention to other important academic, social, and political purposes that are not easily measured by standardized tests.

In addition to the critiques outlined earlier, there are a host of other manifestations of the "market lie" in the federal SIG program. Public education's current fiscal crisis pressures the nation's most impoverished, least resourced schools to opt into the SIG program in order to offset deficits in their basic operating funds. While the program provides temporary financial resources for those schools that are willing—or forced—to participate in turnaround-style reform, it does little to alter the long-term financial and social constraints within which these schools must try to function. The result of these financial pressures is another round of federal policies that continue to reproduce the same inequitable distribution of resources, conditions, and reforms that disadvantage those schools in greatest need of fundamental change. The market-based character of turnaround policies diverts public attention from fundamental questions about adequate, equitable funding and the insidious effects of racially and socioeconomically segregated schools. In doing so, SIG policies and the literature promoting them misrepresent how powerfully students' opportunities to learn are shaped by structural conditions related to poverty, race, and government spending.

Finally, the absence of community voices in the SIG policy and its literature speaks volumes about the lack of democratic input into both the development of these policies and their implementation. While individual cases of community engagement in turnarounds are emerging, researchers and policymakers have been largely silent about this democratic deficit. The result is a policy that is driven almost solely by elites and which excludes the crucial perspectives of those most impacted by the policies—families and educators in turnaround-targeted schools.

Democratic School Turnarounds: Centering More Meaningful Purposes of Education

The federal SIG policy is at odds with a democratic approach to public education, one that frames schooling as a public good, rather than a private commodity. Such purposes of schooling are far broader than profit-based, market-driven ones. The democratic approach creates opportunities for local communities to publicly deliberate and self-govern (Trujillo, 2013). For example, a growing body of rigorous research points to the ways in which community organizations have become engaged in analogous, yet more successful reforms in low-income communities and communities of color (Mediratta et al., 2009; Oakes & Rogers, 2006; Orr & Rogers, 2011; Warren & Mapp, 2011)—the populations that are most likely to be targeted for turnaround.

Researchers have documented how community organizations develop meaningful roles for community members in school decision making, increase social capital within underresourced communities, and help shift understandings about the structural causes of educational inequity in high-poverty communities of color (Delgado-Gaitan, 2001; Renée & McAlister, 2010; Shirley, 1997; Shirley, 2002; Warren, 2001). A national cross-case analysis of more than 140 community organizations identified the specific ways in which such organizations effectively foster cross-community alliances, develop democratic leadership, and improve civic participation (Gold et al., 2004). In-depth case studies have revealed the organizations' impacts on policy and resource-allocation decisions, school-level improvements, and student performance (Mediratta et al., 2009; Renee, 2006; Warren, 2001). More recent research has begun to link community organizing with more equitable school-funding arrangements, effective teacher recruitment and retention, and increased access to rigorous curricula (Renée & McAlister, 2010). Together, these studies suggest a wide range of possible roles for communities in promoting more democratic school turnarounds. Yet, the federal government failed to engage those most affected by turnaround reforms—educators and families in the most racially and socioeconomically segregated communities—in developing and carrying out the SIG program.

Emerging Examples of Democratic Engagement in School Turnaround

The goal of a democratic approach to school turnarounds is providing all students with equitable opportunities to learn, participate in society, and further social change. While there are examples of communities successfully engaging in the turnaround of individual schools (AISR, 2012; Mediratta et al., 2009), more relevant to this chapter are examples of democratic efforts to shape the current turnaround policy. Around the country, organized groups of parents, students, and teachers are pushing for an alternative to this reform.

Over the past several years, community organizers from across the nation have been trying to ensure that the thinking of students attending low-performing schools and their families informs federal, state, and local policies and decisions. First coming together in 2010 as the Communities for Excellent Public Schools (CEPS, 2010), thirty-four grassroots community organizations joined together to influence both the reauthorization of the Elementary and Secondary Education Act and the revision of the SIG program (CEPS, 2012). The coalition proposed three revisions to the federal SIG policy: replace the four mandated turnaround "options" with research-proven strategies to improve teaching and learning; require turnaround schools to provide wrap-around social supports; and engage communities, parents, students, and educators in developing school-assessment processes and improvement plans. As the reauthorization of ESEA stalled, the organizers rechanneled their efforts into a national campaign against school closings and turnarounds, known as the Journey for Justice.

In June 2012, community organizers from the Journey for Justice convened in Chicago and announced their intention to file Title VI complaints with the Department of Education's Office of Civil Rights. The complaints charge that the federal policy is leading to local school closings and layoffs that disproportionally impact students of color and students with disabilities. Building on this action, the Journey for Justice issued a set of demands during a Washington, DC, march in September 2012: a moratorium on school closings, a sustainable transformation model, an investigation of all Title VI complaints, a series of visits by Department of Education staff to impacted cities, and a meeting with President Obama. In response, Department staff agreed to the visits and a meeting in Washington, DC. While the Journey for Justice is very much a campaign in progress, it provides proof that the communities impacted by low-performing schools have a strong desire and clear ideas about how to create successful schools for their children.

At the same time that organized parents and students have been engaging with federal SIG policy, both national teachers unions are also pushing for a more democratic turnaround process. For example, the National Education Association recently launched the Priority Schools Campaign, a collaborative partnership among community members, parents, teachers, and administrators intended to leverage local resources and expertise to cultivate meaningful, sustainable turnarounds in SIG schools serving large numbers of English learners, students of color, and low-income children (Cody, 2012). The partnership aims to learn from community members' wisdom and experience in order to design turnaround efforts that emphasize social justice, teacher professionalism, and reforms that are unique to each community's specific conditions.

In response to market-based policies like the SIG program and parent trigger laws, the American Federation of Teachers is working with grassroots community leaders from across the nation to draft a resolution supporting a "Community Action Schools Program." The resolution calls for a new policy that allows parents, students, community members, teachers, and other school staff at a low-performing school to vote to become a Community Action School. Under this policy, a group of stakeholders would work collaboratively to identify their school's needs and develop and implement a plan for improvement. Importantly, the program requires that "[i]nterventions must be research-based, and focus on instruction, supports for quality teaching, and wrap-around supports for students" (AFT, 2013). This proposal stands in stark contrast to the current top-down SIG policies that focus on laying off school leaders and teachers and leave open many of the details about how to engage the school in improving teaching and learning. Though these community and teacher initiatives are relatively new, they are examples of the ways in which communities can play leading roles in designing, planning, and implementing more equitable, democratic turnarounds.

Recommendations

If we are to truly create a democratic school turnaround policy and, ultimately, democratic schools, the principles outlined in this chapter must be actualized in every step of the process—from defining the problem of low-performing schools, through policy development, to implementation. On the basis of our review of earlier effectiveness studies, high-stakes accountability research, and current school turnaround literature, we outline six connected guidelines for federal, state, and local policymakers to use in developing more equitable and democratic turnaround policies (Trujillo & Renée, 2012). We believe that a democratic approach to education reform requires that policies work toward equity from a systemic perspective rather than rely on the piecemeal approach that dominates the policy process. In the pragmatism of policymaking, compromises are inevitable, but research teaches us that, more often than not, what is compromised first are the parts of a proposal that advance equity (Trujillo, 2013). Advancing these six recommendations as a whole can foster policies that are equitable, democratic, and systemic in their orientation.

First, increase current federal and state spending for public education, particularly as it is allocated for turnaround-style reforms. The schools that qualify for federal SIG grants by definition have low test scores and low graduation rates and serve high numbers of low-income students. Research shows that these are the same schools that also have the fewest resources, such as funding, experienced teachers, and safe and clean facilities, and are located in the nation's most under-resourced cities and towns. As such, the first priority of any equitable education policy must be to increase the amount of federal and state education funding and to ensure that it is equitably distributed. This funding must be at a high enough level to meet educational goals, be targeted to communities and schools with the highest need, and be stable over time.

Second, focus school turnaround policies on improving the quality of teaching and learning rather than on technical-structural changes. Creating policies that treat schools like corporations and students like widgets is not only empirically flawed but also unethical and counter to the democratic purposes of public education. Instead, school turnaround policies should begin by implementing well-documented solutions to improving the quality of teaching and learning in schools: recruiting and retaining qualified teachers, providing cumulative professional development that deepens teachers' knowledge of pedagogy and the communities they teach in, creating local ownership among school and staff and educators and leaders, and granting schools and districts greater autonomy to determine the details of each school's turnaround plans.

Third, engage a broad cross section of schools' communities—teachers, students, parents, and community organizations—in planning and implementing turnaround strategies that are tailored to each school and district context. Logically, any policy aiming to improve schools also must aim to make that improvement sustainable over time. However, sustainability is not automatic and is often a significant part of the failure of education reform (Coburn, 2003). Critical to SIG sustainability is ensuring that school and district leaders incorporate ideas and feedback from teachers, parents, students, and community leaders throughout the development and implementation of the school reform. SIG policy should require that each SIG school create a cross-sector representative oversight body to develop the reform and hold school and district leaders accountable for success. Doing this adequately requires both financial and nonfinancial resources. Soliciting input in multiple formats such as parent, student, and teacher surveys and accessible meetings (varied time and locations; live translation; free child care) is also critical. Creating learning communities among SIG school sites and successful schools in the district could also increase the capacity of schools and districts to sustain reforms at SIG schools.

Fourth, surround persistently low-scoring schools with comprehensive, wraparound supports that stabilize schools and communities. From Community Schools to Promise Neighborhoods, there are many reform models around the nation that document the value of coordinating a web of health, nutrition, and other social service resources to surround schools in high-need communities. SIG policies should encourage these efforts by providing SIG schools with resources to identify and integrate existing community resources into the improvement process.

Fifth, incorporate multiple indicators of effectiveness—apart from test scores—that reflect the multiple purposes of schools. SIG policies should encourage the development and use of better and more methods for assessing schools' progress and working toward academic, social, and democratic goals for their students. This includes measures of schools' development of students' social skills and awareness by assessing students' work in group-based learning tasks, problem-based projects, and curricula that relate directly to students' communities. Measures should be longitudinal and disaggregated by race, family income, and language status as well as by students' access to learning resources. This means that SIG policies should require tracking indicators of education opportunities, including access to highly credentialed teachers and college preparatory and/or advanced courses. SIG policies should also encourage schools to track changes in other measures, such as the reclassification of English learners, suspension and expulsion rates, and the level of democratic participation in the SIG reform. Incorporating these other conceptualizations of effectiveness is another means by which the federal policy can promote more democratic norms and processes in turnaround schools, in place of narrowly market-oriented ones.

Finally, support ongoing, systematic research, evaluation, and dissemination examining all aspects of turnaround processes in schools and districts. As we discussed throughout this chapter, current research on SIG schools is limited. Future funded research should incorporate multiple points of view—including those of teachers, students, and parents— and multiple data points like those described in our fifth recommendation to better understand what schools gained and where they experienced challenges when attempting to turn themselves around. SIG schools would also benefit from research that illuminates the evolution of school and district turnarounds, including the rich historical and social legacies that aid successful turnarounds or thwart them, and that considers how such patterns unfold at the state, district, school, and community levels. Finally, policy should require that research findings be accessible and disseminated to the leaders, teachers, parents, students, and community members engaged in turnaround efforts.

Notes

1. The federal SIG budget was $3.5 billion for the 2010–2011 school year. After this one-time ARRA infusion of funding, the SIG program was funded at $546 million for the 2011–2012 school year and $535 million for the 2012–2013 school year (U.S. Department of Education, 2011).

2. We cite the various reports as relevant throughout the following section.
3. These studies of business turnarounds, which are often reported in case-study formats for business schools, are methodologically lax and prone to exaggerated narratives.

References

Altman, E. (1968). Financial ratios, discriminant analysis and the prediction of corporate bankruptcy. *Journal of Finance, 23*(4), 589–609.

American Federation of Teachers (AFT) (2013). An act to create the community action schools program. American Federation of Teachers Resolution, AFT Executive Council.

Annenberg Institute for School Reform (2012). Profiles in school transformation. Retrieved March 28, 2013, from http://annenberginstitute.org/publication/profiles-school-transformation

Berkeley, M. (2012). A practitioner's view on the policy of turning schools around. *Journal of Education for Students Placed at Risk (JESPAR), 17*(1–2), 34–39.

Bowers, A. (2010). Toward addressing the issues of site selection in district effectiveness research: A two-level hierarchical linear growth model. *Educational Administration Quarterly, 46*(3), 395–425.

Burch, P. (2009). *Hidden markets: The new education privatization.* New York: Routledge.

Center on Education Policy (2008). A call to restructure restructuring: Lessons from the No Child Left Behind Act in five states. Washington, DC: Author.

Coburn, C. E. (2003). Rethinking scale: Moving beyond numbers to deep and lasting change. *Educational Researcher, 326,* 3–12.

Cody, A. (2012). Ellen Holmes: NEA's priority schools focus on teacher expertise, parent, and community involvement. *Education Week Teacher Blogs.* Retrieved May 5, 2012, from http://blogs.edweek.org/teachers/living-in-dialogue/2012/03/teachers_get_a_very_mixed.html

Communities for Excellent Public Schools (CEPS) (2010). *Our communities left behind: An analysis of the administration's school turnaround policies.* Washington, DC: Author.

Communities for Excellent Public Schools (CEPS) (2012). CEPS—About Us. Retrieved May 5, 2012, from www.ed.gov/news/press-releases/obama-administration-announces-historic-opportunity-turn-around-nations-lowestac

David, J. (2010). Drastic school turnaround strategies are risky. *Educational Leadership, 68,* 78–81.

Delgado-Gaitan, C. (2001). *The power of community: Mobilizing for family and schooling.* Lanham, MD: Rowman & Littlefield.

Dowdall, E. (2011). *Closing public schools in Philadelphia: Lessons from six urban districts.* Washington, DC: The Pew Charitable Trust.

Duke, D. (2008). *The little school system that could: Transforming a city school district.* Albany: State University of New York Press.

Duke, D. (2012). Tinkering and turnarounds: Understanding the contemporary campaign to improve low-performing schools. *Journal of Education for Students Placed at Risk, 17*(1–2), 9–24.

Gold, E., Simon, E., Mundell, L., & Brown, C. (2004). Bringing community organizing into the school reform picture. *Nonprofit and Voluntary Sector Quarterly, 33*(3), 54S–76S.

Gunter, H. (1997). *Rethinking education: The consequences of Jurassic management.* London: Cassell.

Hansen, M. (2012). Key issues in empirically identifying chronically low-performing and turnaround schools. *Journal of Education for Students Placed at Risk, 17*(1–2), 55–69.

Hansen, M., & Choi, K. (2011). Chronically low-performing schools and turnaround: Evidence from three states (CALDER Working Paper #60). Washington, DC: Center for the Analysis of Longitudinal Data in Education Research.

Herman, R. (2012). Scaling school turnaround. *Journal of Education for Students Placed at Risk, 17*(1–2), 25–33.

Hess, G. A. (2003). Reconstitution—three years later: Monitoring the effect of sanctions on Chicago high schools. *Education and Urban Society, 35*(3), 300–327.

Hochbein, C. (2012). Relegation and reversion: Longitudinal analysis of school turnaround and decline. *Journal of Education for Students Placed at Risk, 17*(1–2), 92–107.

Huberman, M., Parrish, T., Hannan, S., Arellanes, M., & Shambaugh, L. (2011). *Turnaround schools in California: Who are they and what strategies do they use?* Sacramento: California Comprehensive Center at WestEd, American Institutes for Research, and School Services of California.

Hurlburt, S., Le Flock, K., Therriault, S., & Cole, S. (2011). *Baseline analyses of SIG applications and SIG-eligible and SIG-Awarded schools, NCEE 2011–4019.* Washington, DC: National Center for Education Evaluation and Regional Assistance, Institute of Education Sciences, U.S. Department of Education.

Klein, A. (2012a). *In expensive school turnaround project, questions about effectiveness.* Fort Lauderdale, FL: Florida Center for Investigative Reporting.

Klein, A. (2012b). What's the payoff for $4.6 billion in School Improvement Grants? *The Hechinger Report.* Retrieved October 14, 2012, from http://hechingerreport.org/content/whats-the-payoff-for-3-billion-in-school-improvement-grants_8371/

Ladson-Billings, G. (2006). From the achievement gap to the education debt: Understanding achievement in U.S. schools. *Educational Researcher, 35*(7), 3–12.

Lipman, P. (2011). *The new political economy of urban education: Neoliberalism, race and the right to the city.* New York: Routledge.

Luppescu, S., Allensworth, E., Moore, P., de la Torre, M., & Murphy, J. (2011). *Trends in Chicago's schools across three eras of reform.* Chicago: Consortium on Chicago School Research.

Malen, B., R., Croninger, et al. (2002). Reconstituting schools: 'Testing' the 'theory of action.' *Educational Evaluation and Policy Analysis, 24*(2), 113–132.

Mathis, W. (2009). *NCLB's ultimate restructuring alternatives: Do they improve the quality of education?* Boulder, CO, and Tempe, AZ: Education and the Public Interest Center & Education Policy Research Unit.

McGuinn, P. (2012). Stimulating reform: Race to the Top, competitive grants and the Obama education agenda. *Educational Policy, 26*(1), 136–159.

Mediratta, K., Shah, S., & McAllister, S. (2009). *Community Organizing for Stronger Schools: Strategies and Successes.* Cambridge, MA: Harvard Education Press.

Meyers, C., Lindsay, J., Condon, C., & Wan, Y. (2012). A statistical approach to identifying schools demonstrating substantial improvement in student learning. *Journal of Education for Students Placed at Risk, 17*(1–2), 70–91.

Mintrop, H., and Trujillo, T. (2005). Corrective action in low performing schools: Lessons for NCLB implementation from first-generation accountability systems. *Education Policy Analysis Archives, 13*(48), 1–30.

Murphy, J., and Meyers, C. (2007). *Turning around failing schools: Leadership lessons from the organizational sciences.* Thousand Oaks, CA: Corwin Press.

Nystrom, P., and Starbuck, W. (1984). To avoid organizational crises, unlearn. *Organizational Dynamics, 12*(4), 53–65.

Oakes, J., Lipton, M., Anderson, L., & Stillman, J. (2012). *Teaching to change the world.* Fourth ed. Boulder, CO: Paradigm.

Oakes, J., & Rogers, J. (2006). *Learning power: Organizing for education and justice.* New York: Teachers College Press.

Obama, B. (2011). Remarks by the President at Miami Central High School in Miami, Florida. Retrieved October 23, 2013, from www.whitehouse.gov/the-press-office/2011/03/04/remarks-president-miami-central-high-school-miami-florida

Orr, M., & Rogers, J. (2011). *Public engagement for public education: Joining forces to revitalize democracy and equalize schools.* Stanford, CA: Stanford University Press.

Pappano, L. (2010). *Inside school turnarounds: Urgent hopes, unfolding stories.* Cambridge, MA: Harvard Education Press.

Renée, M. (2006). Knowledge, power and education justice: How social movement organizations use research to influence education policy. Ph.D. dissertation, University of California at Los Angeles.

Renée, M., & McAlister, S. (2010). *The strengths and challenges of community organizing as an education reform strategy: What the research says.* Quincy, MA: Annenberg Institute for School Reform, Brown University.

Rhim, L., Kowal, J., Hassel, B., & Hassel, E. (2007). *School turnarounds: A review of the cross-sector evidence on dramatic organizational improvement.* Lincoln, IL: Public Impact and Center on Innovation & Improvement.

Rothstein, R. (2004). A wider lens on the black-white achievement gap. *Phi Delta Kappan, 86*(2), 104–110.

Rowan, B. (2002). The ecology of school improvement: Notes on the school improvement industry in the United States. *Journal of Educational Change, 3,* 283–314.

Saltman, K. (2007). *Capitalizing on disaster: Taking and breaking public schools.* Boulder, CO: Paradigm.

Shaffer, E., Reynolds, D., & Stringfield, S. (2012). Sustaining turnaround at the school and district levels: The high reliability schools project at Sandfields Secondary School. *Journal of Education for Students Placed at Risk, 17*(1–2), 108–127.

Shipps, D. (2006). *School reform, corporate style: Chicago, 1880–2000.* Lawrence: University Press of Kansas.

Shirley, D. (1997). *Community organizing for urban school reform.* Austin: University of Texas Press.

Shirley, D. (2002). *Valley Interfaith and school reform: Organizing for power in South Texas.* Austin: University of Texas Press.

Staw, B., & Epstein, L. (2000). What bandwagons bring: Effects of popular management techniques on corporate performance, reputation, and CEO pay. *Administrative Science Quarterly, 45*(3), 523–556.

Stewart, M. (2009). *The management myth: Why the experts keep getting it wrong.* New York: W. W. Norton.

Stuit, D. (2012). Turnaround and closure rates in the charter and district sectors. *Journal of Education for Students Placed at Risk, 17*(1–2), 40–54.

Stuit, D., & Stringfield, S. (2012). Responding to the chronic crisis in education: The evolution of the school turnaround mandate. *Journal of Education for Students Placed at Risk, 17*(1–2), 1–8.

Trujillo, T. (2012). The paradoxical logic of school turnarounds: A catch-22. *Teachers College Record Online.* Retrieved October 23, 2013, from www.tcrecord.org/Content.asp?ContentID=16797\

Trujillo, T. (2013). The disproportionate erosion of local control: Urban school boards, high-stakes accountability, and democracy. *Educational Policy, 27*(2), 334–359.

Trujillo, T. (2013). The reincarnation of the effective schools research: Rethinking the literature on district effectiveness. *Journal of Educational Administration, 51*(4), 426–452.

Trujillo, T. (in press, a). The modern cult of efficiency: Intermediary organizations and the new scientific management. *Educational Policy.*

Trujillo, T. (in press, b). Equity-oriented reform amid standards-based accountability: A qualitative comparative analysis of an intermediary's instructional practices. *American Educational Research Journal.*

Trujillo, T., & Renée, M. (2012). *Democratic school turnarounds: Pursuing equity and learning from evidence.* Boulder, CO: National Education Policy Center. Retrieved October 23, 2013, from http://nepc.colorado.edu/publication/democratic-school-turnarounds

U.S. Congress (2010). School Improvement Grants; American Recovery and Reinvestment Act of 2009 (ARRA); Title I of the Elementary and Secondary Education Act of 1965, as Amended (ESEA). U.S. Department of Education. Federal Register 75:28: 66363–66371.

United States Department of Education, (2011, May 1). *An overview of school turnaround.* Retrieved from www2.ed.gov/programs/sif/sigoverviewppt.pdf

U.S. Department of Education, (2012). Guidance on fiscal year 2010 school improvement grants under section 1003(g) of the Elementary and Secondary Education Act of 1965. U.S. Department of Education, Washington, DC.

U.S. Department of Education, (2013). ED.gov school improvement grants press releases. Retrieved September 1, 2013 from www.ed.gov/category/program/school-improvement-grants

Warren, M. R. (2001). *Dry bones rattling: Community building to revitalize American democracy.* Princeton, NJ: Princeton University Press.

Warren, M., & Mapp, K. (2011). *A match on dry grass: Community organizing as a catalyst for school reform.* Oxford: Oxford University Press.

Zavadsky, H. (2012). *School turnarounds: The essential role of districts.* Cambridge, MA: Harvard Education Press.

CONTRIBUTORS

Lauren Anderson is an assistant professor of education at Connecticut College, where she teaches foundations and literacy courses. Her research explores the preparation and practice of equity-minded educators.

Wayne Au is an associate professor at the University of Washington, Bothell, and an editor for the social justice teaching magazine *Rethinking Schools*.

Anthony Cody taught science in a high-poverty school in Oakland, California, for 18 years and served as a coach for another six years. He authors the widely read Living in Dialogue blog at *Education Week*.

Jim Cummins is a professor at the Ontario Institute for Studies in Education at the University of Toronto. His research focuses on the educational achievement of linguistically diverse students.

Curt Dudley-Marling is a professor at the Lynch School of Education at Boston College. His scholarly interests focus on struggling readers and writers and on Disability Studies.

Paul C. Gorski is an associate professor of Integrative Studies at George Mason University's New Century College. He is the founder of EdChange and author of *Reaching and Teaching Students in Poverty*.

Rochelle Gutiérrez researches the roles of mathematics in relation to power, identity, the body, and authority in society; pre-service teachers' knowledge and disposition to teach powerful mathematics to marginalized students; and teachers using "creative insubordination" in their everyday work.

Kevin Kumashiro is dean of the School of Education at the University of San Francisco and president of the National Association for Multicultural Education.

Gloria Ladson-Billings, who holds the Kellner Family Chair in Urban Education at the University of Wisconsin–Madison, focuses on culturally relevant pedagogy and successful educational strategies for African American students and Critical Race Theory applications to education. She is author of *The Dreamkeepers* and *Crossing Over to Canaan*.

Deborah Meier is a senior scholar at NYU's Steinhardt School and a Board member of the Coalition of Essential Schools and FairTest. She spent 45 years working in public schools in New York City and Boston, including highly successful and democratically run public urban schools.

Jeannie Oakes directs the Ford Foundation's work in education. She belongs to the National Academy of Education and is a Fellow of the American Education Research Association, which gave her its 2013 Social Justice in Education Research Award.

Michelle Renée is an assistant clinical professor in the Urban Education Policy Reform program and a principal associate of the Annenberg Institute for School Reform at Brown University.

Katy Swalwell is an assistant professor in the department of Teaching and Learning, Policy and Leadership at the University of Maryland, College Park.

Tina Trujillo is an assistant professor at UC Berkeley. She uses tools from political science and critical policy studies to investigate the politics of urban district reform and policies' instructional and democratic consequences for students of color and English learners.

Kristien Zenkov is an associate professor of education at George Mason University and the author or editor of more than 100 articles, chapters, and books on teacher education and literacy.

INDEX

here's for you," she said, and dragged Guy inside.

Sofia said she needed a cigarette, so she, Mary, the baby and Pinky found an exit door that led to an airless concrete stairwell. Sofia smoked two cigarettes in a row and talked about stuff they could get for Angelyne, strollers and high chairs and teddy bears and juice boxes. Mary felt so miserably tired all she could think of was going back to the loft, though the idea of getting on the bus was making her start to shake. She told Sofia she didn't want anything.

"Party pooper," Sofia said, saying they could go back to the loft in fifteen minutes.

Mary sat on a bench beneath a potted palm in the center of the concourse. Everything in the mall appeared over-saturated, the colors too bright, the music too electric, the shoppers' voices like sudden slashes. Mary felt as though she were being randomly stabbed when she saw Dean walking toward her, wearing a Hawaiian shirt. He was doing a little hula that made Mary wheeze out a laugh, which triggered a sharp pain in her stomach.

"Take her," she choked out, as she doubled over the baby, and Dean tried but couldn't get a grip. The baby started to scream.

"I can't," he said, just as Mary's cramp subsided.

"Shh, shh," she said to the baby.

"Shit." Dean was looking past Mary, who wiped her eyes and saw MeeMee and Guy running for the escalator, and some lady in white lace-up boots that clicked on the marble floor running after them. Dean was already walking in the other direction when Sofia came up behind Mary and pulled her toward the elevator, leaving Pinky standing under the potted palm.

Sofia put three pieces of gum in her mouth as they rode the bus back to Hollywood. When they got near the loft Mary reached for the cord to ding the exit-bell, but Sofia said no; they should stay on until they got to Thrifty's; she could get some stuff for the baby.

"I can't," Mary said, and sucked air to keep her knees from buckling as she got off the bus.

She stood in front of the loft as the bus pulled away. George was across the street in front of the Falafel King, waving her over.

The air in the restaurant was hot and greasy, and made Mary feel as though she were wearing too much clothing. She hoisted the baby higher on her shoulder, trying to find a position on the stool that didn't put pressure on her stitches. As she watched George carve slices of lamb from the spit, a little stream of anesthesia-flavored saliva shot from beneath her tongue.

When George said, "Let me see the little angel," Mary felt her face brighten, and told George that was her name, Angelyne.

"Ah," he said but didn't seem to get it as he

assembled a combination plate and set it on the counter before Mary. The thickness of the aroma made her eyelids droop. George patted his hands together and held them toward the baby; Mary handed her to him. She picked up her fork as George cradled Angelyne and began to sing softly in Greek.

Mary felt a loosening, as if somewhere above her shoulders a spigot of warm water had been turned on: she slumped partway over her plate and ate; the meat tasted elemental, of metal and salt. She could eat this and nothing else forever.

"You going to be able to take care this baby?"

Mary focused on George, then the moving cars on the boulevard behind him. She nodded as she lifted another piece of meat to her mouth.

"Yes? How?"

Mary shrugged; she didn't want to hear this; it was ruining the meat.

"I tell you, you need be clean take care of baby." George was stroking the baby's cheek; Mary saw the heavy hair between each of his knuckles. "I see you kids all day, and I know you here all night half the nights. You can't do that no more."

As grateful as Mary was to be eating, she wanted to throw George's food at his face. She took a last bite that now didn't taste like anything and lay down her fork. She got off the stool and held out her hands for the baby.

"Wait," George said, and with one hand wrapped a double piece of baklava in foil. When Mary took it, he held her wrist.

"You can't take care of this baby, you tell me. We find good home, okay?"

Why was he saying this to her? Was he planning it? The late afternoon sun coming through the window put him in shadow. She couldn't read George's face, she couldn't tell, and then someone in the restaurant was shrieking.

"Stop, stop," he said, pushing the baby at Mary. "You can't do..."

Mary gripped Angelyne to her chest and stepped onto the boulevard, into the street, crossing, her vision tunneling, the tunnel walls throbbing in time with her heart.

Mary stood in the doorway of the loft. MeeMee and Guy were on the floor sharing a forty-ouncer, Guy wearing a sea foam green dress that already had a hole at the hem. Mary watched them drink the beer and thought she needed to give Angelyne a bath; her skin was sticky and she smelled like raisins.

Mary was making suds in the sink when MeeMee's beer breath hit her ear.

"Guy just took it off the mannequin, and this Australian lady who works there is like, 'No worries,' wanting to give him what he wants, thinking this shows how open she is and shit."

Guy stood behind Mary's shoulder, cooing to Angelyne, who arched her back and let out cries that made Mary flinch.

"So he puts on the dress over his clothes, which I think was a bad idea, because now this lady starts to get uppity, and all of a sudden he just blazes out of there." MeeMee smacked at Guy. "Shit, I didn't even know he had a plan."

"Just lucky you fast," he said, then swooped in and kissed Angelyne, which Mary wasn't so keen on, not with the beer and whatever else Guy was doing. She unsnapped the baby's tiny hospital undershirt, feeling the deep softness of her skin.

"Wow," she said, touching the baby's stomach, her arms, dipping her finger into the tiny palm, scarlet and wrinkly. MeeMee grabbed Guy's shoulder when she saw the cockroach-size scab from what was left of the baby's cord, and Guy said how his sister had saved the umbilical off her baby and ground it up and put it in a leather pouch she wore around her neck.

"Is that like Santeria?" asked MeeMee, still staring at Angelyne's scab.

"Why you always saying shit like that?" asked Guy, shaking off MeeMee. "Like, why you think my family would be messing with that devil shit? My sister's Baptist, all right?"

Guy did a duck-and-bob motion with his little head, which, with the dress, Mary thought made him look like a lady in an old-fashioned play.

"What are you getting all bitchy for? You got your period or something?" MeeMee put her arm around Guy. "I'm the one almost got busted, you running like some little girl and not even telling me you gone. That shit's for amateurs. Now come on and let's do you up."

Mary watched MeeMee push Guy toward the bathroom. At 5'10", she was taller than he was, with a great big ass and a huge head. Her hair had suffered a lot. She'd tried to dye it white when Mary did hers, but it didn't take well to the bleach and came out orange. She told everyone she didn't care, but Mary was there when MeeMee shoplifted a bottle of Nice & Easy and tried to get her own color back. Now it was real stiff and stuck out at unnatural angles, because she'd also had it straightened, at some salon near where her mom lived in Inglewood. MeeMee'd go hang with her parents every few weeks, clean up and get clothes. Her dad even gave her a lift to the loft once. He'd come in with a tan windbreaker and a trimmed mustache, like he was bringing his daughter to camp. Sofia was there, saying how the loft was a really good place to be, and how they didn't let guys up, so it was almost like a sorority, and MeeMee's dad kept saying, "Is that right?" and asked if he could take the girls out to lunch. Sofia said thanks, she couldn't, she had to get over to the wax museum, where she had a job restructuring John Wayne's nose, which had melted in the recent heat wave. She used her hands for emphasis, touching MeeMee's dad on the arm when he commiserated about the heat; he was a bus driver so he knew. MeeMee and Mary didn't say anything; they knew Sofia didn't have a job and was on a speed binge and wouldn't have eaten a peanut if you paid her, and anyway, going out with her now probably wasn't a good idea; it was the tail end of the rocket, they didn't know when she'd crash. But Mary was seven months then, and ravenous, and hoped MeeMee's dad would say, "Well, how about you two?" but he didn't. It didn't matter, because when he left he gave MeeMee three twenties, and MeeMee spent it all that night on food and booze, so Mary ate, and the ones like MeeMee who liked their beer and vodka, they drank.

Mary lowered Angelyne into the water. She didn't splash her hands the way Mary pictured she would, but just lay back in the water looking peaceful, and Mary thought, if I do what I'm supposed to do with her, she will be like this every day. Mary cupped her hand and poured water over Angelyne's stomach, and Angelyne opened her mouth and panted, and her fist pounded the water. Mary thought this meant Angelyne liked it, and Mary smiled her first real smile since delivery and poured more water on the savage cord. Angelyne's eyes got very wide, then crinkled up, and she opened her mouth and let out a cry that drilled into Mary so hard she thought she might puke.

"No, no, sssh," she told the baby, but Angelyne kept on until Mary wrapped her in a towel and sat on the bed and pulled out her breast, which had started spurting milk. The baby ate, but fussily, letting the nipple slip from her mouth to cry then rooting around for it again. Mary tried to position herself so that the nipple was facing directly into the baby's mouth, but that made her neck hurt, and she thought about a hot shower and wondered if the water in the bathroom was working. She didn't know she was falling asleep until she heard Guy say from far away, "Girl, the shit's not going to fit over your butt. And why did we just spend all that time doing me up if I wasn't going to wear it?"

Mary's eyes felt full of grit as she focused on Guy. He had on a lot of make-up: rouge, lashes, lavender eye shadow, purple lips. Mary thought, he needs some hair, just as Guy pulled a silky brown wig from his purse and slipped it on his shapely head. It was cut on the bias, falling long on one shoulder and high at nape of the neck. It was an amazing transformation, not so much because of the hair, but because of the delicate way Guy nestled it into place. Everything fit now. With Mary's eyes heavy and the baby's rhythmic sucking, she felt as if she were being pulled into a dream.

"You look beautiful," she said, not knowing she had planned to say it.

Guy looked at her from beneath his lashes, and tucked the hair behind his shell-shaped ear.

"A gift. From a friend," he said, the emphasis on the last word. He was receiving an infusion of hope from the woozy look Mary was giving him; her look said he was the person he imagined himself to be. "Very expensive."

Mary's vision blurred, but she felt she had to tell him, to tell him, "You're lovely." Guy let out a trill and Mary saw his face bloom and soften, and the loft fall away behind him in a cascade of green and silver, the hum of electric music coming from somewhere.

"Mary, we going down by the Clown-Mart. You want to come?"

Mary heard MeeMee's voice like an echo. What? she thought, what is she asking me? The humming sounds got louder, and MeeMee's voice became a puddle, and Mary felt someone lay her head on a soft pillow, a warm blanket drifting on top of her, and she looked up and saw Guy's face floating above her, smiling like a good prince.

CHAPTER NINE

Roach stood in front of the Falafel King cracking sunflower seeds with his teeth and spitting out the shells, one of the tricks he'd learned growing up outside Sacramento, where there were fields of sunflowers, tomatoes, almond and plum trees. His grandpa grew plums for a big prune conglomerate, and Roach ate as many prunes as he ever would before he was seven years old, when he and his mom and his little brother Jamie lived on the farm. His grandpa would take Roach driving through the plum fields, row after row of trees until you could see nothing of the rest of the world. After checking for blight, his grandpa would stop the truck and look serious, turn to Roach, who was called Joseph then, and say, "Are you ready?" Roach would nod seriously, climb onto his grandpa's lap, and hold the steering wheel in his two fists. His grandpa would work the shift, and they'd run the rows, making a loop at each end, until his grandpa said, "Now, that's good driving," as Roach took them all the way back home. Jamie had been extra jealous, but his grandpa said his turn was coming, soon as he turned six. It was their expectation that when they became old enough to work, they would work, like their grandpa, which was especially good because their mom hadn't been too well. She stayed in the house most of the time, and didn't come to meals anymore. A hired woman cooked for him and his brother and grandpa, and she seemed to be spending a lot of time there, which was okay with Roach; she had smooth hands that smelled like talcum powder and would take time on his earaches and show some enthusiasm when he came home with a high mark. His mom couldn't do that anymore, because "she needs rest," his grandpa said.

Right before Jamie turned six, their grandpa had a stroke and was put in a home after it was decided his daughter couldn't take care of him. They stayed at the farm while it was up for sale, but the house had become a dark, rambling place where the boys foraged for themselves and as often as not slept in the barn, saying it was fun, but really it was to get away from their mom, who was so completely silent. When the farm sold, his mom moved them into a city, to a motel court where the only place for him and Jamie to play was the parking lot, and the manager didn't like that, so they stayed inside and watched TV, or went out by the pool, but they weren't allowed to go in without an adult, so they'd lead their mom out there and sit her in a chair and she would stare as they swam. His mom was an amazing starer. There were times when she would stare for days, and no matter what he and his brother did, she'd stare. In the beginning, they'd tickle her feet, or do something bad so she'd notice and scold them, but she'd just say, "Be good, now," and keep staring. She didn't seem to eat and she never cooked, so Roach started getting food from the vending machines, and doing the laundry at the motel machines. He no longer asked his mom for money; he knew where it was, a stack of tens and twenties in the rose silk lining of her suitcase. Roach took the money he needed, and kept the small change for himself and Jamie.

When his mom started sleeping for days, Roach got scared. He didn't want to leave the room, in case something happened. He made Jamie stay with their mom when he went to the closest store, and bought as much food as he could carry. He'd mix packets of oatmeal with tap water and serve it to his brother, and they'd eat oatmeal and watch TV while their mom slept. Roach knew they weren't going to school, but he didn't know how long they'd been there; maybe it was still summer. When the truant officer came knocking, Roach tried to explain his mom was sick, but the lady said she needed to speak with her anyway. His mom looked genuinely bewildered, standing in the motel room door in a white t-shirt and panties, her face mottled and puffy. She looked at Roach and asked, "You haven't been going to school?"

They never did go to school there, because that day their mom packed like a robot, stuffed all their things into the station wagon and drove until nightfall, when she pulled into a field and parked. They sat there in the cold car for a half-hour before Roach asked, "Is this where you want to go, mama?" but she didn't answer. Roach and Jamie got out of the car and explored in a fifty-foot radius, ate a packet of dry cocoa mix, and crawled into the back of the car and went to sleep. In the morning, their mom was still staring out the window, and when Jamie said he was hungry their mom turned her face to them with her mouth tensed and open like a scream she couldn't get out and it scared the hell out of them. Jamie started to cry, and Roach just sat there looking at her, then started asking, just so it wouldn't be so quiet, "Mama, are you okay? Mama..." But filling up the car with sound scared him, and he knew if he kept it up he'd start crying, so he unlatched the back door of the station wagon and stood in a world of birds and bugs humming all around. Then he went around to the front, pushed his mother over on the car seat, and drove the station wagon around the field in a wide circle. It was bumpy, and seemed to jolt his mother enough so that she said, "Stop," and got out of the car and stared at the horizon all day while Roach and Jamie played. Jamie forgot while they climbed trees, but Roach was always watching his mom, not climbing as high as Jamie in case his mom gave some sign of moving, which she didn't, even when the sun began to set, and Roach and Jamie were starving, having gone through a box of saltines and some spray cheese by noon. Roach wanted to go into town, but he couldn't bring himself to say so. He was terrified that if he said something his mom would fall completely over the edge she seemed to be standing on. That Jamie was whining and making a mess of the car didn't matter; Roach knew it wouldn't affect her as much as one peep from him, so he didn't say anything. He got his and Jamie's sleeping bags out of the car and lay them on the ground, then found a blanket and told Jamie to give it to their mom. Jamie considered this a mission, and sneaked up behind her but lost it near the end and started to cry, so that Roach quickly and noiselessly took the blanket and tossed it on his mom's shoes and grabbed Jamie by the arm and got him into the sleeping bag, where the younger boy cried himself to sleep, but Roach stayed up until the moon was high, watching his mom just stand there, trying to stay awake so he could protect her.

He knew he'd failed when he woke to the sound of voices, and there was a cop car with its lights off but the radio on. Roach could hear the low crackle of a female voice on the radio, and there was a cop standing in the dawn talking softly to his mother. She was looking down and not saying anything, and when the cop looked over Roach quickly closed his eyes and realized, in that second, that this was how he failed her, hiding when he should get up and beat up that cop, so he opened his eyes, but the cop was already walking to his car, getting on the radio, and a cyclone started in Roach's chest; he was losing everything as the cop pressed his thumb on the handset and told the woman at the other end that they had a DWF with two minors, and would be bringing them in.

"Oh, and Marge? Call Social Services when they open."

"Copy."

Roach watched as the cop's shiny black shoes made their way to him, saw the scratchy blue fabric round over the knee that squatted in front of him.

"Morning, son." Roach looked at him, not knowing his huge gray eyes were trembling. "My name is Officer Riley. I'm here to take you and your brother into town for some breakfast. Would you like that?"

Roach didn't say anything. He wriggled out of the bag, still wearing his clothes.

"And your brother here. Should I wake him up?"

Officer Riley asked, so that Roach could smell the coffee on his breath and knew the man had already eaten breakfast.

"Jamie. Get up," Roach said, and pulled his sneakers over his dirty socks. Jamie whined until he rolled over and saw the cop, and his eyes got very wide. For the first time, Roach saw how young his brother was, noticed the wet lips and round cheeks and hated him for these, for being so little and helpless when they were in such huge trouble. And, of course, Jamie let Officer Riley help him roll his sleeping bag, but Roach did his alone, and tried to block out everything and concentrate on his mother, who was sitting in the front seat of the station wagon with the blanket on her shoulders and a thermos between her legs. But there was too much other stuff, too much noise to get back to that place where, if he concentrated, he could save her. He was trying to concentrate when Officer Riley patted him on the shoulder.

"Don't worry about the car, son. We'll come for it later," he said, and went and got Roach's mom and led her slowly to the cop car, where Jamie was already, looking at the squawk-box, and Officer Riley made him get in the car and their mom got in, too, with the blanket still on her shoulders, a dark green army blanket that had been an emergency car blanket, in case, his mom had told Roach a long time ago, they ever wanted to stop and have a picnic, or if they had a breakdown. Roach watched the side of his mom's head, her gold-and-brown curls matted, and remembered lying on her bed when they'd first moved to the farm, her letting him and Jamie softly pull on those curls and watch them spring back. This morning, he left his mom with that blanket on her shoulders at the station with some lady, who told Roach they were "gonna take good care of his mama" and, having already failed her, and being tired and sore from trying to lie awake all night, Roach had eaten pancakes with Officer Riley at the Redwood City Diner, though not for one minute did he forget his fatal error.

Roach looked at the sunflower seed husks building up on the sidewalk near the massive thigh of a girl called Maggot. She was pale and fat, her heavy calves laced tightly into stomp boots she'd detailed with crescents of pea-size aluminum studs. She had her hair shaved off at the sides and a stud in her tongue.

Roach looked at Maggot's humped back; she was eating somewhere, that was for sure, though Roach had no idea where; he didn't hang with Maggot much, didn't like her, always sprawled on the sidewalk in front of the Falafel King, too lazy to even stand. He looked across the street and saw MeeMee and the light-skinned queen she hung with coming out of the loft.

"Got any weed?" Maggot asked, not looking up. Roach spat another seed that landed on her shoe.

"Fuck you, man," she said, as Roach crossed the street. He ran low to the ground until he came up right behind MeeMee and throttled her.

"Roach! Don't go sneakin' up like that, now," she said. Roach held up his hands in surrender, and nodded at the queen, who was looking at Roach from beneath these long eyelashes.

"Looking good, Guy," said Roach, making Guy blush beneath his make-up. Guy could see Roach was exactly between being a boy and a man, the hairs on his lip not yet stiff, his chest probably still smooth.

"We going down by the Clown-Mart, Roach," MeeMee said.

The statement made Guy feel as though he'd been covered with a lead sheet. He stole a look at Roach and thought, he'll split now, but Roach kept walking east with them on Hollywood, and because of this, Guy felt their value had tripled.

The Clown-Mart was one of Miralee's new spots, so Roach hung with MeeMee until Guy got in a new Toyota mini-van. It didn't surprise Roach, the people who slowed down and blinked expectant eyes at him and his friends. During the day the kids scattered between La Brea and Gower were extras to give the street the proper cast for the tourists. At night Roach saw the stars creep out, brilliant and hard, the kids who would do anything. Lit by the neon on the marquees, they watched the needs churn down the boulevard and crash onto the sidewalks, spilling cash and collateral for the next day.

"Bet he don't make more than thirty," MeeMee said as she sucked a sunflower seed Roach had given her. "Them Asian guys is cheap."

"Uh huh." Roach was watching Miralee, sitting catty-corner at a bus stop with a limp arm over the back of the baby's stroller.

"Where you going?" MeeMee called, watching Roach dodge the traffic.

Roach stood behind Miralee, noticing how her v-neck gapped out, and that she didn't have on a bra. He reached around and gently patted her shirt to her chest; she didn't react. The baby sat two feet away, chewing on the rim of a soda cup. Her little face was all lit up and filthy, and Roach thought, someone should wash her face. There was a grimy aqua diaper bag hanging from the back of the stroller, but Roach had a feeling he wouldn't find much in there for the baby.

When the bus pulled in, Roach stepped back a few feet and watched. Miralee woke up, blinked her eyes, looked as though she were going to say something, then began to nod again. Some people who got off the bus noticed her. A middle-aged lady shook her head and tucked a dollar in the baby bag. Miralee mumbled, but the bus's leaving killed the sound, its exhaust clouding her and the baby one more time.

Roach stood behind Miralee as she coughed in her sleep, and he put a sheath on the ache he carried for her. Then he took the cup out of the baby's mouth and rooted in the bag and came up with a bottle of juice, which he smelled before giving to her.

Roach didn't see Freddy in the doorway of the SRO hotel across the street, sitting on the hard seat of his stolen black bicycle (which he called The Stallion). Freddy's eyes became slits as he watched Roach re-cross the street to stand with that bitch MeeMee; she had a mouth on her and he would close it if she ever got in his face again, fucking black cunt. And what the fuck was Roach doing touching his old lady? If he found out she was fucking him, he'd gut her like a fish. Don't be messing with Freddy, he said to himself as his bony foot pressed the pedal; he spun the bike across the street, plucked the buck out of the baby bag and took off down Vine.

CHAPTER TEN

Mary opened her eyes. She wasn't covered with a soft blanket, but Guy's army jacket. She tucked the jacket around the baby and waddled to the bathroom. Rinsing her underwear in the sink, she saw in the mirror that the skin around her eyes was puffy, her hair was sticking out in little platinum poofs; she couldn't remember the last time she brushed her teeth. She cupped cold water on her face until her skin felt taut, raked water through her hair, patted it around her neck and ears and dried herself with her shirt. Better. She was also hungry, and as she passed Angelyne wondered if it would be okay to leave her just to go out and find some food.

Mary sat on the window ledge and saw Maggot hanging out, as usual, and Sofia. Sofia had a large Thrifty's bag slung over her shoulder and was giving a cigarette to Henry, an older guy with four dots tattooed on his face like compass points. Henry was always trying to stand near Sofia, who talked to him like she talked to everybody, but Mary kept her distance. The old ones like Henry scared her, with their caked-on dirt and their infirmities and eyes that looked coated in snot. The drinkers didn't scare her as much; they were sloppy and slow, always drunk or hung-over with a black eye or a dislocated shoulder from fighting or falling down. They'd talk at you for hours, if you let them, and they usually smelled really bad, like piss and rotten fruit, but they were okay. Roach had told her, they're only fighting themselves. But Mary wouldn't go near the junkies if she could help it. Sometimes they wanted to hang or party, or said they'd turn Mary on to some quick cash, but she wouldn't do it. They were skinny and mean, and a lot of them were sick. When Mary first came to Hollywood, just seeing them caused what felt like hot jolts of electricity in her legs, which Mary took as a warning to stay away. But Roach explained they weren't as mean or bad off as they looked, it was just their scam, honed and made into a career. For instance, he said, this guy Tommy, he had a real bad limp, like he was missing six inches of one leg. He washed windows in the parking lot of the Mayfair market in the daytime, smoked crack at night, and had been able to live this way for ten years. And

Roach swore the guy's leg was fine, that it was his gig, that bad leg; but the thing was, after all these years, the guy couldn't stop limping.

"How do you know?" Mary asked Roach. It had been a windy day in early spring. She'd only been in town a month, and they were sitting on a bench in Poinsettia Park.

"He told me," Roach said, lighting Mary's cigarette.

Mary took a drag. "Maybe he's lying. Maybe something bad really did happen to his leg and he wants to pretend it didn't."

Roach retracted his head a little to inspect Mary. "How'd you get so cynical so young?"

"What?" Mary laughed, not wanting to admit she didn't know what cynical meant. "Anyway, I'm not so young. I'm thirteen."

Roach squinted and called her a baby and grinned when he said it. She thought he might kiss her then, but he said, "Let's go," and they smoked a joint as they walked away from Hollywood, down Highland, until they were on a street called Olympic that Mary had never seen. She asked Roach if this was where the Olympics had been, but he said he'd only been in Hollywood nine months, so he didn't know, but he didn't think so.

"You been in Hollywood your whole life?" he asked.

Mary shook her head. "A month. Mostly, I was in San Francisco. With my mom." Mary leaned down and picked a dandelion. "She died, though."

Roach let things be quiet for a minute. "That's bad," he said.

"Yeah." She stayed quiet for a minute, too. "Want to know how?"

"If you want to tell me."

Mary stared at the dandelion and pulled out its threads. "She was hit by a car and both legs broke, and then they got infected, because it's really cold in San Francisco and we were outside a lot then, and she couldn't stand the itching, and was ripping off the bandages and stuff." She bent the dandelion's stem and flung it. "Her legs got so swollen the doctors said they'd have to amputate them. But she died before they could do that."

Roach watched Mary wipe the milk-sap on her pants. Her hand was as small as a little girl's; he took hold of it and petted the knuckles. "At least you know she's not going to be in any more pain."

Mary blinked. Roach watched the sun spark off her dark blue cracked crystal eyes. Doll's eyes.

"I guess," she said.

They walked in silence through the residential streets, winding up in front of a duplex with a "For Rent" sign.

"'Upstairs unit'" Roach read. "'Two bedrooms, two baths, big kitchen. Must see.'" He took three big steps up the sloping lawn to the front door.

"Roach, don't," Mary said, as he depressed the thumb lock. The door opened. He smiled at her and mouthed, come on. She looked down the street one way, then scooted through the door behind him.

The small vestibule broke to the right, up a semi-circular stairwell, past a long window that smelled like window cleaner. Roach put his ear to the upstairs door, then knocked softly.

"Roach..." Mary said. She was so nervous it was making her want to pee.

He turned the knob and let them into a living room with shiny wood floors and no furniture.

"Not bad, not bad," Roach said, taking Mary's hand and leading her through the apartment. The kitchen was narrow and dark, and in the refrigerator was a box of cheese crackers, which Roach grabbed and brought into the back bedroom. He and Mary sat on the new gray carpet eating crackers, surveying the space and discussing the best place to put the bed. They smoked another joint and lay down, and Roach propped himself on one elbow and kissed Mary; his hip was halfway on hers and she was extremely excited, more than she'd ever been, and they took off their pants and made love and fell asleep.

Mary woke up first. Even though Roach's weight had cut off circulation to her leg, she didn't move. She wanted to stay as they were, imagining they'd just moved in and all the stuff they would buy to make it nice. When Roach woke up, Mary wanted to suggest they stay the rest of the night, but didn't. They got dressed in the dark and walked back to Hollywood, Mary with her arms crossed over her chest because she was cold. Roach gave her a little kiss when they got back to the boulevard, and took off someplace with Top Jimmy, and Mary didn't kiss anyone else for a month.

Sofia looked up to the loft. From the window, Mary saw her eyes jumping around and wondered where she was in the cycle of speed and recovery. Mary moved her fingers to her mouth, and Sofia nodded. She said something to Henry, handed him the Thrifty's bag, and slipped around the corner by the shoemaker's. Mary watched for two minutes until an LTD slowed and made the turn, and forty minutes later Sofia was walking into the loft with a takeout sack from Rallye's.

"How'd you get all the way down there?" Mary asked, pushing four French fries in her mouth.

"I had the guy stop," said Sofia. "I said my sister just had a baby and I needed to get her some food."

"Must've added to the romance."

"He'd already gotten what he needed." Sofia pulled the tomato off her cheeseburger and popped it in her mouth. "Even paid for the grub."

They were sitting amidst a pile of baby stuff from Thrifty's. There were diapers, hoodie towels, a can that went moo when you turned it over, a tube of ointment.

"Manolo says you put this stuff on the bellybutton, and that will help it heal," Sofia said.

Manolo was the night manager at the Hollywood Thrifty's. He was from Venezuela and made a point of being gentlemanly and attentive to the girls, especially Sofia, who took care of him in the rear of the store, in a dingy room off the men's john with a wall of tiny lockers, one cracked-up Naugahyde chair and a sign that read "Worker's Compensation—Know Your Rights." Manolo and Sofia usually did it standing up, his breath in her ear. If Sofia brought anyone with her, they had to wait outside the store, that was the deal; Manolo said he didn't want kids walking around when there was only one employee on the floor. And Sofia could never show up with a boy; Manolo said it wasn't because he was jealous but because he knew a boy would steal from him.

Manolo knew; he'd seen Sofia steal from him twice. The first time, she'd been wearing a pink top, no bra, and he'd let her get away with a tube of mascara, but the next time, he took her by the arm just before she got to the front door.

"What?" she said, jerking away as he pulled her toward the back of the store. She was taller than he was.

"You be quiet."

"But these are my sunglasses," she said, and realized

the moment she did what an idiot she was, and felt Manolo's grip become less intense, and saw he was trying not to smile.

When they got to the back room, he sat down in the chair and made her stand in front of him. He told her he was going to call the police, but she said, please don't. He asked her if she was sorry, and she looked at her feet and nodded and handed him the glasses. He laid them on his lap, and told her she could have them, if she wanted. She looked up, and saw he was nervous. She got on her knees and lay her hand on the glasses and felt his erection, then began to open his fly but he said no, first pull up your shirt. He stroked himself as he stared at her tits; to him, they were perfect, just-full, with clean-rimmed nipples the color of pomegranates. He grabbed Sofia's hand, and as soon as she touched him, he came. Manolo felt his face get hot, and went quickly into the men's room for some paper towels to wipe himself; he'd made stains on his tan work trousers, and quickly asked God that his wife wouldn't recognize them for what they were, she who always scrubbed every particle of dirt, a laundry fool, he thought, but a good wife. He tucked in his shirt and went out to Sofia, but she and the glasses were gone.

Sofia came back about once a week after that, every time she needed something substantial; she wasn't going to do it just for lip gloss. But she liked being with Manolo; he was quick and gentle, and hearing his accent was like a little vacation. She could tell he was falling for her. One time, he gave her a pendant from the jewelry counter, a gold heart with a tiny amethyst in the center that Sofia hadn't really liked. She'd asked if she could trade it for a carton of cigarettes, but when she saw the hurt in Manolo's eyes, she laughed and said she was kidding, and held up her dark hair so he could clasp it on her, which he did, still pouting but loving the way the hair curled down the nape of her neck, and afterwards they had intercourse for the first time, Manolo panting in Spanish as he came.

Sofia had been eager to go to Thrifty's; she wanted to surprise Mary with bags and bags of baby stuff, but realized when she got there the speed had about worn off. Standing on the corner of Sunset and Gower, with the sun setting and the wind making her sweat freeze to her skin, she looked toward the brightly-lit store and thought she shouldn't go in; she was starting to white-out and her legs were doing the sewing-machine thing. She pressed her diaphragm to the concrete bus bench and leaned over until she caught her breath.

Inside Thrifty's the air was frigid and moving. Sofia's teeth began to chatter, and she realized she had BO and hugged herself to keep her armpits covered. She didn't see Manolo at the registers, so walked straight to the deodorant aisle and was trying to decide which one to use when she heard his voice. He was behind the film counter, counting out change for a lady. Sofia stared at him, thinking, I'll only stay if he sees me in the next minute. She was still looking his way when she reached for a stick deodorant and knocked over the row. Manolo looked up in manager-concern and indicated he'd be with her a minute. She was picking deodorants off the floor when he came up to her and before he could ask, she began telling him she didn't need anything for herself, but for the baby. Manolo nodded seriously, saying he had three kids and if he didn't know what a baby needed, nobody did. Sofia stayed one step behind as he pushed a shopping cart and tossed in diapers and bottles and tubes, and she thought, as he explained about the ointment for the cord and the *coulo*, what a good father he was. She began to cry; she never wanted to leave the Thrifty's; she wanted to be Manolo's wife and have everything she needed. Manolo dropped the diaper rash cream in the cart and asked, "Linda, why do you cry?" and put his hand on Sofia's cheek. "You are hot. You are sick?"

Sofia shook her head; she couldn't tell him the truth, that she hadn't slept in two days, that she was sick, yes, but not with anything he could fix. She let Manolo give her a box of tissues and walked through the aisles behind him until the cart was half-full. She wanted to have sex with him, but he said, "Get these to the baby. They are famously impatient," and let Sofia out the side door into an alley, where she luckily ran into Top Jimmy and this big alcoholic Indian they called Chief, and Sofia traded Jimmy a box of baby wipes for two bumps to get her going again.

CHAPTER ELEVEN

Mary sat on the windowsill, watching Sofia fight herself in her sleep. She was on the mattress by the window, arching her back and frowning and letting out jagged cries before her body would go slack again. Mary was glad she didn't do speed. She looked toward the mattress near the bathroom, to make sure Angelyne was still asleep, then turned back to the action across the street, a dozen homeboys the cops had squatting like hens in front of the electronic store.

Mary knew the boys probably hadn't been breaking in, that it was just some excuse the cops gave so they could harass them. You'd have to be an idiot to rob a store on Hollywood and Wilcox; there were seventy-five cops a day trawling the street, giving the kids a hard time, saying, "Where do you go to school?" and "You think it's funny? We'll see who's laughing when I have my size ten up your ass." All the kids had spent time at the cop shop, Hotel Wilcox, the playpen, but the cops couldn't hold them; they were too young, or the crimes couldn't be proven; how do you prove soliciting if the john's already driven away? The girls didn't think it was a crime, anyway; they figured they were allowed to do what they wanted with their bodies. The cops barely looked at them when they were hungry, but when they made money, here they came, staring at the kids' cheeseburgers like they were evidence.

Mary saw one of the cops kick a homeboy's foot out from under him so that the kid landed on his side all curled up. The cop watched him try to roll upright, then tipped him back over with his nightstick. Mary felt her cheeks flush. She remembered when she made the trip downtown to see Dean after he got arrested for disorderly conduct, which they could legally hold him for since he was eighteen. She'd taken a number and waited on a bench in a big room with a lot of women speaking to each other in Spanish and little kids lying on the floor. The overhead lights were off but it was still hot. When Mary pushed in the center of her tank top to soak up the sweat, the Mexican woman next to her lifted her own meaty arm to reveal the giant wet spot spreading down her dress.

After an hour Mary's number was called. The clerk pushed the paper number onto a spike while looking at Mary, who sensed she was supposed to do something else.

"Who you here to see?" the woman asked, which was when Mary realized she didn't know Dean's last name. The woman leaned back and said something to the worker next to her, who laughed.

"You see that staircase?" the clerk asked. Mary turned to look where the woman was looking, a wide set of marble steps at the far end of the room. "Fill this out and bring it on up there." The clerk passed Mary a blue piece of paper with a lot of questions on it. "You also need to show them ID."

Mary pushed through the revolving door. The sun outside was so strong she had to close her eyes against it. In the center of the courtyard was an iron statue of an eagle holding a paper in its claws, its wingspan shielding people Mary thought might be lawyers because they had on suits. One was a lady tapping the lapel of one of the men she was talking to. Mary bit her nail and thought she might ask the lady about the blue piece of paper; if it was necessary to get Dean out, but the lady and the men were laughing in a way that didn't seem interruptible, and the sun was making Mary light-headed, and she didn't see that the lawyers had walked away until they were almost inside the courthouse. Mary didn't have ID, anyway. She took the bus back to Hollywood and stood behind the shoemaker's with Roach. He said he was sure Dean would be out soon; the jails were too crowded to hold a guy just for making too much noise. Mary was making her hair into a little braid when a cop car stopped in the mouth of the alley and a tall cop with huge shoulders started walking toward her, making Mary feel as though she needed to pee.

"Let's go," he said, and pulled her and Roach by their arms onto the boulevard. The kids in front of the Falafel King moved back a few steps, and the tourists slowed to see what was going on. Mary said, "Why are you doing this?" and the cop looked down at her cut-offs and said, "Vagrancy," then pushed her into the back of the squad car and left the door open, Mary wondering what vagrancy meant and if she'd done it. She had to stay in the car while they kept Roach outside in the sun. She watched the big cop get right in Roach's face and tell him if he were Mary's pimp, he would personally see to it that Roach was charged as an adult.

"You could be eleven for all I care. I can make it stick," the cop said, while his Asian partner stood by the car tapping his nightstick in his palm and staring at the kids in front of the Falafel King. Roach didn't say anything, except that they should let Mary go. The big cop looked at her crotch and said, "Why? You losing money?"

Mary put her head between her legs and screamed,

"Why are you doing this!" which made the Asian cop bang his nightstick on the hood. Mary felt the reverberation run through her body, and as the cop insisted Roach was a disease infecting little girls, she let go of her bladder, not all the way but enough to wet the seat. The cops didn't notice when they pulled her out of the car, but Mary felt bad because they pushed Roach in and seated him right where she'd been. She confessed this to Roach when he got out the next day, but he said he hadn't felt anything, and actually thought it was funny, "definitely a girl's way of getting revenge."

They had sex for the second and last time that afternoon, in the Wilcox Avenue apartment of some woman Roach said he knew.

"She works during the day but said it was cool for us to come up." Mary wondered whom he meant by "us." The place wasn't very nice, one room that smelled like smoke, with a bedspread hanging where the bathroom door should be. Mary sat on the floor by an open black futon. She was nervous and concentrated on picking cigarette butts off the carpet and putting them in an ashtray.

"Don't worry about that," Roach said. He flopped on his stomach on the futon. "Come here."

Mary crawled to Roach, and they began making out, him on top. She felt his hipbones press into her; she wrapped her arms around his neck and they took their time, and it felt good to be warm and alone and wanting to do it, not rushing with Dean in some vestibule, or lying beneath a scratchy bush at Poinsettia Park where you were only ever covered on three sides.

Afterward Roach pulled the comforter over them and Mary lay with her head on his chest. He ran his fingers through her hair, which was still long then, and laughed again about her wetting the seat.

"You're so funny," he said, and they kissed some more, until Roach said he was hungry, so Mary went to the fridge naked and found some cream cheese and crackers, and looked at Roach to see if it was okay. He nodded. She spread cream cheese on the crackers and arranged them on a plate and balanced the plate on her fingers like a waitress.

"I believe that's my order, miss," Roach said, and Mary brought them to him in bed and they watched game shows and cuddled until there was a bang on the door. Roach looked at Mary and put his finger to his lips, until the banging came again, and they heard Dean asking, "You in there, bro?" Roach grabbed his clothes off the floor and so did Mary, and when they were rearranged Roach opened the door, and Dean came in with a twelve-pack and hugged Roach and shouted, "They can't keep a good man down!" There was now a lot of movement in the tiny apartment. Dean was in high spirits, grabbing Mary around the waist and giving her a toothy kiss, which tasted funny after Roach's and the cream cheese, and Mary wondered whether Dean could tell, so made herself busy making more crackers and listened as Dean and Roach retold their run-ins with the law, and Dean pulled off his tank top and peeled back a bandage to show a new jailhouse tattoo on his chest, a scabbed-over patch he said was two hands in prayer.

Mary looked down at the cops still holding the homeboys and shouted, "Why don't you *popos* go back to the station!" Then she ducked.

She was watching a flashlight beam scan the loft's windows when Sofia pushed onto her elbow and tried to focus her one open eye. "What's going on?"

"Sshh." Mary was laughing, pressing her hands to her lips so she wouldn't wake Angelyne, who was already awake, her face turned toward her mother's voice.

CHAPTER TWELVE

MeeMee dropped her big purse by the front door and a can of potato chips rolled out. "I should have popped his ear right through his fucking head," she said, as Mary watched the can roll across the floor. The baby's hands flinched, maybe because MeeMee was yelling and banging while Guy stood completely still, his face bent toward some distant point of air. Mary saw the whites of his eyes were the color of tobacco spit.

"You listening to me? Shee." MeeMee yawned and started pulling at a tuft of her hard hair. "Mary, you got any that cream left?"

Mary didn't know what MeeMee was talking about, but it didn't matter because MeeMee was already crawling onto the mattress with Sofia.

Guy didn't move. Mary could see his lipstick had

become a memory, a faint rosy stain from nose to chin. A long shred of crinoline hung from the hem of his dress.

"Did you have a good night?" she asked.

Guy didn't answer. He pulled off the wig. Mary thought his real hair looked as though it had been sifted with ash, it was so dry, and she felt the opposite, full of liquid. She asked if he'd watch Angelyne while she went to the bathroom.

Guy tried to make the mattress move not at all as he sat down. He watched the baby's fingers twitch in her sleep; she looked so clean. He wanted to lean down and smell her, but thought it might not be right. Not that he was filthy, it had been an easy night; the man had wanted to suck him, that's all. Guy had hiked up the dress and let him, watched the man's sleek black hair swing, listened to the sloshing and congested grunts. Guy told the man when he was about to come, in case the man wanted to move, which he did. He pulled off his mouth at the last second and gave a quavery cry as the semen hit his cheek and forehead. Guy swallowed a "sorry" but the man looked completely calm, head tipped back, lips parted as the come rolled over his brow bone. Then he opened his eyes and backed against the driver's door. Guy looked away. The man pulled a baby wipe from a dispenser and twisted the rearview mirror and cleaned his face. Guy asked if he wanted anything else, and the man put on his glasses and held out two twenties.

"It's better if I let you out here," he said, with no trace of an Asian accent, and Guy opened the door of the mini-van and stood in the alley. He'd wanted to walk away first, to show off his dress a little, but the man quickly put the car in reverse. Guy stood by a dumpster and watched the tail lights move west on Santa Monica Boulevard, past a bus shelter on the corner of Cahuenga, where three hustlers ducked their heads to see into the passing cars.

Guy walked the two blocks back to the Clown-Mart. He had blisters on both heels by the time he got there. MeeMee was waiting on him, and they went across the street to the China Bowl and ate, Guy pretending he didn't see the Mexican boys eating at a booth in the corner, hissing "*Chupar me pinga!*" and sucking in kisses.

"I think all y'all beaners best be going back to Echo Park," MeeMee said, pointing her plastic fork at a boy wearing a blue bandana tied nearly to his eyes. "And don't you got like six babies waitin' in your Section Eight?"

The boy squinted and lifted his chin at MeeMee. "Yeah, I do, and all of them could fit in that condo you call an ass."

MeeMee went to get up but Guy held her arm.

"Let's just go," he whispered, and walked toward

the exit, his hem netting bits of spilt rice, the boys shouting "Faggot!" so that the nervous cashiers placed their hands over the order mikes. The boys threw ice cubes at Guy and MeeMee as they left but there was no other trouble, though he did have to listen to her talk about it all the way up Vine.

Guy looked as though he were about to fall asleep when Mary came out of the bathroom. She looked at Angelyne, curled inside a terry cloth pajama with a pull-string at the bottom. She thought she looked cold and asked Guy if she could keep using his jacket to keep the baby warm. He nodded. Mary crawled onto the mattress and asked Guy to turn out the light.

Roach stood in the doorway, letting his eyes adjust and then travel from one mattress to the other. He hadn't come up yesterday, thinking Mary might need to sleep, which she hadn't done in two days. He was trying to close the door without making any sound when he saw Guy on the couch, the pink neon of the Pacific Theater across the street reflecting on his face.

"Hey." Roach sat on the windowsill facing Guy, who was still wearing that dress and was also drunk, judging from the trouble he was having getting the tip of his cigarette to connect with the match. "How you doin'?"

Guy closed his eyes and leaned forward with his arms spread, a move meant to show Roach that life was wonderful.

"Okay, there," Roach said, fast enough to catch Guy's shoulder and keep him from pitching forward. He saw the bottle of schnapps on the floor.

"Want some?" Guy asked, not looking up, wondering if Roach would sit next to him. Roach did. The schnapps felt like silver syrup in his throat. Guy's hand went to his own Adam's apple as he watched Roach's go up and down.

"You want a cigarette, Roach?"

"Nah," he said, though he lit a match for Guy's. Seeing the match glow on Roach's face, Guy felt his crush move urgently; here they were, smoking like friends. He brought the bottle to his lips and looked at Roach from beneath his fake lashes.

"What did you do tonight, Roach?" He liked saying Roach's name.

"Let's see. I met up with Top Jimmy, and we went over to this chick's house and had some food. Then we saw a nasty fight in front of the Spotlight."

"They're always fighting there, Roach."

"Man, you know it. There was this one huge fag— sorry, man." Guy waved it away. "This huge guy in an evening dress, and he was screaming at this old guy in a wheelchair. The tranny was pretty fine, I mean, she had a good build, and she was young, and she's throwing this fit because this fat guy in the wheelchair was talking to some Mexican fag, who's going in and out of the bar every couple of minutes, saying something smart, but the tranny just shut him down, she was going to beat the shit out of him, and the guy in the wheelchair is just hanging his head, listening to all this, like he's been a bad boy and now he's gonna get it, until finally the tranny is crying, and saying, 'Nobody loves you like I love you,' and 'Who's the one takes you to the clinic? Me, that's who,' and all this shit, and then starts pushing the wheelchair, and the guy in the chair is saying, 'But I haven't finished my drink!' and the tranny is saying how she'll fix him one at home, and the Mexican guy comes out with a couple of his friends and they start catcalling after them, and the tranny literally leaves the guy in the wheelchair in the middle of the street, and takes two steps with her fist out—she's got this massive forearm—and the Mexican guys jump back into the bar like fleas, and the guy in the wheelchair is yelling because this car wants to get by and is honking like three inches away from him, so I come up and move him out of the street, and the tranny looks at me all hot, like I'm trying to take her man, so I say, 'Lady, I'm just trying to be a good Samaritan,' and she smiles and says, in this real high voice that is the opposite of the voice she's been screaming in, 'Thank you for taking care of my husband. He's getting on in years,' and she pushes him toward Sunset. Man, it was freak show supreme."

Roach took another sip of the schnapps, and it

seemed to Guy that Roach's hand lingered as he passed the bottle.

Roach got off the couch to stretch. "There any food here?" He opened the fridge just a little so the light wouldn't wake Mary or the baby. He saw a bag of Rallye's fries, which tasted worse cold than they did hot, if that were possible, and a bottle of grape juice. His lips were purple when he got back to the couch.

"You stay down by the Clown-Mart?" Roach asked.

Guy could smell the juice, thick and sweet.

"Not long," he said. His voice came out too loud, making Sofia moan in her sleep. "Never takes too long."

"Nope." Roach looked over at the girls. When they tricked it bothered him, but they had to, they had to make money. But when guys did it that was their choice. They must want to, because he never did and he was still eating.

Roach put the grape juice bottle on the floor and walked to the john. There was brown scum on the bottom of the tub, a few empty plastic shampoo bottles in the corner and a pair of bloody panties wadded next to the toilet. Roach looked at the panties as he peed, and was about to flush when he heard the lock on the bathroom door. He stood with his dick in his hand and his back turned, listening as someone inched toward him. When he or she got right behind him, Roach peered under his arm and saw Guy;

he was out of the dress, in jeans but no shirt, sitting with his knees tucked under him, looking at the floor. His hand touched Roach's calf.

"Okay?" he asked, so softly Roach barely heard. Roach turned his face to the wall, not knowing what to say, but also anticipating Guy's hands on him. They came first to Roach's waist, wrapping around and petting the hair on his stomach, and further down, and Roach was already hard when he let Guy's hand wrap around his cock. He heard himself suck air as Guy pivoted and took Roach in his mouth and began sucking with an urgency that felt good, too good. Roach looked down at Guy's tiny bobbing head, which kind of killed the sensation, so he threw back his own head to feel good again, and heard a little cry leave his mouth, which he tried to cover by clearing his throat. He knew he didn't have long and still couldn't decide whether he wanted this, and at the last moment before he was going to come jerked himself loose, so that Guy fell over on his side and smacked his head on the porcelain tub and started to groan.

"Sorry, man," Roach said, and went to pick him up, then didn't.

Guy stayed curled up on the floor.

"Sorry," Roach said again, and stepped over him.

Roach stood over Mary, telling himself that if she woke up, he'd lie next to her; if she moved at all, he'd speak to her. But she didn't, so he softly said her name, and she sat up and took his hand and pulled him onto the mattress. Her eyes were closed, and he started running his finger over her cheek.

"I'm too sore," she whispered, and Roach was ashamed she thought that's what he wanted.

"Go back to sleep," he said, and buried his face in her chest but kept his eyes open. He was waiting to hear Guy come out of the bathroom.

Guy told himself he could sleep on the floor, it was okay, but after a while he was chilled through and as silently as possible stood and looked into the loft. A little daylight was turning the long windows that faced the boulevard gray. Guy saw Roach curled around Mary, and the baby asleep on his jacket, and the other bed full of two girls. He walked to the couch and pulled a towel around his shoulders and smoked and felt dirty and cold to the bone, and as though he'd never fall asleep.

Roach watched Guy's head drop forward, until his neck formed a right angle to his chest, and heard him start to snore, a man's sound amidst all the women. Then he went back to watching Mary. Her bleached hair was curling behind her small ear; everything about her was small except for her breasts, which were pressing against him. They felt hot. Roach moved back and touched Mary's shirt. It was wet.

"Look," she said, and Roach watched her lift the

shirt and unsnap the bra, so that one breast popped out. She squeezed it, and Roach saw a pearly needle of milk shoot out of her nipple.

"God," he said. "That's so wild."

Mary rolled over and got Angelyne, placed her on her right breast while Roach tasted her left. She lay looking at the ceiling, smiling because milk flowed only to the baby, whose tongue did not stimulate her the way Roach's did. Mary's heart beat so hard she could see the baby's head bounce up and down.

"Kiss me," she said. Roach crawled up to her face. He tasted sweet.

CHAPTER THIRTEEN

Miralee lit the pipe. The baby was screaming, on and fucking on, and Miralee thought, get me through this pipe, dear Lord, and no more; I'll fix her stroller and clean her up and we can all sleep. She pulled hot smoke into her lungs and held it, until Freddy pushed her down on the bed, planting his palm in her chest and sucking on what she coughed out. He grabbed the empty pipe and looked at it, then tossed it on the spread and said she was greedy and when was she going to get the checks started again?

Miralee stared at the ceiling, smelling the chemical resin of the pipe and wanting more but knowing she wouldn't get it; knowing if Freddy did head out it would be to take care of himself, even though she'd been the one who got money for the room, standing all day in front of the 7-Eleven trying to tell people they didn't need Pampers and milk but money.

"I'll be back," Freddy said, hoisting his suspenders over his bare shoulders, then keeping silent for that slice of a second that meant he was going to snatch the pipe. Miralee scrabbled her hand on the spread and grabbed it.

"Like I fucking need it," Freddy said, punching the mattress near Miralee's face. "Like I can't make a pipe out of any piece of fucking garbage I find. Keep your fucking pipe."

He took his bike and left the door open, letting in a night breeze so sharp Miralee's body spiked with gooseflesh and she cried out once, then relaxed.

"Thank you, Jesus," she whispered, and turned to see the baby. The backboard of the stroller was broken, so Miralee pulled the comforter partway off the bed and made a pallet on the floor, where she laid the baby, who whined and kicked twice, then put her thumb in her mouth and stayed quiet. Thank you for that, too, Lord, thought Miralee, dragging herself back to the mattress. Her lungs felt like scratched aluminum, each breath making them feel bent to the breaking point. She closed her eyes and courted the night's first version of sleep. It would only last a short time, this feeling of floating through black space. It was almost the same feeling she got when she prayed, because she was a Christian now, she'd converted a couple of years ago, when she moved back in with her mom. Her mother, who'd moved herself and four kids from Rosario, Texas when Miralee was six, who'd stood by her through the trouble in high school and after, the arrests, but Freddy she would not abide, would not let him in her house after that first time, when he stole from her purse.

"He is no good, Miralee," she'd said. "You tell me he is good, that he is from hard times, and that he will change, but he will not change. I know this thing, Miralee, I know. He is not welcome here."

Miralee had promised her mother many times that they were cleaning up, promised that if she would just let Miralee get the checks sent to her house, she and Freddy could get their own place. Her mother agreed, twice, and when Miralee failed the second time she stopped taking her collect calls. Miralee staged tantrums on her mother's small front lawn, tearing up the scrubby grass while her mother sat in the darkened living room staring in the opposite direction, telling her younger daughter that the girl outside was no longer her sister, and to stop peeking through the curtains.

Miralee didn't intend on ever seeing her family again, until she turned up pregnant, and Freddy cooked up a plan to steal her mother's car, which he felt Miralee could legally sell, her having the same name. Miralee had watched him kick at the dumpsters in the parking lot of the motel they were in, yelling that she'd better follow through because he wasn't about to support her ass and a baby, too. Standing on the balcony with the sun splitting open her head, Miralee nodded out of exhaustion until Freddy broke a bottle and said he might as well just slit his throat right now, or did she want to, because that's what she was doing. The weekend manager came out and said he was going to call the cops if Freddy didn't settle down, and Freddy threw the bottle at the dumpster and took off. Miralee hid in the room until the Chicana housekeeper who always said Miralee reminded her of her cousin unlocked the door, and Miralee asked if the girl could give her a ride home.

At first, it was all Miralee could do to sit in her mother's living room with the curtains closed and the TV on, fidgeting and sweating, her body screaming, her veins feeling like freeways teeming with white cars from the future, metallic and racing, slicing her to ribbons from the inside. When she retched nothing came out. Her mother came home on her lunch hour every day and stood with pursed lips and a heart like a blood-bag in the doorway of the kitchen, watching Miralee sweat through the sheet she'd tucked over the cushions on the couch. She'd make a lunch and leave it for Miralee, and in two weeks time, Miralee was gaining weight and showing an interest in keeping clean. Her little sister Christina cut

Miralee's hair so it looked like her junior high graduation photo, put little blobs of gel on the ends so it
curled like it used to, and her cousin brought over
maternity clothes, which were enormous for Miralee.
She needed to gain weight, that's what her friends
from high school said when they visited, their tod-
dlers playing at the edges of the room, pressing their
sticky hands to the floor-to-ceiling mirror feathered
with gold. Her friends, all of them nineteen with
wide rear ends and visible blackheads, did Miralee's
nails and listened as she told them what it was like
on the street, with a guy ten years older, a guy who
didn't call after that first week, not after Miralee's
older brother Robbie, who was a cop, took the phone
from Miralee and told Freddy he'd put a restraining
order out on him. Miralee had sat on a kitchen chair,
her hands pressed between her knees, listening to
Freddy yell through the receiver, wanting to know
what charges.

Robbie said, "Statutory Rape."

"But she told me—"

"I don't care what she told you, *ese*, I'm telling you,
you come around her, I'm sticking your skinny ass
in jail."

Robbie hung up. He shook his head at the coffee
his mother offered, and knelt in his uniform before
Miralee.

"I'm not gonna do that again. You understand me?"

Miralee bent her neck to stare at his shoes. He caught her chin.

"Don't hide on me, little girl. You see this?" He pressed his hand to her stomach; she was five months now. "You mess up this baby any more than you already have, and I'll put you in jail. And I'm not talking no kiddie jail, like where you used to go. You go to the big house downtown, baby or no."

He stood up, kissed his mother, and was out the door before Miralee had a chance to say what she'd said a thousand times: who made him everyone's fucking father?

Miralee's mother made her start coming to mass. It was a big church and she hadn't been in six years, but her mother told her not to worry what anyone said. Sitting inside all that stained glass, with mostly old ladies singing songs she didn't know, Miralee felt as though she were the only person in the church God was scrutinizing, as though there was a direct beam from heaven to Soto Street. The icons around the room scared the hell out of her; they were all crying or bleeding or had their clothes ripped up. How did those crazy people get to be statues? Miralee wondered, and then thought, maybe it's people in really bad shape who wind up being closest to God, because once they atone for their sins, God looks on them more favorably. Maybe He knows their road is harder than for people who are naturally good.

After her third time at mass, Father Mark shook Miralee's hand and said it was good to have her back, and wondered if she could possibly stay after mass one Sunday.

The following week, Miralee helped Father Mark lead a Bible class for eight-to-ten-year-olds. She stood in the basement rec room, pointing to the day-glo "Just Say No" sign and said it was true, that the kids didn't want to wind up like her. They looked at her stomach and laughed, thinking that's what she meant, but she said no, for this she was grateful, and started to explain something she wasn't sure was true, that the baby was a gift from God, and that He gave her the strength to go on without drugs, ever again. One kid raised his hand and asked if drugs came from the Devil. Miralee looked at Father Mark, who said, "'The enemy that sowed them is the devil; the harvest is the end of the world; and the reapers are the angels.'"

Miralee understood the reference no more than she had when she was in Bible class, but she figured that was what God was about, a force just beyond your capacity to comprehend, because He was God.

After class, Father Mark took Miralee to the rectory kitchen, and Miralee remembered the time she'd been there before, when she was little and Robbie forgot to pick her up from religious instructions, and she'd sat with this old nun who stirred canned milk into Miralee's tea, even though Miralee said that wasn't how her mom made it.

"What was her name again, Father?"

"I'm not sure, Miralee. I've only been here four years," he said, taking a box of chocolate donuts off the top of the refrigerator. "For nine years before that, I was in upstate New York."

Miralee took a donut. "How'd you know you wanted to be a priest?"

"Well, I guess I didn't, but I had faith." Father Mark drank from a little kid-size can of apple juice. "You know Miralee, faith isn't about believing in God and poof, that's it. It must be renewed every day. The deliberate act of renewal is itself the way to keep clear the path to God."

Miralee picked a few crumbs off the counter with her finger. "Like making sure the table is clear so it'll be ready when you have to set it again?"

"Good analogy. The one I used to use in Buffalo was, like shoveling snow, but that never gets a big response in Los Angeles."

At Sunday dinner, Miralee imagined herself full of light, but her mother and sister and brothers ate their pork without noticing. She kept trying to steer the conversation to religious topics until her brother Hernando, who was twenty-two and an account executive for a cellular phone company, held up his hand.

"*Hermana*, chill on the Jesus stuff while we're eating."

"But that's just exactly what you're not getting, Nando," she said. "He has to be a part of life every day in order to keep the path clear to him. It's like shoveling snow."

Hernando stopped his fork midway to his mouth. "*Mira*, the only snow you ever shoveled was up your nose."

Their mother clanged her knife on her plate. "That's enough, Hernando."

"Okay, Ma, but look at her, in her condition, telling everybody how to believe in God. Little sister, we never stopped believing in God."

"Cut it out, Nando," Robbie said. Hernando pushed his plate away and balanced on the back legs of his mother's gilt-edged dining chair. He stared at Miralee, and his stare was like a heat lamp; she could feel the radiance melt off her, and her gut fill with the same thick white paste she thought she'd gotten rid of for good. She looked down and let the tears plop onto her plate.

"Go lie down in my room," her mother said.

Miralee lay on her mother's bed and let tears roll down her cheeks and into her ears, and after crying for five minutes she asked God to help her, to help her clear a path to Him. She said Our Fathers and Hail Marys until her skin buzzed and she began to feel high, which made her want to call Freddy, tell him his life was wrong, and that she'd figured out how to make hers right. But thinking about Freddy gave her a ticklish feeling in her throat, the same as a craving for crack, which made her cry all over again. She grabbed her mother's pillow and bit the corner and sucked until it was pointy and wet; she was afraid to move, afraid she would never be safe anywhere but this bed, and did not know she was falling asleep until she felt her mother stroke her hair off her forehead, a luxury Miralee leaned into as if she were a kitten.

"Come have some ice cream," her mother said.

Miralee wound up eating a big bowl that kept her awake until late, so she watched infomercials and then a Christian show beamed from a massive crystal cathedral. The silver-haired priest spoke about how we all fall down, but that Jesus is always there to pick us up, and he spoke of the scene on the plaque Miralee's mother had in her bathroom, the one where the man sees the footsteps of his life in the sand, and Jesus's footsteps are always beside his, except during the hardest parts of the man's life, when there is only one set of prints, and the man cries to Jesus, "How could you have abandoned me in my times of need?" and Jesus says, "Oh, my son, during those times, I was carrying you." The silver-haired TV priest said all Jesus asks in return is that we make Him our personal savior. There were video screens showing the audience praising Jesus and crying; the people all looked as though they knew they had a lot to be sorry for, but now that they'd repented, they were part of this glorious future.

Every night after her mother and sister went to sleep, Miralee watched this show with the sound low. She learned the priest wasn't a priest, because he wasn't Catholic, but he welcomed everyone, all you had to do was speak some words, which one night Miralee did, standing in front of the TV, the blue light making her nightgown transparent.

That last time at mass, Father Mark read from Proverbs. "'Wisdom is the principal thing; therefore get wisdom: and with all thy getting get understanding... for the way of the wicked is as darkness: they know not at what they stumble.'"

Miralee felt fortified. She knew God would not have made Father Mark choose this sermon if she hadn't needed to hear it.

After services, Father Mark shook hands good morning. "You look well, Miralee. Bigger."

Christina patted Miralee's belly. "She eats ice cream every night, Father. I told her the baby's going to come out 31 flavors."

"Enough." Miralee's mother face was very lined that morning. "She's up half the night, Father, watching the evangelists."

"I'm not," Miralee said.

"Don't tell me no, Mira. Don't start again with the lying!"

Miralee did not know what she had done wrong, but her mother's nostrils were flaring, and her dyed black hair looked severe against the soft umber tones of the church.

Father Mark put a hand on Miralee's mother's shoulder and asked if she'd like to speak about this in his office. She gave a curt nod and told Christina to wait in the car.

"Did you convert, Miralee?" Father Mark had his hands folded on his desk. Her mother held a Styrofoam coffee cup showing her brown lipstick and two bites marks.

"No," Miralee said. "I mean, I said words, but it's all God, right? Is it a different God or something?"

Father Mark spoke slowly. "It's not that it's a different God, Miralee. Christianity only recognizes one God. It's simply a different way of honoring Him."

"Is it the wrong way?"

"Yes, it's the wrong way," her mother said. "It's a religion that says, 'You beat your wife last night? Oh, that's okay, you ask for forgiveness and you're clean.'"

"But... isn't that the same as confession?" As soon as Miralee said it, she saw the ruptured vein beneath her mother's eye, the one she said got worse with each pregnancy, begin to fill with blood.

"Miralee, I think what your mother is saying, and

you can correct me if I'm wrong, Mrs. Rosales, is you've been raised Catholic. You have an investment in this church, and it in you. We'd like to keep you in the flock."

All Miralee could think of was a bank commercial she'd seen for the past month, saying they didn't want to lose their good customers, so they were offering incentives, and like the actor in the commercial, Miralee asked, "What do I get if I stay?"

"You get a place to have your little *pendejo* baptized, that's what you get!"

Father Mark blinked. "Mrs. Rosales—"

She held up her hand. In this position, Miralee thought her mother looked like a Spanish queen, someone with the power to behead you.

"I'm sorry, Father, but I know what I am saying. She will run from one thing to the next, with no respect for anyone else."

"How can you say that? Haven't I been good? I've been home almost two months!"

Her mother turned on her so fast Miralee thought she was going to get hit, but her mother just stared, and as she did, Miralee felt an unfamiliar two-inch wide split of ice run down her spine. She watched as her mother with great precision placed the coffee cup on Father Mark's desk.

"Two whole months." Her mother stood, pressing her purse to her stomach.

"If you'd like to come and talk, I'm here anytime," Father Mark said. Miralee's mother closed the door behind her.

Father Mark's voice sounded muffled as he asked if Miralee would like to help with Bible class. "It's the little ones today. Might be good practice for you."

Miralee went outside. She saw her mother's car in a far corner of the lot. The heat was making everything shimmer, and she couldn't tell whether the car was moving toward her. It was. Christina was in the passenger seat, reaching out her hands to Miralee as the car passed and turned out of the lot. It felt odd, knowing her mother was leaving, but Miralee forgave her right away. She sat on the church steps and said her Our Fathers and Hail Marys and knew that comfort was available to her anytime. And since she'd been back with Freddy, this had really turned out to be true; all she needed to do to get things— except for drugs, because they were a sin—was pray. For instance, if she'd been standing outside a long time, and it was raining or people just weren't feeling charitable, she prayed, and it seemed like every time, she got what she needed. Which told her she was doing the right thing. But it was more than that, it was the faith she felt when the baby was sleeping and Freddy was gone, and she got to lie alone in the dark, knowing she was saved.

Miralee woke up cold and dirty. Freddy was still

out, and the baby was asleep in her stroller; she must have climbed in there herself. Miralee regarded her with a tenderness that came only now, in the middle of the night, when there was a little distance between days. Though Miralee's bones hurt to the point of breaking through her skin, she moved her arm toward the baby's face and touched her cheek. It was sticky. Miralee lay back on the bed and asked God for the strength to get out of bed and wash herself and the baby. It took an hour, during which Miralee smoked Salems, hoping Freddy would walk in with some crack but knowing he wouldn't. She finally rousted herself and turned on the tub, and though she was exhausted and felt like crying when the baby cried, she got them both undressed and in the tub. Miralee realized she smelled very bad, so let the water run out and started filling it back up with very hot water, so hot it made the baby scream, and Miralee screamed back, "Then stand outside!" and stuck the baby on the floor. The baby crawled up and held onto the side of the tub, bobbing on bent knees and watching Miralee take a bath.

Though her skin felt burnt, Miralee washed every part of herself, shaved under her arms, leaned her head back and let the water soak her caramel hair. When the water had cooled down, she grabbed for the baby, who tucked up her legs in anticipation of pain, but Miralee wasn't strong enough to hold her up and in she went with a plop, and didn't fuss; the water had cooled to the point where Miralee grew chilled. She got out and sat on the toilet seat, a thin motel towel around her shoulders, smoking and watching the baby splash and letting the ash of the cigarette fall on her thigh, which looked skinny and red. Miralee pulled a wash rag off the sink, wiped her thigh, and tossed it into the tub. The baby watched it float and went back to trying to put the spigot in its mouth, which was when Miralee saw the scabs on the baby's forehead, and remembered she'd taken a tumble a few days before, trying to crawl out of her stroller in front of the 7-Eleven. A woman in an orange Volkswagen had just driven up, and saw the baby fall, and ran into the store and bought gauze and disinfectant, and handed them to Miralee, who was too high and took a long time trying to figure out how to open the bandages. The woman watched for a minute then said, "Here, let me get that," and knelt by the baby, who'd drawn a crowd at this point. She took the baby's head in her hands and dabbed the scrapes with peroxide, then blew on them when the baby cried, and taped on the bandage in what looked to Miralee like a medical ballet: the woman's hands moved with such grace and certainty that when she finished, Miralee looked at her with half-closed eyes and said, "That was beautiful." The woman had stood there, the bandages in her hands, looking at

Miralee. Then she went back in the store and came out with a junior first aid kit.

"You should change the dressing later, about… when it gets dark," the woman said. Miralee took the kit in her limp hands. "Thank you, thank you," she whispered, as the woman knelt in front of the baby and showed her a banana, and broke off a chunk. The baby gummed it, then tried to feed it to the woman. "No, no, for you," the woman said, and handed the baby the rest of the banana and lingered as she ate it.

Miralee got herself and the baby to the 7-Eleven by noon; she wanted to hit the lunch crowd; if she asked in Spanish sometimes the laborers felt a little solidarity, though mostly they looked at her and said nothing; she could tell, from the silent stares of the Central American boys, that they didn't feel pity for her; they knew she was making her own problems. She'd only gotten two dollars, which she and Freddy were already arguing about when a man and woman from Family Services swung their city car into the parking space directly in front of Miralee.

Miralee made a show of looking through the baby's bag for ID. She had a terrible headache from smoking a lot the night before and none yet today and wanted to get this over with. She and Freddy told the story about how they'd come down from Sacramento for a construction job that had fallen through, and they didn't have any family here so they were staying at the motel next door, trying to make money until he could get another job. The man and woman asked the same questions they always asked: "Are you on drugs?" "Is this baby being cared for properly?" "Do you understand we could take this child away from you right now?" and Miralee said no, no, yes, I understand that, and then cried from frustration because they were detaining her longer than they ever had. The social workers asked how the baby got the cut on her head, and Miralee said she fell two days ago, and there was a woman who could attest to that. They asked the woman's name, but Miralee said she didn't know. Was she supposed to know? And except for the bandage (which Miralee had thought about changing, but decided not to; she could never have done it the way the woman had) and the dirty clothes, the baby looked okay, cooing and playing looky-loo with this homeless guy called Weird Al. Freddy and Miralee were given a summons that said they had to call Family Services within seventy-two hours to report whether they'd found work and where they were living, and were told to move along if they didn't want to get arrested for panhandling. Freddy took hold of the black bike's handlebars while Miralee gathered what Pampers and food they'd been given that morning, and they pushed south on Cahuenga, Weird Al trailing them, saying, "That was close. You don't want them to take your kid, no way," but as soon as they got to the corner, Weird Al stopped and pretended to be concerned with the belt that held together his army knapsack. He confined himself to the streets adjacent to the 7-Eleven. Sometimes Freddy called him on it, saying, "You scent these four corners or something?" Which made Al, a crumpled man with zero-color hair, mumble and look away. But Freddy didn't bother with Al this morning; he was pissed off and thinking the baby wasn't worth what she brought in.

Freddy rode ahead of Miralee and the baby to the corner of Cahuenga and Hollywood, and stood in front of the check cashing place. Miralee said something about making a sign but Freddy told her to shut up, he was thinking. All he knew right now was he had to take a dump, so he told Miralee he'd be back and rode east on Hollywood, to a construction site, and found a Porto-San. He didn't want to leave his bike outside, so he hauled it in. The john was steamy and the bike didn't quite fit, so Freddy had to hold the door closed with his hand, with the bike chain biting into his arm, so that by the time he finished he was sweaty and more pissed off, and snapped at Miralee when she asked again if she should make a sign.

"Why the fuck do you keep asking me? If you want to make a sign, make a fucking sign! What are you, retarded?"

The words hit Miralee like spit, absorbed before

she could wipe them away. The baby clapped her hands as Freddy looked past Miralee, then rode off fast. Because she was watching him leave, she didn't see the LAPD car pull up behind her. The doors opened and a tall black cop with bulging arm muscles and a pale Latin cop with oiled black hair stepped out and walked a semi-circle around Miralee, staring at her from the feet up, before going into the pizza parlor. Miralee felt a rumble in her stomach she thought could be hunger, and her eyes met the Latin cop's as he chewed, and held up his slice to her, like a man offering a glass of champagne. Miralee didn't respond; the cop shrugged and ate. When he came out, he didn't bring her anything.

"You eat today?" he asked, working a toothpick around his mouth and, Miralee thought, glancing at her crotch. "That baby eat?"

Miralee lied and said yes, and the cop told her, good, then she had no reason to be hanging around here. Miralee hoisted the baby bag higher in the stroller and pushed west, to the Falafel King. There were only two people hanging out, a fat girl who flashed her tongue stud at the baby, and Roach's friend Top Jimmy, who Miralee saw was all cranked-up. She went with him to the alley by the shoemaker's and did a line, which woke her up fast; she wasn't used to crank. She and Jimmy talked about how their situations might be fucked up, but at least they were living how they wanted, and Miralee thought she'd found a really good friend until she felt herself whiting out, and heard Top Jimmy's voice coming as through a tunnel, "Mary Lee? Mary Lee..."

Top Jimmy thought he should take her up to the loft, but his foot was badly swollen and he couldn't carry her and the baby, so he lay Miralee down on the ground and decided to make her comfortable, but with what? His eyes darted to the dumpster; he couldn't face it this early. He wasn't Popcorn Guy, this filth-encrusted man who foraged every morning in the bins behind the theaters, stuffing worn garbage bags with cold popcorn. Jimmy and Roach had followed him one time as he marched barefoot up Highland with the bags slung over his shoulder, his lips fluttering in silent conference as he moved past the motorists on their way to work; had seen him crawl into his burrow by the underpass that led to the Valley and shove handfuls of popcorn in his mouth, grinding the hulls and spitting out chaff, and then start to dig a hole.

Top Jimmy took off his sweatshirt and made a pillow for Miralee's head. He looked at the baby but decided to leave the stroller where it was as he limped back to the boulevard. Maggot didn't want to help him.

"Why should I?" she droned from her designated spot in front of the Falafel King. But she followed Top

Jimmy. When they got to the dumpster, they saw a stain under Miralee's mouth.

"Gross. She puked on your shirt," said Maggot.

Miralee heard her, and wanted to say, I'm okay, but she couldn't lift her head; she pictured her neck like the bent stem of a flower. She managed to sit up, but her head still hung all the way down, her chin jutting so hard into her chest her neck felt hyper-extended. She could sense Top Jimmy and that girl standing above her, waiting for her to do something, but she was disconnected from her voice; it felt like a pancake lying low in her belly and no matter what she did, she couldn't get it to rise. With great effort, Miralee brought the pancake up an inch, and on the descent it compressed two syllables of air that came out, "M'okay."

Maggot shifted her feet. She wanted Top Jimmy to get her stoned, but knew if she said something now he'd tell her to fuck off, so she waited, a flesh pylon between Miralee and the early traffic on Wilcox.

Across the street, a freestanding hut rolled up its service window, and the dusty smell of cumin roiled out in an ochre smoke. Chiles were sizzling in a cast iron pan as an Indian couple, he in Western clothes, she in a sari, prepared for the lunch trade. Husband and wife were both oily and stout, streaked with red like their food, hair grizzled with gray, exposed ankles rocketed with spider veins. They were jolly, like parents always glad to see grown children, no matter what the news, and regularly chatted with their customers, many of whom were not happy to be there. The local papers commented on the dicey location, but also on the authenticity of the cuisine, which brought interlopers to the area. Some would wait for the food with the engines of their luxury cars idling, marveling that they were paying only $5.60 for lunch, and let Pankaj carry the take-out boxes to their cars, whereupon they'd become alarmed and say, "Not on the seat!" because it might tip, and that kind of food stains so badly, plus the smell lasts forever. Pankaj would watch the driver spread newspaper on the floor of the car, or pop the trunk, and give a wink, waiting for Pankaj to acknowledge his or her cleverness. Pankaj would bid them good journey and commit the face to memory, for who can forget the gift of a meal, the communion of putting food into another human being? But it didn't matter, because these people only ever came once.

Pankaj planted sun umbrellas in the two outdoor tables. The shade let him see what was going on in the alley across the street. He recognized the boy with the bad foot, who looked very white and sickly, stooping to say something to a woman on the ground. Pankaj craned his neck to see if she were conscious, and caught the skin of his finger in the clamp that held the umbrella. He cursed briefly, and

Madhu looked through her little portal, hearing her husband over the sounds of the cooking pots. She followed his eyes and saw the stroller, and the back of a wide woman. She said something in Punjabi. Pankaj shrugged and walked back to the hut for the napkin holders.

"You want me to get you water or something?" Top Jimmy asked Miralee. At least they weren't asking anymore if she could hear them, they'd asked three times before Miralee was able to groan, "Uhn huh." She could produce only small sounds, which bothered her only because she was being asked to speak. She finally took to moving her head, with all the imprecision of a sack tied to the end of a stick, which was enough for Maggot.

"She's okay," she said. "Yo, Jimmy, let's get stoned."

Jimmy told Maggot, "In a minute," and squatted near Miralee, though squatting made his foot throb. "You want me to find Freddy?"

Miralee thought about this, she felt she had the leisure to, and no, she didn't want Top Jimmy to find Freddy, she was content where she was; she shook her head loosely.

"You. You there."

Top Jimmy deliberately did not turn. It was an art, ignoring one's reflexes, but the voice across the street kept on. "Young man!"

Jimmy turned. Pankaj was standing on the curb

opposite, waving Jimmy over. "Please come here."

"I can't, man. She's sick."

"I know that, young man. I'd like to speak with you about this."

Top Jimmy looked at Maggot, and saw her mouth hanging open in disgust. He got to his good foot and hop-stepped across the street. "What is it?"

"What's wrong with her?" asked Pankaj.

"I don't know." Jimmy looked away. "She just... passed out."

Madhu spoke to her husband rapidly in Punjabi.

"Yes, yes," he said to her, and to Jimmy, "Then let us bring her out of the sun."

Top Jimmy found himself following the man across the street. Pankaj stooped over Miralee, and placed a broad palm on her shoulder.

"Miss, I am going to pick you up. Please don't be afraid."

Miralee was not afraid, but she was limp, so limp she laughed, though only she could hear it.

The girl was lighter than Pankaj thought she'd be, and he easily supported her as Top Jimmy leaned onto the handles of the baby stroller.

"Grab my sweatshirt," he told Maggot.

"I thought we were going to party," she said, as the men and their human cargo crossed the street.

Pankaj lay Miralee down with her head toward the rear of his pick-up truck. He pulled one of the sun umbrellas out of its housing and balanced it against the tailgate so the shadow fell across Miralee's face. Pankaj moved aside as Madhu walked from the hut.

Miralee heard the swish of Madhu's sari, smelled its dusty perfume as it brushed against her hair. Madhu pressed a cold cloth firmly onto Miralee's forehead. The cloth crackled as the dried verbena leaves Madhu used to bring down a fever were crushed; Miralee felt a singing cold that was tolerable and smelled the fragrant drops of water that rolled down her temples and into her ears. Madhu continued to press the cloth, and as she did it seemed to Miralee that her own neck recessed, it was a tube of white plastic pressing into the truck bed; the image so preoccupied her that the voices were no longer asking anything, they were merely tonal.

"Is she on drugs?" Pankaj asked, not expecting a truthful answer, but figuring he had to ask. Perhaps the young man would realize the seriousness of the situation.

"I... don't know," Top Jimmy said. "Maybe."

"And the baby. Is she yours or hers?"

Top Jimmy looked at the baby, who had her hands wrapped around the restraining bar of the stroller. "Not mine."

Pankaj realized he was not going to get any more information from the young man, and looked for Madhu, who was carrying a cup of tea. She held it toward Top Jimmy. He looked at the tea and mumbled, "Thanks," though he wasn't sure he could get it down. But he did wrap his hands around the mug and let the warm seep in. It felt good, like a mini hot bath. He set down the tea, took off the fingerless black bicycle gloves he always wore, and was shocked to see how pink and wet his hands were. He carefully picked up the mug and drank a small sip, and felt the liquid roll down his chest and directly into his cock. He had to pee, but he didn't move; he'd stay all day on the bed of the warm truck before he moved.

"What you want me to do with this?" Maggot was standing at the curb, Jimmy's vomit-soaked shirt dangling from one finger. "I'll throw it in the fucking trash."

"Just give it to me." Jimmy held out his hand.

"No. You come here."

Jimmy sighed, and skipped on one foot to Maggot, who pulled the shirt away. "I thought we were going to party," she said.

"I didn't say that."

"I helped your ass out. I came and watched her."

Top Jimmy started to feel sick himself, like the tea might come up. "Maggot, just chill, all right? Maybe later."

She threw his sweatshirt on the sidewalk, and gave it a kick. "You want your shirt, you diseased motherfucker?" She kicked again at Top Jimmy's shirt.

"Miss! Miss, you must stop this!" Pankaj was on the curb with them, a dishcloth in his hands. "You cannot fight here."

Maggot and Jimmy stood like two tension wires, hers humming, his black and slack, almost extinguished.

"If you like, I'll give you lunch." Pankaj said, his eyebrows rising. "Yes? Would you like to eat?"

Ten minutes later, Maggot and Jimmy were sitting at the white plastic table, with plates of chicken and lentils and yellow rice before them. Maggot chewed with her mouth open, but Jimmy just moved the food around. When Maggot finished, she pushed the plate away and walked off without saying anything to anybody, and Jimmy was the beneficiary of a warm wind that blew down from the Hollywood sign. He put his bad foot on Maggot's chair and let the chill under his skin turn to prickles and dissolve into the air.

He looked at the baby. Madhu had pushed the stroller to the back door of the hut; the baby was chewing on some puffy bread and watching Madhu cook. As she cooked, she spoke to the baby in Punjabi and English, and for some reason this made Top Jimmy choke up, because in ten minutes these people knew how to take care of a baby that wasn't even theirs. Top Jimmy knew if he started crying it would be a long one, and what a ludicrous image that was, sitting here bawling, maybe even having the guy come out and put a hand on his shoulder. The idea made Top Jimmy laugh, and with the laugh the bilious smell that came when he hadn't eaten in a long time, so he shut his mouth and looked down at his food. He slowly wrapped a very small piece of chicken in a shard of the puffy bread, and looked at it. Then he put it in his mouth and started to chew. Food. It felt alien and took a long time to break down. Swallowing was hard; the masticated clump felt like a matchbox car moving down his throat, no other cars on the road. It made Jimmy so exhausted, that one bite, that one step toward a life based around eating and sleeping, that he almost reared back from it, almost tossed his plate and made for the alley. But he saw Miralee watching him eat and she looked as though she were smiling, so he thought, okay, and carried his plate to the truck and sat near her. He made another roll-up and brought it to her mouth, which she opened. They kept eating, first her, then him, until the food was done and Jimmy was wiping a finger on the waxy paper plate, and registering a unfamiliar fullness that made him want to sleep. He wanted to lay down next to Miralee in the shade of the Indian shack and take a nap. That was simple, wasn't it? Wanting to sleep after a meal? But it was not an option. He wasn't sick like Miralee. Oh, he was sick, but it wasn't an emergency; his infected foot wasn't going to stop traffic and bring concerned citizens asking, what happened?

When Top Jimmy felt the food start to bubble back up, he thought he'd better go. But he heard the squeak of the stroller wheels and watched as the baby came toward him and Miralee, a piece of brown cake in each hand. Pankaj was pushing her, and smiling; he and the baby were in collusion in this offering. Despite the fact that this was TV stuff, Miralee and Jimmy smiled when the baby handed them each a piece of cake; the pantomimed thank you Pankaj expected was subdued, it was just cake, but still the baby clapped when Miralee pushed herself onto her elbow and took it. She broke off a piece, and handed the rest to the baby, who chewed it into a mass of crumbs that fell into the reservoir of other crumbs in the seat of her stroller, stuff she ate later, or molded into paste balls with the sweat of her small hands, so that the stroller took on a fermented smell, and her skin wore a balm of food from the 7-Eleven.

Miralee stretched, the armhole in her baggy t-shirt dipping low, so that Jimmy inadvertently caught a peek of one tit. He looked away, and a little squirt of saliva shot out from under his tongue, and for a second time he thought he might cry. He tried not to think about sex at all. When he peed, he didn't look down, afraid of the crust and the strong smell. It became a game: stand against the wall, stare straight ahead, pee; tuck in, breathe. He had no access to girls, anyway. The last time was Wendy. They all thought she was a freak, because she talked to herself and wore long skirts and hung onto a crochet hook like it was her baby doll. Roach called her "Hook," but Jimmy didn't. He thought she looked like some kind of princess, with a lot of honey-colored hair cascading over her shoulders. She'd shown up in late summer, wandering up the boulevard in the sunshine, smiling and chatting to herself, digging in trash bins like it was nothing. But she didn't really need to; Jimmy noticed people were always giving her stuff; he once saw a woman hand Wendy a bag full of balled yellow yarn, and thought, they try to save the ones who are best off. It made him wonder where he was on the chain. But he noticed Wendy broke that chain, crocheting little squares the size of pot holders, which she'd give to the worst off, a dusty angel of mercy offering micro-blankets. Jimmy lived in dread that she'd give him one; that she was somehow in charge of sorting. He held his breath whenever she passed, her eyes shining and staying on him until he'd grow uncomfortable and look away and hide his bad foot behind his good one. But she never gave him anything.

"I think Hook's got a thing for you, man," Roach told Jimmy one afternoon, as they watched her glide down the street; you couldn't see her feet moving beneath those skirts. Roach told Jimmy he thought

Wendy looked like one of those old-time ghosts you see in the movies, "the ones who are real sad because their whole family has been wrongfully killed, and they're stuck in this mansion until some living person can understand them."

The *El Ninos* had blown cold the fall after Wendy showed up. By midnight, everyone scrambled for cover; finding squats early or standing behind the plate glass of the Falafel King watching soda cups whip down the boulevard. But Top Jimmy didn't feel right inside; he'd lost the sense of being welcome. Roach still had it, and Jimmy was okay going places with him, but alone, he couldn't. He felt he'd gone past being invisible to being a negative.

By October, Top Jimmy resigned himself to the spot under the freeway, though it was far, past the area where everyone hung out, on the other side of Gower. Every night, he'd pull his sweatshirt around his ribs and walk east on Hollywood, past the abandoned theaters and empty construction sites. The walk hurt his foot, but he did it, heading for the green 101 freeway sign, which looked a mile away in a snowstorm. He'd put his head to the wind and aim for his midpoint, the Ford dealership, whose elevated blue sign threw a circumference of white light. And one night, sitting in its radius, was Wendy. From two blocks off, Jimmy knew it was her; no one else wore skirts like that. He stopped walking, and on the wind came a tiny scrap of voice. The voice became a series of notes and gaps that Jimmy wanted to hear more clearly, and he walked toward Wendy despite what he saw in her hand: a little yellow square. He would face it, even if it meant he had to take the square in his teeth and tear it, and when he was standing before her, his sweat freezing to his pitted chest, Wendy held up her hand with the square in it. As Jimmy reached for it, she grabbed his wrist and pulled herself to standing, and started talking close to his face, her voice buzzing like a transformer. He couldn't understand what she was saying, but thought maybe it because of was the wind, and let her walk next to him through what looked like a nuclear winter, white litter flying and everything that wasn't rooted to a foundation blowing away.

Wendy climbed after Jimmy between the chainlink fence and the retaining wall, and through a narrow maze that widened into a small shelter beneath the freeway. Now that Wendy was here Jimmy saw the shelter in a different way, and he went back into himself and was ashamed anew. But immediately she started talking, run-on strings of words that filled the shelter and forced the violent rushing of the cars overhead to the background. Listening to her, Jimmy felt relaxed. He made a fire and unfolded the broken foam rubber pallet.

Insulated and alone with her, he felt calm enough

to try to decipher what Wendy was saying, but after two minutes decided the sounds did not translate to words and ceased looking for the code. Wendy sang as she unwound a blanket from beneath her skirts, and spread it on the ground. She carefully pulled from her mesh bag a box of crackers and a can of sausage, which they ate beneath the sounds of the cars passing overhead. When Jimmy got up to feed the fire, Wendy wrapped the blanket around herself, so that Jimmy anticipated the extra coldness of being shut out, until the sound of her voice made him know she wanted him to crawl in with her. He slowly lowered himself, feeling only one bad pang from the foot, and let her wrap the blanket around his shoulders. She kissed Jimmy's cold cheek, and her soft lips made the blood pour into his own rough blue lips, and he turned his face to her, and saw she was as clean as if she'd been rolling in snow. He would've crawled into himself then if she hadn't pulled him to her, and taken his hand and led it beneath her skirt; he let himself kiss her as his hand explored her thigh, it was enough, it was more than enough. He closed his eyes and let the warmth from her and her blanket and her voice slough off the layers of what hurt him, and as she took off his clothes, he began to cry, the tears running through the dirt on his face, and when her hand went to his penis, he looked down, and saw that he was pink down there, that he was still good.

Miralee felt the food coming back up, all over the back of the nice man's truck. It made her scream, this cycle of food and no food, sickness and no sickness. Madhu came running out of the hut, and took Miralee by the shoulders, saying she was going to call an ambulance. Miralee grabbed the front of Madhu's sari, her hands clawing the silk and leaving it wet, and said, no, call Father Mark. Miralee flopped over on the back of the truck bed and began fumbling though the baby's bag, pulling out shreds of paper.

"He's at Our Lady of Guadalupe Church, in East Los Angeles. Please tell him Miralee needs help, that's me. Tell him to come get me."

As Miralee stuffed the papers back, she saw all the action around her stop. Madhu did not run for the phone. Pankaj stood holding a rag but made no move to clean up. Jimmy stood over her, the baby reaching for the leg of his pants. And then Miralee felt a bubble pop in the back of her skull, and saw the already-bright day get brighter, exploding from a pinhole in the center and burning its way out. Miralee let out an animal cry so high it could not be distinguished from the noise of the universe, into which Miralee felt herself burst, a trillion atoms flung and sparkling in the air.

Jimmy pushed the baby fast down Hollywood. It was four o'clock, his least favorite time of day, still hours of heat to go and no place to hole up and hide, and he was crying because he was scared. When Madhu started to scream he'd gotten the baby out of there, he didn't know why, he didn't know what he was going to do with her, he just kept pushing the stroller as fast as he could, which didn't seem to make the baby happy. She was twisting in her seat, throwing down her bottle every three steps, and bending to pick up the bottle meant Jimmy had to crouch, which made his foot hurt. He picked up the bottle for about the ninth time in two blocks, and was about to hand it back when he saw Wendy standing in front of the Thrifty's, eating pastries from a pink box. She smiled at him, and he pushed the stroller to her and released the handles. Wendy cooed at the baby, broke off a piece of a Danish and handed it to her, and tried to give a piece to Jimmy, who shook his head. He already felt sick, and was thinking about what he needed to do when Wendy handed him the cake box, took the stroller, and started to push. Jimmy watched them move across the parking lot, heard the squeak of the wheels getting smaller, little bottle rockets spiraling out and away, until Wendy walked out of the lot and down Gower. Jimmy thought about following her; in his mind he saw himself dragging behind her at a distance of fifty feet, then one hundred, still able to hear her humming, and the baby squealing in harmony, until Jimmy was a full block behind and knew he wasn't going to catch up. But Jimmy didn't actually move; he stood with the pastry box open, and picked one frosted almond off the top of a Danish and put it in his mouth. The sweet simplicity of it made his bladder open, and he peed himself, right there in front of the Thrifty's, which both relieved and horrified him. But did it matter? He was close to the underpass, he could get there, he could lie there and dry out, it was okay, he wasn't Popcorn guy; he just needed to dry out.

CHAPTER FOURTEEN

Sofia was boiling water for cocoa when she heard someone try to use a key to get in the loft.

"*Zut*," said a man, pushing open the door and walking in. There were two people behind him, a couple wearing fashionable black clothes that looked like uniforms.

"Who are you?" the man asked Sofia. He had an accent, and did not seem mad.

"We..." She turned off the pot of water and looked at Mary. "We live here. I mean we're staying here."

The fashionable couple looked at the man, and said something in French; he answered, then looked at Sofia and smiled, sort of.

"You have ze lease?"

Sofia heard her voice through the throb of her heart, asking Mary, "Do we have a lease?"

"I have to get her," Mary whispered, going to the mattress and wrapping the baby.

The man crossed to Mary, and looked down at Angelyne.

"He is yours?"

Mary nodded.

"Gazou gazou, cute baby," the man said. He turned to Sofia. "You have one-quarter hour to get your things, then I call the police."

The man and the couple stayed in the doorway, making quiet comments and softly laughing while Sofia put her clothes in a garbage bag, and Mary gathered her and the baby's things.

"Ca va, okay," the man said, when the girls had their belongings and were standing in front of him, as if waiting for a signal. "And if you think of coming back, you may think again. Okay, goodbye."

Sofia carried one of Mary's bags down the steps and pushed open the door to the street with her back. It was unbearably bright outside, and the sun bounced off the baby's white blanket and into Mary's eyes.

"I need something to drink," Mary said, feeling like she couldn't get enough air. As she slid down the face of the building Sofia reached and pinned Mary's shoulders, trying to keep her upright.

"Wait, just wait," Sofia said, using her foot to push her bag under Mary and get Mary sitting.

"Bend over a little more!" some dude shouted from a passing car.

"Fuck you!" Sofia shouted back, and hearing the tears in her voice, shouted up to the loft's windows, "Fucking French assholes!"

Sofia looked at Mary, in the ripped pink shirt, the stained army pants, half-collapsed over the baby. What day was it, Saturday? Manolo didn't work today. Okay. Sophia took a breath and said to Mary, "You stay with the stuff, okay?" Mary nodded into her own lap, and kept nodding as Sofia took off up Wilcox.

When Mary opened her eyes she was looking right into the baby's face. "It's okay," she said, using the corner of the blanket to dab at some dribble. When her legs fell asleep Mary dragged her and Sofia's bags to the corner in front of Playmates, where it was shady and also where she could see if anyone was hanging out in front the Falafel King. She hadn't seen Roach in days, and someone had told her that Dean had been arrested again. Mary sat on her garbage bag and thought about going downtown, to the courthouse, an idea that exhausted her.

"Get up."

Mary opened her eyes and saw Sofia flipping forward the passenger seat to a long purple American car. "Let's go," Sofia said.

Mary held tight to the baby as she ducked into the back of the car. It was airless in there, and part of the leather from the roof was hanging down. The driver had his arm across the seat back, and as Sofia crammed a bag into the back seat, Mary could see sparkling beads of sweat nesting in the man's blue-black arm hair.

"It's all going to be good." Sofia was in the front seat, looking straight ahead. "Larry's a producer."

Larry spit some air through his lips and gunned the engine to make the light.

CHAPTER FIFTEEN

After doing two weeks in juvie, Roach went straight to the loft and found a lock on it, and a sign saying trespassers would be prosecuted. He backed away from the door, wondering who would rent such a dump, and stood on the corner across from the Falafel King. It was very early on a Sunday, the boulevard still empty except for the heavy punk slogging up the street toward him.

"Got any pot?" Maggot asked.

Roach didn't say anything.

"Where you been?" she asked.

Roach was hungry, and decided to use part of the $25 they'd given him upon release for some real food, but didn't want Maggot trying to horn in. He bet that girl could eat.

"Lock-up," he said.

"Down Wilmington?"

"Nah, Pacoima."

"What for?"

Roach rubbed his face.

"You see they locked up the loft?" she asked.

"Yeah, I seen that," Roach said, thinking he'd head to the Hollywood 8. Sometimes Miralee got up early to go to church. Maybe he'd walk over with her.

"So why'd they arrest you?" Maggot asked, trying to stay alongside Roach.

"Just some shit with Dean. He was holding something for somebody and got busted and I was with him."

"He go to Pacoima with you?"

Roach didn't know exactly where Dean went, but heard it was Wayside Honor Rancho, and that he might not be coming out for two years. "Nah."

Maggot was huffing to keep up. "You heard about that girl with the baby?"

Roach kept walking. "Mary?"

"Nah, the other one. With that old guy."

Roach stopped. "Miralee?"

"Yeah, that chick," said Maggot, her eyes taking on the gleam of someone about to tell a good secret. "She bought it the other day. I saw it, I was there."

Roach's pulse started banging in his throat. "What are you talking about?" He heard his own voice; it sounded mechanical.

"Right at that Indian restaurant," said Maggot. "She was with your buddy Jimmy, I guess they were both pretty high, and she started puking all over the place and then she croaked."

Roach's throat closed, he couldn't breath.

"It was a fucking mess. She was in the back of the guy's truck…"

Roach began to run.

"Where are you going?" Maggot took two flat-footed strides after him, her big arms flopping. "Okay, then." She crammed her hands in her pockets as she looked down the empty boulevard, trying to decide which way to go.

Roach ran to the motel; the Indian woman was not on duty, it was still the young night guy, who told Roach he didn't know what girl he was talking about. Roach wove his fingers through the security grate.

"She's got a baby, and her husband is this sort of older guy. With a bike?"

The night guy told Roach to please remove his fingers from the grate, and that it was against policy to give out information about paying guests. Roach looked at the guy sitting all safe, took a step back and kicked at the grate until his foot throbbed and the guy was yelling into the phone.

Roach walked fast with his head down to the Indian restaurant. It was closed. He went across the street, to the alley behind the shoemaker's, sat next to the dumpster and put his face in his hands. He couldn't sit still. He got up and screamed.

"Shut the fuck up down there," some lady yelled, probably Mona in her shitty, shitty apartment. This was her fucking fault; he would've been around if it weren't for her lame-ass fucking weed.

"You shut up!" He looked for something to heave at the window, and found a can of spray paint. It came down and hit the ground, black paint hissing from the broken tip. Roach scrambled for the can, and slid on the seat of his pants to the dumpster. He took off one of his socks and balled it and crammed in the nozzle and pushed until paint soaked the sock. He held the sock to his face and breathed, wondering what would happen if he shot the nozzle directly into his nostril, but before finishing the thought he was having a dream, little white ghost faces spinning like rags in a bottomless black dryer, their voices hollow and pleading as they went round and round. Roach stared into the vortex; that was where he wanted to go, that's where he wanted to go. Slumping to the ground, only a small piece of Roach knew he was gagging, and he didn't want that piece, he was trying to let go of that piece and was almost there when he heard a voice—his voice?—from far away saying, "It's okay, I'm okay," as Chief hauled him up by the armpits, telling him to walk, saying over and over, "You need air, brother. Air."

CHAPTER SIXTEEN

Mary knew if she looked out the window and to the left she'd see the Christmas decorations on the lampposts on Hollywood. But she didn't look because she wasn't dressed yet, and LA had turned cold. The baby was asleep on the floor between the bed and the window, in the car seat she'd gotten from the clinic. What Mary had really wanted was a stroller, but the woman, who told Mary she was her "caseworker," said there was a waiting list and to come back after the holidays. Or did Mary have a relative she could ask? The woman did not look old but had frizzy gray hair and wore a dress that looked like it was from Africa even though she was white, and she had a way of asking, kind of looking serious and friendly at the same time, that made Mary think the woman was trying to get information. Mary had looked at

Angelyne in the car seat; she looked cozy, and Mary told the woman, who said to call her Judy, that she was okay, she was staying with friends.

Mary stared at the ceiling and wondered how long she could stay in Larry's apartment. He didn't even let her go in the kitchen if he was asleep, and she couldn't turn on the TV until he was gone, which was never before noon. She just had to lie there while he slept and also keep the baby quiet or Larry would curse and, one time, punch the bed.

Larry's cell phone rang with the theme from "Star Wars." He pulled open the bathroom door and glared at Mary, though she hadn't moved. He stood with a towel around his waist, his hairy stomach swaying toward her.

"Yeah," he said into the phone. Mary heard the tinkle of a woman's voice.

"Is that Sofia?" Mary gathered the sheet around her. "Can I talk to her?"

"Yeah," he said. Mary held out her hand; Larry batted it away. "Yeah, yeah, two."

He closed the phone and grabbed Mary's wrist. "What are you doing, hah?" He pulled up on her arm until she was on her knees. "Sofia's working, you understand working?" He threw her arm back at her. "Of course you don't."

Mary held her wrist. She had to get out of here. Her voice already sounded far away when she asked,

"But are you going to see her today?"

"This is your business?" Larry slipped on his gold watch and kept his eyes on Mary. She pushed back on the bed. "Let's go," he said.

"No." Mary backed toward the wall.

"You're ready."

"I'm not." Her voice squeaked up. "You said my mouth."

"No more mouth, I'm sick of your mouth."

"I'm too sore, I just had a baby." She had to get out of here.

"What the fuck does that mean?" Larry let the towel drop. "My mother had eight kids in nine years so obviously my dad was able to fuck her." He grabbed Mary's chin, his face so close she could see the holes around his whiskers. She tried to hide under the blanket. Larry threw the blanket on the floor and flipped her over.

"Please, please, not so hard." Mary heard her voice vibrating as Larry kept on. He came and collapsed on top of her, which made a big whoosh of fluid shoot out of Mary's vagina. Larry jumped off the bed and stood at its edge watching the pool of blood and mucus spread on the black sheet.

"Shit," he said, and before he shut himself in the bathroom, Mary saw his eyes would not meet hers.

She was glad he was scared, and after he left she was going to take a long bath, even though he'd told her she couldn't. Her body felt as though she'd gone through a washing machine with a bunch of rocks. She curled on her side. Angelyne was still sleeping. That was good. Mary looked at the ceiling and wondered if she'd just been raped. She wasn't sure you could call it that since Larry let her sleep here.

He came out of the bathroom doing his belt.

"Get yourself something to eat," he said. He tossed a ten dollar bill that sailed onto the bed, grabbed his car keys, and split.

So Mary had ten dollars, for food and diapers and bus fare and whatever else she needed. She needed a different place to stay. Roach had told her, "You can always find a place; you're a girl." But she wasn't a girl; she was two girls. She remembered reading in a book MeeMee had that "two can travel as easy as one," but that was written by a black lady a long time ago and she thought, Mary did, that maybe black people were able to handle hardship, they'd been getting dumped on for so long, maybe they'd built up some thick genetic skin. Maybe they were able to do what they needed to do. Mary didn't yet know what she needed to do.

She heard the baby coo. Angelyne was awake, staring at Mary with both thumbs in her mouth. Mary picked her up and laid her on the bed. She watched Angelyne flex her legs and blow spit bubbles, which made Mary smile; she sat there naked and watched the baby kick and kick, and picked Larry's towel off the floor and started to wipe herself, under her arms, around her crotch, and then she started scratching where she had another one of those sores. She pinched around its edges, coaxing the blister to a head until she felt a tiny pop. She looked at the wetness on her fingers; it was just water. Then she changed the baby.

ABOUT THE AUTHOR

Nancy Rommelmann's articles and profiles have appeared in the *New York Times Magazine*, the *LA Weekly*, the *Los Angeles Times*, *Reason* and other publications. The idea for this novel grew out of her non-fiction work, which often explores the story behind the story when it comes to Los Angeles's more interstitial populations: LAPD officers and the refuge that is the cop bar; the itinerant inhabitants of a Sunset Boulevard motel; the workaday lives of a Mexican gardening crew in the Hollywood Hills. To find these and other stories, visit www.nancyrommelmann.com.

CPSIA information can be obtained
at www.ICGtesting.com
Printed in the USA
BVHW082319221019
561842BV00006B/74/P